MW01231680

Reinventing THE RIGHT

CONSERVATIVE VOICES
FOR THE NEW MILLENNIUM

Edited by

ROBERT WHEELER & JOHN AMBLE

Copyright © 2009 Robert Wheeler & John Amble
All rights reserved.

ISBN: 1-4392-6735-9
ISBN-13: 9781439267356

To our families.

TABLE OF CONTENTS

Editors' Note ix

Introduction – Reinventing the Right xi
Our Conservatism

I. Liberty and Justice for All 1
Judicial Philosophy and Representative Government

II. Permission to Speak Freely 19
The First Amendment as the Cornerstone of American Democracy

III. Disarmed is Dangerous 29
A Fresh Take on the Second Amendment

IV. Free to Believe 41
A Secularist's Defense of Religious Liberty

V. Locking the Bedroom Door 55
Government, Sexuality, and Society

VI. Extending a Hand 65
Strengthening Volunteerism in America

VII. True Multiculturalism 77
Shattering the Walls That Divide Americans

VIII. Voices of the Damned 89
A Rights-Based Analysis of Abortion in America

IX. Liberty and Stewardship 99
Going Green the American Way

X. Powering America 119
Enduring Solutions to the Energy Problem

XI. Live Free or Die 139
Principles for a 21st Century Healthcare System

XII. Freedom to Choose 163
Reestablishing Excellence in American Education

XIII. Serve and Protect 175
A Federalist Approach to Police and Crime Policy

XIV. Yes, Unless 187
A Just Approach to Immigration

XV. Navigating the Shoals 203
Building a Conservative Foreign Policy Worldview

XVI. Reclaiming our Foreign Policy 221
International Organizations and American Sovereignty

XVII. This We Will Defend 239
A Principled Approach to National Security

XVIII. Free Men, Free Trade 251
Embracing the Virtues of Globalization

XIX. Dissolving Collectivism 267
Taxing, Spending, and the Rights of Man

Conclusion – Reinventing the Right 281
The Way Forward

Acknowledgements 287

"It was the cause of America that made me an author."
-Thomas Paine

EDITORS' NOTE

It is the nature of political writing that not everyone will agree with each point of view espoused or every argument made. Usually, opposition to a piece is spearheaded by those on the other end of the political spectrum. There remains an unspoken assumption that all on the left will agree with any argument made under the banner of liberalism and that all on the right will necessarily accept the views of any conservative commentator.

This is not the case with *Reinventing the Right*. Some conservatives may not agree with every conclusion reached in the pages that follow. Indeed, we, the editors, may disagree with some of the policy prescriptions outlined in this book. Some essays may even be more palatable to self-described liberals than to others who accept the moniker of conservative.

Despite this, all the essays are bound together by a set of fundamental values. Each chapter aims to apply our country's founding principles – individual liberty, free markets, and equality before the law – to contemporary policy areas that dominate public debate.

The project was born of a desire to reclaim these ideals for conservatism and demonstrate their power to reshape American governance in the new millennium. *Reinventing the Right* is the culmination of the efforts of fifteen young Americans who joined us to articulate this vision. Other conservatives may apply these values differently to particular public policy areas and thereby reach different conclusions than we do. We welcome the debate that results and view a plurality of opinions within the movement as an asset that will ultimately make conservatism, and America, stronger. If this work can provide a catalyst for such debate and, in so doing, strengthen the principles that have defined America's history, then we will have done our part to truly reinvent the right.

Robert Wheeler and John Amble
Editors

REINVENTING THE RIGHT:
Our Conservatism
by John Amble and Robert Wheeler

The book you hold is not a political manifesto. It is neither a partisan attack, nor a partisan defense. Rather, these pages contain a series of philosophical essays, each based on a broad set of unified principles – principles whose history is deeply interconnected with the story of America itself. We firmly believe that these principles hold the key to both unlimited opportunity for individual Americans and the realization of our country's boundless potential. Collectively, the principles promoted herein form the basis of our shared conservative philosophy.

The writers of the essays that follow are not academicians nor are we politicos. We are not scholars in a professional sense. We are students and soldiers, teachers and artists, lawyers and laborers. Our backgrounds are varied, and our unique paths have led us each to adopt a common set of beliefs. Namely, we believe that the principles upon which our country was founded are as relevant and essential to America's ongoing success today as they were more than 220 years ago. In 1787, with our young nation at a critical crossroads, our government was given direction by the events and deliberations that took place in the Pennsylvania State House in Philadelphia. This gathering of proud, hopeful, energetic Americans inspires awe to this day. We channel their pride, their hopefulness, and their energy, as we humbly attempt to apply the principles that they so eloquently laid out in the Constitution to the issues that our nation faces today.

The Founders set out to create a new system of government, one unlike any the world had yet seen. It was an experiment reliant upon individual liberty as its cornerstone. A simple look at the text of the Constitution suggests a strong inclination on the part of the Framers to create in the document a defense against any future threat of tyranny. They wrote positive limitations on the domain of the government into the Constitution itself. In doing so, they set the stage for unprecedented success. Indeed, the Founders' experiment resulted in the most prosperous, diverse, and powerful society in the world's history. In order to build upon this legacy, we seek to rediscover their experiment by reclaiming and reapplying the principles they laid out more than two centuries ago. It should be noted, then, that ours is not a new philosophy. Rather, it is a return to the philosophy upon which our country was built.

There is in America a movement whose ideological underpinnings differ dramatically from ours, one that is often in opposition to conservative positions on contemporary political issues. The movement may be called liberal, progressive, leftist, or any other variety of names. We've chosen not to belabor ourselves in semantics, as many of the terms have become too politicized to allow for an issue-based discussion regarding America's future. That said, we must articulate one critical difference between the opposing ideologies. The strength of our belief system lies in its founding in the principles that helped America achieve the pinnacle of political, economic, military, and cultural supremacy. Conversely, opposing philosophies have no such founding, and as such they fail to offer clear solutions to the myriad issues our society faces. In fact, the actions and rhetoric of our philosophical counterparts suggest a belief that our nation's foundational principles no longer apply.

In order to give the reader the necessary perspective from which to approach the chapters that follow, we should note the current political situation. Recent developments give the strong impression that conservatism as a movement has lost ground in the national political arena. We urge caution to anyone who might infer from these electoral results that conservatism's value is waning. We hope these essays show that conservatism is alive and well in the United States, and that it is the philosophy that offers the best chance of solving the current problems we face. Our conservatism is the best path toward reestablishing America as a nation of prosperity and opportunity.

We are not so naïve as to posit that our country today could be efficiently governed by our eighteenth century government. Rather, our position is that the principles best suited to serve as the foundation of our political system remain the same. Unfortunately, they have fallen victim to a systematic process of erosion, which has been marked by a vast expansion of the domain of government. This continuing trend has become accepted by the bulk of our country's populace as a natural evolution, a sentiment that is as false as it is dangerous. The expanding province of government necessarily yields a reduction in the rights of individuals, for politics in this sense is truly a zero-sum game. Consider as a simple example the case of taxation: every dollar paid in taxes results in a dollar that cannot be spent as the individual taxpayer sees fit. This zero-sum concept marks the struggle for all political rights. As the government's role expands, it deprives individuals of their right to make decisions for themselves. Sadly, this trend robs our society of many of its greatest assets – creativity, innovation, and individual determination – those elements of the human spirit which, when unencumbered by government interference, propelled our nation to greatness.

We recognize that in any nation in which power originates with the people, government policies and priorities will change as political winds blow and public opinion shifts. With this we have no quarrel. In fact, we hold it up as a testament to the responsiveness of our particular brand of republican government. But the set of principles upon which our nation was founded has been cast aside, and our original system of government has been transformed into a complex behemoth, heavily involved in formerly private areas of life. This fact has made it virtually unrecognizable in comparison with its original form. Our current system allows for – and indeed facilitates – government intrusion into homes, schools, businesses, and places of worship. Within just a few generations, Americans have seen the limited federal government envisioned by Madison assume the roles of mass employer, public contractor, commercial bank, financial investor, farmer, industrialist, retirement advisor, healthcare provider, spiritual leader, and parent. None of these are enumerated in the Constitution.

America today faces many challenges: our economy has plunged into a recession; our military is in the midst of protracted conflicts in faraway lands; the threat of terrorism is as acute as ever; our social security system is on the brink of collapse; and we consistently increase spending on healthcare and education, only to watch both programs become less competitive with those of other countries. And this list is far from complete. We are at a critical juncture that requires an honest, open discussion about the best direction for our country. We sincerely hope that this book helps to spur dialog and bring about such a discussion. We fear continued movement toward a point where habit dictates that we look to the government for solutions to an ever widening range of problems. We believe that it is time to halt this trend and rejuvenate our political system by reapplying the principles and the virtues upon which our country was founded.

This, then, is the heart of our big idea. Our philosophy proudly proclaims that the only right and proper function of our government is to secure, promote, and protect the individual liberties of its citizens. We firmly believe that any philosophy which repudiates the primacy of the individual in favor of the tyranny of the collective will inevitably obstruct our nation's progress. We abhor any such philosophical restriction of our potential, both as a society and as free, American individuals. In our country today, too many government actions are seemingly based on the premise that each American cannot be trusted to exercise rights on his or her own. Our argument refutes this notion and claims just the opposite. We submit that individual rights are to be protected, that they are too sacred to belong within the province of government. This is the concept and moral value that we hold dear: that a government guided by the sole purpose of protecting individual freedoms is both morally superior to other forms of government, and also stewards over a more prosperous, diverse, and happy society than can be achieved under a government guided by any other principle. This compendium of essays seeks to paint a picture of a society where the philosophy we espouse guides government's policymaking. We seek to create a vision of a society that enjoys the many blessings of individual liberty. This is the essence of our conservatism.

In working to effect a restoration of conservative principles, we face an undeniably difficult task. Government expansion is by nature self-propagating. It is the product of the emergence of the belief, among citizens and intellectuals alike, that a better life for the American community lies just beyond the government's current reach. Failure to solve our country's problems with government programs leads to calls for bigger programs with greater reach and larger budgets. However, once a person is forced to abrogate any individual freedom to the government, it is a freedom he will rarely get back. At some point the realization of this fact must lead Americans to accept that a government response to each problem we face may not provide the solutions we truly need. There must be a restoration of the fundamental faith in man that led our founders to hold up the idea of individual liberty with such reverence that it formed the very core of our nation's birth and development. We've compiled this collection of essays in the hopes that we may play even the smallest role in returning to the individual those rights that have been stripped from him and taken by the government.

Each of the essays that follow applies the tenets of our conservatism to a specific policy area. As a diverse group of young Americans with a wide variety of backgrounds, our writers proudly acknowledge that the only attribute shared across our ranks is a deep faith and abiding adherence to conservative principles. This fact underlies our confidence that conservatism is the best philosophical fit for a population as diverse as America's. We sincerely hope that this book contributes to a better public understanding of the principles we espouse. These essays serve as a collective statement of our willingness and our intention to stand up to the destructive movement toward larger government and further disintegration of individual freedom. We bring to this endeavor pride in America, hope for a bright future, and the energy that abounds in a country where an optimistic group of young men and women can take a stand such as ours.

I. LIBERTY AND JUSTICE FOR ALL:
Judicial Philosophy and Representative Government
by Chris Tiedeman

"I intend to go right on appointing highly qualified individuals of the highest personal integrity to the bench, individuals who understand the danger of short-circuiting the electoral process and disenfranchising the people through judicial activism."

- President Ronald Reagan.

"We therefore have a clear question about which institution, a legislature or a court, is relatively more competent to deal with an emerging issue as to which facts currently unknown could be dispositive. The answer has to be, for the reasons already stated, that the legislative process is to be preferred..."

- Justice David Souter in *Washington v. Glucksberg*

Reinventing the Right seeks to serve as a timeless expression of our nation's values while also providing a contemporarily relevant discussion of the direction of liberty in America. This book strives to explain why the Twitter generation should support the application of conservative principles to the problems our society faces. This particular essay discusses the judiciary – how and under what lens laws affecting faith, free markets, and a strong national defense are judged. It offers an alternative to the current judicial paradigm where standards are all too often ephemeral and the courts are all too seldom held to task. While canons of statutory interpretation and sentencing guidelines may not drive voters the way that social justice, war, or abortion do, the method by which the judiciary examines each of the other topics in this book may have a more lasting and profound effect on those issues than the legislative debate that codifies the public policy in the first place.

Frequently, a discussion of judicial philosophy immediately leads down the path toward topics of abortion, gay marriage, or other "hot-button" social issues. As such, it is nearly impossible to utilize high profile US and state Supreme Court decisions to motivate an intellectually honest discussion on the significance of judicial philosophy to concepts such as liberty, or the benefits of conservatism to our generation. These hot-button issues are critically important and are addressed in the other essays in this book. But because of the passions they inflame, these decisions can cloud an honest and dispassionate debate on the judiciary. Sadly, such issue-based politicization has made the judiciary's function itself clouded and less dispassionate. My hope with this essay is to articulate a judicial philosophy based on principles by addressing the judiciary outside of the context of most controversial political issues that seem to lead people only to political conclusions.

The Founders demonstrated immense foresight and wisdom by establishing the judiciary as the third branch of our government, equal to the legislators who make laws and the executives who enforce them. The role of this co-equal branch of government is to render judgments when laws are broken or when good-faith legal conflicts arise between members of our society. In many of this book's chapters, authors may question whether or not government should have any role at all in a particular public policy area. Such an argument clearly has no place here. A "public" judiciary is a critical, perhaps inherent, function of any government that promises to safeguard the rights of its people.

Our founding fathers had a particular conception of the American judicial branch. Alexander Hamilton argued for a judiciary with a limited mandate in Federalist 78:

> *Whoever attentively considers the different departments of power must perceive, that, in a government in which they are separated from each other, the judiciary, from the nature of its functions, will always be the least dangerous to the political rights of the Constitution; because it will be least in a capacity to annoy or injure them. The Executive not only dispenses the honors, but holds the sword of the community.*

The legislature not only commands the purse, but prescribes the rules by which the duties and rights of every citizen are to be regulated. The judiciary...may truly be said to have neither FORCE nor WILL, but merely judgment; and must ultimately depend upon the aid of the executive arm even for the efficacy of its judgments.

Starting from this perspective, the important question for those who believe in individual liberty and free markets is not whether the government should provide for a judiciary, but rather what that judiciary should properly judge. A judiciary limited to its intended functions provides a critical defense of individual liberty and free markets, concepts espoused throughout this book. Such a restrained judiciary can mean the difference between the protection and the banning of religious and political expression. It can mean the difference between the confidence of individuals and businesses in their rights as property owners, or the fear of confiscation at the whim of government. It can mean either a fundamental respect or court imposed disregard for contractual agreements. And it can mean the difference between a society in which citizens feel safe from any threat, and one in which the government itself is a threat to the people.

The philosophy that a judge takes to the bench is not an issue that drives the politics of a generation. Perhaps this is because when many of us were young, we generally held a matter-of-fact view of what a judge *is*. This view has informed our broader belief of what the judiciary *should be*. It is as black and white as the robes and shirts most judges wear. The role of a judge is precisely the role that Hamilton outlined: to plainly and simply make judgments. And they are to do so based on what the law is, not based on what they wish the law to be. Even Justice Souter, known for his judicial activism, acknowledges that "the legislative process is to be preferred" for determining the contents of a nation's laws. The reasons for this preference are extensive and important and will be addressed. But judicial philosophy only deserves the attention it gets here because of the existence of a differing school of thought, that the legislative process is not to be preferred, and perhaps should be supplanted or ignored.

The alternate theory is the philosophy of judicial activism – that judges should seek to use their rulings to craft public policy. But under our form

3

of government, the legislative process is very clearly designated as the mechanism by which public policy is crafted. If Americans on the political left believe the courts should make policy, then they need to be prepared for the opposite effect – for politically conservative judges to strike down liberal laws with which they don't agree. The same is true for conservatives who believe the courts should make rulings which would effectively alter our laws. Accepting such judicial activism requires the corresponding acceptance that legitimately passed laws of a conservative nature will be thrown out by liberal judges. (For the sake of clarity, I should note that a politically conservative judge is not necessarily the same as a judge who has a conservative judicial philosophy, as I will explain later).

What's more, unless you truly believe in the omnipotent judiciary implied by the theory of judicial activism, a conservative judicial philosophy should seem especially critical if your policy views are contrary to every one of those expressed in this book. Otherwise, with judicial activists on the bench, your policy views can be deconstructed by the courts as quickly as they were erected – with no deference to the legislative process or repercussions for the jurists. In other words, if you believe that judges are the ultimate arbiters, unconstrained by a sense of duty to consider only what the law is rather than what they wish the law to be, you had better be prepared to accept the striking down of your own priority policies by the courts.

We live in a hyper-political environment, made more so by the advent of the Internet, the 24-hour news cycle, and social media platforms. The descendants of America's revolutionary pamphleteers have a virtual megaphone today because of Facebook, Twitter, LinkedIn, and the endless array of blogs. The starry-eyed philosopher can be published because economies of scale now allow for it. There might be a kneejerk negative reaction to the term "hyper-political," but I use the term to describe a positive development in American democracy. At the risk of spewing a series of clichés, the only thing better than free and open speech in political discourse is freer and more open speech. Information is power, and we live in a country where the lack of access to sufficient information has been reduced as a roadblock to individuals' developing their own political beliefs. Rather, the primary obstacle is sifting through and managing the exponentially growing quantities of information readily available. In short, in today's political debate, even the voiceless have a voice. Today more so than at any time in history, the winning argument will be that which is presented and debated most effectively.

Because of the ubiquity of information, it is more likely than ever that the legislative process will reflect the will of the electorate. Regardless of your political leanings, the side that has its legislative priorities enacted into law should rightly be concerned that its legislative successes might be overturned by an unaccountable judiciary for no other reason than that the judges happen to favor a different outcome. In this context, such a judgment is a blow not just to a particular policy initiative, but to the very concept of a legislative process.

We live in a new world where ideas are exchanged and debated at the speed of light. In these pages, you are reading about a diverse set of issues like energy, taxes, national security, healthcare, freedom of speech, and national defense. All of these issues will be debated extensively in the context of our political campaigns, as well as in the virtual cloud of the blogosphere, twitterverse, and on innumerable Facebook pages. The hope is that the free and open exchange of ideas will lead not only our policymakers, but the citizenry generally, to the best possible policy prescription on these issues and others.

Whether we get to the "best policy" through that debate or not is irrelevant, however, if an unelected, unaccountable group of judges simply select a different prescription (within the limits of pre-established constitutional protections, which we should be equally nervous can be set aside unilaterally). It is the fear of our voices being silenced and our rights being stripped that requires this book to include an essay on conservative judicial philosophy. Such a philosophy is essential to maintaining the sanctity of our unalienable rights, upon which our free society is based, and on which all of the other issues, regardless of your political ideology, depend.

Whether you are pro-life or pro-choice, you had better ultimately believe in a conservative judicial philosophy. Whether you believe in relying on market mechanisms to protect our environment or you believe we need command and control regulations, fines, and taxes, you had ultimately better believe in a conservative judicial philosophy. Whether you believe in low taxes or the redistribution of wealth, you had ultimately better believe in a conservative judicial philosophy.

The Constitution penned by our forefathers is imperfect, as are the laws passed by our legislators and executed by our governors and presidents. Both consist of mere words that are subject to interpretation and misunderstanding. Wording can be crafted sloppily or filled with vagaries and inconsistencies. And words can be deliberately twisted and spun to arrive at meanings far different from their intent when originally drafted.

In response to this characteristic of the law, the subject of statutory interpretation and construction has developed into an entire field of study. Many first year law students take classes in statutory construction on top of traditional courses such as torts, contracts, property, and criminal law. Over time, a list of rules, or canons, has developed to define different ways for judges to interpret both the Constitution and individual laws. Volumes have been written on these canons, which can be split into three broad categories. Textual canons have been designed with the goal of helping one understand the actual text of laws; again, words are only as perfect as those flawed individuals who draft them. Substantive canons have developed over time to interpret language to attain certain policy goals. And canons of deference have evolved to lead one to interpret a statute in a way that does not violate a higher level of law – the Constitution, for example.

The problem with statutory construction as a field of study is that a moral equivalence has emerged between differing views of statutory interpretation. Textual canons based on interpreting the actual meaning of the words have become one of a menu of options by which law students are taught to interpret laws. Substantive canons are supposed to guide us towards an interpretation based on social values or specific policy goals, which may lie outside of how the statute or constitutional provision actually reads. These substantive cannons remove certainty and specificity from the judiciary's role. In short, they open the door to activism and close the door on accountability. Our judiciary is effective only when it is blind and dispassionate, as intended by our founders, so all parties are treated fairly and justly. Allowing for interpretations that subjugate justice to the policy goals of judges necessarily creates a judiciary that arbitrarily takes sides. This, by definition, is not just.

I wrote earlier that there is an innate understanding that the job of a judge is to do just that: judge. John Roberts, Chief Justice of the US

Supreme Court, has likened a judge to an umpire calling balls and strikes. That is, judges should make judgments based on what the law is, not what they wish the law to be. It would not make much sense for different umpires to apply wildly different strike zones or for one umpire to have different strike zones for each batter based upon personal preference. In much the same way, our laws are drafted for the citizens to follow and for judges to judge impartially and dispassionately with regard to the policy implications of the law itself. Regardless of one's political views, the belief that a judge should deviate from the content of the law in making judgments is contrary to our natural view of the role of judges and must be reigned in. In many ways, the development of the field of statutory interpretation has done nothing more than to create a menu of justifications for judgments that disregard "what the law is."

Our legislative bodies are designed to be deliberative and reach policy-oriented objectives. Shouldn't there be an expectation that the statutes created through such a process will be interpreted as they read?

The counter-argument, of course, is that if the individuals who make laws and the words that they use are both flawed, then the laws they create may very likely be flawed as well. These flaws, it is argued, require corrective action by the courts. The problem that arises is that an expectation of judicial review to achieve a policy objective has created a significant moral hazard in the legislative process. Laws are not necessarily flawed and in need of judicial correction simply because lawmakers are flawed. In fact, the opposite is just as likely true: that the anticipation of judicial activism has resulted in more and more laws that are flawed from the start.

Judges who adhere to substantive canons use their position on the bench to morph a statute according to their personal preference, regardless of the original language of the law. This creates a strong disincentive for legislators to utilize clear and concise language as they craft policy. After all, recent history suggests that the courts will apply a law as they see fit, regardless of how well the legislature articulates its true intent. This book is written by individuals who believe in liberty and the inherent benefits of free markets. There is an expectation that if policymakers who hold similar values win election, they will craft legislation that comports with the values they espoused to get elected. I assume the expectation on the left is similar.

Equally important to crafting legislation that comports with our values is doing so in a way that clearly and concisely defines what the law is to do and how it is to be applied. Elected officials should consider themselves bound by our democratic process to craft legislation that articulates specific rules and guidelines. Knowing in advance that, ultimately, an unelected body may interpret the legislation as it sees fit has created a perverse incentive to legislate themes rather than specific policy prescriptions. Unfortunately, this naturally leads toward a greater need for a menu of interpretive tools, which creates a greater incentive for sloppy and vague construction. The solution to this problem is to ensure that no matter who wins election, the laws they craft will be applied by the courts faithfully, as written.

In 2007, Minnesota's legislature passed the "Freedom to Breathe Act," which placed a ban on smoking in places of business, including bars and restaurants. Within the law, they placed a vaguely written exception for "theatrical performances" that has since been the subject of controversy and litigation. Bars and restaurants allowed for what they considered "theatrical performances" among their patrons. They then allowed the patrons to smoke cigarettes in the establishment based on the exception explicitly crafted into the law. On July 14th, 2009, a Minnesota Appeals Court upheld an earlier District Court ruling that found a bar owner guilty of allowing smoking in a public place, a petty misdemeanor that carried a $300 fine. The bar in question and other bars around the state of Minnesota had been staging "Theater Nights," in which they allowed patrons to smoke.[1] The law reads:

> *"Sections 144.414 to 144.417 do not prohibit smoking by actors and actresses as part of a theatrical performance conducted in compliance with section 366.01. Notice of smoking in a performance shall be given to theater patrons in advance and shall be included in performance programs."*

Bars followed these provisions as written and allowed for smoking by "actors" in the performance. "Theater Nights" were theme nights established by the bar owners in which patrons acted in amateur theatrical productions. This allowed patrons to smoke in the establishment while complying with the language of the law. Clearly, this statute was sloppily written, leaving it open to the whims of the judge. There is no legal definition of "theatrical performance," and the court seemingly did not feel compelled to provide one. Since art exists in the eye of the artist and without a specific definition of theatrical performance, what expertise did the judge have to say what was theater and what was not? Some have argued this was simply a clever way for bar owners to avoid legislation affecting their places of business. But whether or not this is the case is inconsequential in a world where judges are allowed to be policymakers, because citizens cannot expect legislative certainty anyway.

In this situation, essentially unaccountable judges arbitrarily decided what they thought a theatrical performance to be. If we believe this to be an acceptable ruling, consistency dictates that we accept other arbitrary definitions based on the whim or wish of whoever happens to be behind the bench. A better alternative would have been to rule the statute unenforceable and ask the legislature to rewrite the law. Or, the judge could have allowed these establishments' "theatrical performances" to proceed and thereby avoided making an arbitrary and capricious ruling.

The movement from a judiciary focused on what the law is toward a judiciary more concerned with deciding what the law should be has, unfortunately, politicized this decidedly non-political branch of government. While the judiciary is part of government, it is supposed to be separate and not influenced by politics. Such influence strips all parties that come before a court of their chance to obtain a just result.

How judges are selected has also become a political hot-button issue. I don't intend to take a specific position in this essay on the subject of whether the judiciary should be elected, appointed, or selected by some hybrid of the two. Such a topic could easily be the subject of a separate, lengthy essay. Suffice it to say that an election of judges, in and of itself, does not necessarily lead to politicization of the judiciary in the traditional sense of the word. Nor does the pure appointment of judges by elected individuals shield the judiciary from politicization.

If a judge adjudicates cases based on what the law is, rather than the political outcome a differing interpretation of the law might achieve, his work becomes necessarily apolitical. This is true regardless of how he might have attained his position. But over time, more and more judges have sought to adjudicate specific political outcomes based on what they wish a law to be. This naturally has resulted in a politicized judiciary where a judge's political beliefs affect the decisions he or she makes. This is where we find ourselves today.

Such a politicized judiciary has given birth to an extensive debate on the method of selecting judges, distracting lawmakers from important discussions of tax policy, the environment, healthcare, public safety, or national defense. Advocates of judicial appointment cite expensive elections and the worrisome prospect of judges' accepting endorsements from interest groups and political parties. In Missouri, general elections have been replaced by "retention elections." Under this system, judges are initially appointed. At the end of their term, the question posed to Missourians is, "shall Judge X be retained?" If the citizens vote yes, the judge remains on the bench. If voters believe the judge has not lived up to their expectations, the judge is voted out of office. When the judicial branch co-opts the role of policymaker, close scrutiny of the politics of a particular judicial candidate is required. But some get the issue exactly backwards and proclaim that any close examination of our judges' political beliefs is itself the cause of the politicization of the courts.

In 2005, then Appeals Court Judge Sonia Sotomayor said, "a court of appeals is where policy is made."[2] According to the Associated Press, because she was aware that she was on tape, Judge Sotomayor quickly added, "I should never say that *because we don't make law*." Judge Sotomayor was later selected by President Barack Obama and confirmed by the US Senate to fill a spot on the Supreme Court. Is it any wonder that judges face aggressive electoral challenges when even those considered qualified to serve on the Supreme Court of the United States hold a view that they are there to decide what the law should be, rather than interpret what the law is? In this situation, did the politicization of the judiciary occur when the judge herself said she believed it was her job to reach a political conclusion? Or did the politicization occur when people reacted to those statements, questioning her fitness to serve as a dispassionate arbiter of the law? It is clear that America's judiciary has been politicized by those very judges who believe our courts are "where policy is made."

A growing number of judges believe that it is perfectly acceptable to use the bench to advance personal policy positions. Conservatives might question a liberal's fitness to serve on the court not because that person holds liberal beliefs but because, in our politicized judiciary, those beliefs actually affect how a judge applies the law. With a politicized courts system, ensuring that a judge's politics conform to the legislature's own politics is *necessary* to ensuring that laws are applied as intended. This is the nature of the judiciary's politicization and has drawn the ire of many conservatives. The result of this has been a significant backlash against of those in the judiciary who would be policymakers.

It should come as no more of a surprise that a movement against a political judiciary has developed than if fans and players protested a big league umpire who decided to make his strike zone larger than that established by the game's rules. Yet as that movement against a political judiciary has evolved, many in the legal establishment have questioned both the movement itself and the motives of those who advocate for a judiciary that judges rather than one that makes policy. But their arguments are marked by hypocrisy, as they use our commonsense perspective of a judge's responsibility to argue that politics should play no role in judicial appointments, while simultaneously advancing the notion that politics *should* inform judicial rulings. Holding both beliefs is both nonsensical and intellectually dishonest.

The politicization of the judiciary has taken two significant forms. First, policymakers have sought to limit citizen involvement in campaigns where states have established the election of judges. Secondly, the nomination process for Senatorial candidates has seen an elevated priority given to how the candidate would vote on judicial nominees.[*]

In areas where state and local judges stand for election, there has been a significant increase in passionate campaigns to elect judges. Both advocates and opponents of our conservative judicial philosophy are playing a larger role in judicial campaigns than at any time in history.

A recently decided US Supreme Court case demonstrates the contentious nature of judicial elections. The court's narrowly structured opinion required that a state supreme court judge recuse himself in a case where one of the parties had contributed $3 million to his election effort (*Caperton v. A.T. Massey Coal Company, US Supreme Court 2009*). Legal thriller author

---

[*] This is because Senators are charged with confirming or blocking the President's judicial appointments.

John Grisham addressed this same issue of judicial campaigns in his 2008 novel, "The Appeal." And in Minnesota in 2002, a rule that had blocked judicial candidates from accepting certain endorsements or discussing judicial philosophy during their elections was overturned (*Republican Party v. White, US Supreme Court 2002*). These examples are provided not to take a position on the merits of judicial elections, but to highlight that they exist and have become a very important part of the political debate. State legislative and (perhaps ironically) judicial branches around the country are addressing "the issue" of judicial elections. Policies are being proposed and implemented to limit and regulate how candidates and citizens express their views in these elections.

Federally appointed judges and justices have not escaped the political environment that has grown out of the increasingly prevalent theory that judges are policymakers. While they don't stand for election, the appointment process has grown into a media spectacle. The US Senate is charged with confirming federal district court, appeals court, and Supreme Court judges and justices. Many senatorial candidates find themselves spending significant time addressing how they will vote on judicial confirmations during their own election bids. Judicial philosophy is becoming an increasingly important issue for candidates who seek both legislative and executive office. These candidates for executive and legislative office stand to develop the laws that the judiciary is charged with applying. One would think that candidates for such jobs, regardless of their politics, would support a judiciary that makes rulings based on what the law is, not based on what it wishes the law to be. Sadly, this is not always the case.

An expectation has emerged, most prominently among the political left, that candidates will support judges who pursue policy goals from their positions on the bench. The nomination of a federal judge is an immensely important process and we should demand that our policymakers examine the judicial temperament and philosophy of those who stand to be given lifetime tenure. But judicial confirmations have taken on a decidedly political tone, and often take a significant amount of time that could be devoted to more salient issues. As the judiciary has been increasingly politicized by judges who seek to be policymakers, the nomination process itself has become increasingly political. And if judicial activism is the accepted judicial philosophy of the day, then it is only right that the confirmations have become politicized.

In order to guarantee the judiciary's ability to continue in its critical role of safeguarding our rights, we must seek a means to diminish the politicization of judicial elections, state judicial appointments, and the nomination process for federal judges. Intellectual honesty requires that we acknowledge that any effective method of doing so will include a curtailment of the growing trend of appointing judges who believe their role exceeds that intended by our nation's founders.

In contrast to the modest branch that Hamilton envisioned, the judiciary's power has grown over the years exactly because some judges are willing to utilize the courts as "a place where policy is made." In the case of an elected legislature (where policy is *supposed* to be made), legislators have a clear voting record and must stand for election on a regular basis. This allows legislators' performance to be assessed based on the policies they advance. The judiciary is far less accountable, it is under significantly less scrutiny, and the actions of a judge are often not as clear as those of a legislator who must vote yea or nay on a specific issue of public policy. In many ways, this is a good thing. The role of the judiciary is inherently analytical and requires an intellectual process that should exceed comparably simplistic legislative mechanisms. Again, as Justice Souter said, *"The answer has to be, for the reasons already stated, that the legislative process is to be preferred."* However, when the judiciary consists of individuals who believe that the courts provide a better means of creating policy, the lack of scrutiny and accountability presents a much more serious concern than if our judges were simply "calling balls and strikes."

As I wrote earlier, political conservatism and a conservative view of the judiciary are not one and the same. That said, most conservatives would opt for a judiciary that "calls balls and strikes" rather than a judiciary that believes "the court of appeals is where policy is made." Most conservatives would support such a system even if a particular decision it enables does not advance a politically conservative end. This is because our judicial philosophy fundamentally affirms the freedom of the populace to determine society's organization while an activist philosophy inherently infringes on the will of the people and places individual freedoms in the hands of unaccountable, omnipotent jurists.

The same cannot easily be said about today's political left. More and more, liberals have trended toward utilizing the courts as a policymaking mechanism. This is perhaps a function of America's generally conservative government relative to the rest of the world, even when the balance of power swings to the left. Leftist support for activist judges is demonstrably true based on the trend toward pushing a policymaking judiciary as a political issue in liberal-leaning political primaries.

Whether we are looking at the judiciary in the context of criminal law, civil law, or the defense of constitutionally guaranteed liberties, this should be concerning. Our legislatures write criminal codes to protect citizens' liberties from infringement by other people. This is the context in which laws against murder, rape, robbery, and a laundry list of other crimes have been developed. Judges, in these instances, are supposed to apply criminal statutes defined by the legislatures, while defending all parties' constitutionally protected liberties. Judges who do not apply laws as written risk failing to protect innocent citizens from criminals. And they risk incentivizing criminal behavior by creating uncertainty about the application of our laws. If criminal punishments go beyond what a judge personally believes should apply to certain crimes, the legislative mechanism is the appropriate one to fix this problem.* Judges in these cases are better suited to run for the legislature than they are to be members of the judiciary.

Likewise, our civil law system exists to resolve good-faith disputes between parties. This system is where contracts between parties are enforced, property rights are protected, certainty in commercial transactions is guaranteed by rules, and civil sanctions are established to protect us from harm that might result outside of the criminal context. This system is wrought with abuse by judges who refuse to apply the law openly and evenly, preferring instead to pursue goals by using their power in ways that vastly exceed the proper limits of their responsibilities.

For example, if asked to choose between paying for a product or receiving it for free, any rational person would prefer the latter option. However,

---

* This is true as long as the criminal punishments in question do not violate constitutional principles. If they do, then the judiciary is the appropriate institution to correct the injustice. This is an application of the "hierarchical canon" mentioned earlier – a legislature cannot create law that violates a higher classification of law (in this case, the Constitution). If it does, the courts should strike it down but the justification for such a ruling is not the whim of the judge. Rather, it is the existence of a higher level of law that takes precedence.

in our society, we expect that if one goes out to eat, goes to a movie, or shops for a car, there should be a cost. In California, a group of consumers saw it differently. They denied the right of their wireless phone carriers to charge fees for early termination of service contracts, despite the fact that they had signed agreements consenting to the charges. Most wireless carriers argue that because they subsidize the cost of wireless devices for consumers, they need to charge a fee should the customer leave for a different carrier before the contract period expires. As such, acceptance of a service contract allows consumers to pay less for phones. Early termination fees may raise passions with people who would rather not pay them, just as the cost of a movie ticket might anger someone who would prefer to go to the movie for free. But the fact remains that consumers are easily able to avoid these fees simply by choosing not to sign a contract with a carrier who charges them, using a traditional wire line, or utilizing a prepaid phone service. Ignoring the terms of the contract freely entered into by both parties, a judge ruled in 2008 that the mutually agreed upon fees are not legal.[3] The judge further decided that one carrier must repay $18.2 million to consumers in collected fees.

We can have differing feelings regarding the cost of any particular product or service. The "public policy" of prohibiting early termination fee agreements provides a glaring example of egregious judicial overreach. Even if such a restriction of corporate and individual freedom were justifiable (which it is not), the legislative branch, not the judiciary, is the institution that should codify it. Imagine a situation in which a judge ruled it illegal for sculpture to be sold for a profit (recall earlier I wrote about judges ruling on "theatrical performances," if the example seems absurd), or that it is illegal to charge for the installation of solar panels. This is the slippery slope on which we tread when we allow the whim of the judge to subvert the traditional role of our courts. We risk undermining the very system of private property and individual liberty that have made possible America's rise to the pinnacle of economic, political, and cultural success.

Websites such as stupidwarningssite.com mock the consequences society faces because of a fundamental disrespect for the role of the judiciary. A warning placed on an iPod shuffle to protect from liability reads, "do not eat." On an iron, a cautionary label reads, "do not iron while clothes are on body." These are placed on products at a cost to consumers because of a judiciary run amok. Perhaps the penultimate example of a judiciary run amok comes not from a ruling, but from a lawsuit filed by a judge himself. A Washington DC Administrative Law Judge sued his drycleaner for $54 million because they lost his pants.[4]

While the DC judge lost the case, it is supremely indicative of the problems we face that such a frivolous suit would have been filed in the first place by someone who should have a far higher respect for the proper role of the judiciary. We might laugh at ridiculous warning labels, and anecdotes about frivolous lawsuits can be hysterical. But as long as we allow a critical function of government to be transformed into a caricature that completely undermines the intent of our founders, we pay the price in the form of lost liberty, decreased safety, and foregone prosperity.

Ongoing developments in technology make for an increasingly hyper-political environment in which political messages can be communicated to the masses at the speed of light. In political and legislative campaigns, even the voiceless now have a voice. Blogs, social networking sites, and technology yet to come have created an environment where information is nearly perfect (not perfect in the sense that all information is always correct, but perfect in the sense that an evaluation of the plethora of evidence can help us arrive at a correct and informed answer). The resulting empowerment of the citizenry has created widespread enthusiasm and participation in both the political and policy debates.

Conservatives have always been advocates for the type of judiciary that citizens viscerally understand and naturally expect. One doesn't need to be taught that a judge's job is to "call balls and strikes," because that is the role by definition: a judge should judge. Unfortunately, too many politicians, many of whom are found on the left, have recognized the political advantage of the judiciary as a public policy ally. An entire field of study has developed in our law schools to provide the justification necessary for judges to become policymakers who advance agendas that fail to garner either legislative or popular support.

But, deep down, even archetypes of judicial activism know and understand the correct function of the courts. Justice Souter was one of the leading activist liberals on the court. Yet when evaluating the role of the judiciary in one of his judicial opinions, Souter wrote, "We therefore have a clear question about which institution, a legislature or a court, is relatively more competent to deal with an emerging issue as to which facts currently unknown could be dispositive. The answer has to be, for the reasons already stated, that the legislative process is to be preferred…" And Justice Sotomayor qualified her statement that appeals courts are where policy is made by saying, "I shouldn't say that because we don't make law." She understands the intended role of the American judiciary, even if she does not feel bound by it in her career as a jurist.

It is time that we require our judges to do more than simply pay lip service to the sacrosanct role of our constitutionally defined courts system. It is time that we demand that these judges and others act accordingly in their roles as arbiters and guarantors of Americans' rights.

Today, unprecedented access to information and a citizenry that is engaged in the political process mean that election results and the legislation that follows is more likely than ever before to be the result of real debate and popular sentiment. But judiciary examination of each of the other topics in this book may have a more lasting and profound effect on those issues than the legislative debate that codifies the public policy in the first place. Activists of all political stripes should be able to count on a court system where well debated legislative activities are not overturned by an unaccountable judiciary. Those who advocate for a policymaking judiciary should be cautious lest they get that for which they wish.

We can all learn a history lesson from President Ronald Reagan on judicial philosophy and its importance as a foundational and driving principle. He understood the way we all inherently do, that judicial activism poses a real danger of short-circuiting the electoral process and disenfranchising the people. Our hope is that this same philosophy will help engage a generation of powerful voices armed with Twitter, Facebook, and other technologies yet to be developed. Now more than ever, we are armed to demand a judiciary limited to calling "balls and strikes." Now more than ever, we can protect our electoral process from being short-circuited and our voices from being silenced.

Chris Tiedeman is a principal with Weber Johnson Public Affairs, a general public affairs and political consulting firm headquartered in St. Paul, MN. His extensive experience includes providing public affairs, legal and political guidance to a wide range of clients, from major companies, to prominent national public figures and international political parties. Prior to his current position, Chris served as the Director of Government Affairs at the Center of the American Experiment, a Minnesota-based free market think tank. Chris received his BA from St. Olaf College and his JD from the University of Minnesota Law School.

II. PERMISSION TO SPEAK FREELY:
The First Amendment as the Cornerstone of American Democracy
by Christian Camerota

Conservatism needs to be rearticulated for a new generation. To accomplish this effectively, it is important not to seek a return to the past but to pursue a vision for the future, a vision built on the values whose primacy history has evinced. The right to free speech is arguably the most recognized pillar of freedom in America; it is the foundation of every democratic nation and a requirement for any society intent on pursuing truth. Democracy, after all, is about self-governance and demands that its populace elect, monitor, and replace its representatives as it deems necessary. In such a society, the value of information is paramount because information empowers a citizenry to assess its government and ensure it remains accountable and effective. As a nation, then, it is vital that we maintain our freedom of speech precisely because of the critical role it plays in allowing our democracy to flourish.

In their book, *The Elements of Journalism*, Bill Kovach and Tom Rosenstiel write, simply, "information created democracy."[1] They continue by saying, "...history reveals an important trend. The more democratic the society, the more news and information it tends to have."[2] This observation forms the basis of this essay's central theme: governance of the people, by the people, and for the people is predicated upon a citizenry's ability to freely exchange information and opinion. The freedom of our speech, not coincidentally protected by the very first amendment of our Constitution, is what makes this governance possible. The open exchange of information that results from this freedom allows well-crafted government policies to be enacted that reflect the aggregate will of America's diverse population. In this way, free speech enables effective self-governance.

A failure to clearly define this right, however, can easily result in a dangerously superficial understanding of it and a subsequent loss of its potency. When misunderstood, it may even *inhibit* effective self-governance. So what does "free speech" mean in contemporary America? The First Amendment does not place the onus on government to provide a platform for citizens to voice their opinions. It does not demand or deem that every opinion is equally valid. It does not mean that private institutions can be prohibited from restricting the speech of their members. Rather, it guarantees that individuals not be forcibly prevented from expressing their opinions, while also requiring that they provide for themselves the platform to advance the positions they espouse. Finally, the First Amendment should prevent the government from restricting individuals from utilizing their own money and property to advance causes they see fit. Collectively, these ideas represent the most critical components of the constitutional right to free speech, a right that is no less important to the maintenance of democracy today than it was at our nation's founding.

Having defined the right to free speech in these terms, it should be clear that the spirit of this principle transcends time. The challenge appears when it is subjected to the pressures of a complex and rapidly changing world, as it has been many times in the past and will continue to be as our society progresses. Contemporary discussions of free speech include everything from pornography to political contributions. With the advent of the Internet, even the most common means of exercising this right continue to evolve, from public protests that no longer take place in the public square but on Facebook, to the application of libel laws in the blogosphere. But the most significant impact that the Internet's rise has had on free speech can be seen in the state of our nation's press.

A free press provides the most visible example of the First Amendment in action. Over the course of history, the press has assumed the role of finding, vetting, and publishing facts for public consumption. The press is undoubtedly a collection of businesses intent on making money. Yet it is this need to satisfy consumers that encourages news outlets to strive to disseminate concrete information upon which readers, viewers, and listeners can base their opinions and move to action. Over time, however, this noble mission has been complicated by external pressures, both monetary and ideological. Disciplines like public relations, marketing, and advertising often occlude or muddle truth and infuse it with biases, ulterior motives, and sensationalism. While the press has always been required to strike a balance between reporting facts and entertaining its audience, it often seems that today entertainment trumps reporting. Some lament this fact, yet the continued popularity of Bill O'Reilly and Keith Olberman suggests that many people want some editorializing in their newscasts. Seen in this light, many changes in the nature of "the news" – whether in paper, television, or electronic format – are in response to market pressures and the rapid technological progress we have seen over the past few decades. The key to the press's enduring success lies in the hands of the people; throughout history, if they felt their needs for information were not being met, they invented new methods for obtaining and providing it. In effect, this is democracy at its best: an informed citizenry acting to ensure its needs and desires continue to bet met.

The proliferation of the Internet, concurrently, has challenged the dominance of traditional news organizations, which face unprecedented market pressures from web-based news sources and aggregators. In the name of truth and transparency, this is largely a good thing since people enjoy greater access to information than ever before. Yet, many lament the changes taking place, clinging to a nostalgic view of the Sunday morning newspaper and the evening network newscast. They clamor for government intervention to ensure that these institutions, long America's most prominent defenders and guarantors of democracy, be saved through subsidization. The problem these voices fail to recognize is that government assumption of particular pieces of the media would inevitably compromise the autonomy and objectivity that make these organizations so useful in the first place.

Richard Perez-Pena, in an article entitled *Websites that Dig for News Rise As Watchdogs*, writes about contemporary journalism that, "information is now a public service as much as it's a commodity. It should be thought of the same as education, healthcare."[3] But consider the current state of these other public services. It is no coincidence that as healthcare and education become increasingly intertwined in a large governmental network, they also become increasingly ineffective, weighed down by enormous costs and stultifying webs of bureaucracy run amok. Maintaining efficiency in government is one of the chief tenets of conservative thought, largely because as government grows, it becomes less manageable and, therefore, less representative of the public it is meant to serve. The media provides one of the most powerful tools for a free citizenry to hold its government in check. The thought, then, that it should be subsumed and subsidized by the government is patently dangerous.

The challenges faced by society as traditional media sources struggle is only compounded by the belief that government is responsible for fixing all of society's problems. Many argue that government should coerce changes that at a particular moment might be considered "necessary." This is folly, especially in terms of a free press. Revival and maintenance of a free press will not come through a government subsidization of ailing media outlets. The solution is precisely the opposite. As Barry Goldwater writes in his work, *The Conscience of a Conservative*, "only a philosophy that takes into account the essential differences between men, and, accordingly, makes provision for developing the different potentialities of each man can claim to be in accord with Nature."[4] This philosophy is captured in the wonder of capitalism: that the most resourceful entities are the ones that succeed. So, it is not a national tragedy that many traditional news organizations are shrinking under the weight of difficult financial times and disappearing because of their archaisms. Instead, it is almost an inevitability of sorts, a process of economic natural selection. Long have newspapers, magazines, and television stations been the only sources for news. Because of their past commercial successes, many have come to rest on their laurels, resist innovation, and revel in the luxury of their temporary monopoly on the information business.

It is not that traditional news outlets have unfairly been forced into the red. It is that they have not been resourceful enough to remain in the black. Today's news producers, whether they are enormous conglomerates or autonomous bloggers, must find new ways to monetize their services. Only those that capitalize on their offerings deserve to remain viable. If their potential is exhausted, then so is their public utility, and they deserve to disappear. They are left with a simple choice, predicated on Goldwater's idea of humanity best served by philosophies that "make provision for developing the different potentialities of man." In short: innovate or disintegrate.

That is the monetary aspect of the changing state of media in society. The ethical aspect is more complex but is tied to the same principles. Again, quoting Goldwater, "Every man, for his individual good and for the good of his society, is responsible for his own development."[5] If our democracy's development depends on the circulation of credible information and people's ability to act on it, what happens when such information becomes harder to come by? What happens when sources become slanted, objectivity is occluded, and the truth becomes an elusive ideal?

The answer, simply, is that it is the individual's task to make sure he or she provides him or herself the information to make intelligent decisions. The wrong answer is embodied in the Federal Communication Commission's (FCC) 1949 "Fairness Doctrine." The policy, largely aimed at curtailing the rise of polemical talk radio shows, established an obligation for news organizations to present controversial topics evenhandedly without editorializing. In concept, it seems a somewhat reasonable idea – in fact, there may even be a market for a news source that freely chooses to embrace this concept. In practice, though, it is a violation of one of our primary, unalienable rights as citizens of the United States. It is not the government's role to silence voices, just as it should not be tasked with providing a platform for them. Opinions, after all, are expressed within the context of a free and open market of ideas. If there are no willing consumers for these opinions, government interference will only serve to create artificial markets and lend a sense of legitimacy to those ideas that cannot obtain legitimacy on their own merits.

The Reagan administration ultimately did away with the Fairness Doctrine in 1987 for exactly these reasons. But, interestingly, there is support among some politicians today for reinstituting the policy, mostly as a means of combating vociferous partisan assertions and criticisms. Would this really serve our nation's best interests, though? Would silencing popular voices or amplifying illegitimate ones, all in the name of supposed objectivity, really allow every American the power to exercise his freedoms and take responsibility for his own development? It would absolutely not.

The principal danger we face when the government is allowed to select winners and losers in the marketplace of ideas is that such a right will ultimately evolve into outright censorship. No government need admit to censorship for it to exist. Once we accept a government's right to enhance or degrade any voice in the name of an ideal such as equality, it will inevitably employ this right to justify even blatant censorship. For an example, we can look to China. In 2009, the Chinese government sought to require that all computers sold there be outfitted with censoring software.[6] Known as "Green Dam," the program was intended to filter out "vulgar" content like pornography that the government deems unsuitable. It is not difficult to imagine that such software, though originally targeted only at obscenity, could ultimately be used to fortify the Chinese government's already worrisome tendency to censor a variety of other material, such as politically sensitive items or reports on human rights abuses. This sets a dangerous precedent, one that reminds us just how likely "Big Brother" scenarios might become if individual liberties are not closely guarded.

In fact, one might question if filtering out pornography is in the citizens' best interests at all and leads us to yet another embodiment of free speech: the right to freely express opinions and publish material that might not be universally popular. Would outlawing pornography create a more subversive and dangerous black market for it? Is it within the government's purview to prohibit free men and women from freely choosing to experience a very real part of the human condition? If pornography came first, what might follow? Political cartoons? Government dissent? Were Green Dam software proposed in the United States, it would not only be a violation of our fundamental laws and truths, it would be an affront on the quality of our lives and characters that we have worked so hard to build. As well, consider that in censoring speech and deeming certain issues objectionable, we risk anything being labeled as such afterward. Are we prepared to allow the government to determine what is or is not too objectionable for free Americans to view, hear, read…or even to think?

This question becomes increasingly critical as technological advancement makes the material many do find objectionable more prevalent and more accessible every day. Many are pushing for legal restrictions aimed at curtailing the Internet's relative lawlessness. Yet, this lawlessness is precisely why the Internet has flourished. With few bureaucratic hurdles to navigate, the Internet has become something of an electronic documentation of the whole of human knowledge and a safe haven for proclaiming our convictions. What once may have taken months of research to discover now lies just a few keystrokes away. What once may have been shared only among a few friends can now be writ large for all to see and hear. And were it not for the provision in the Bill of Rights that protects the free spread of information, such innovations could be nipped in the bud, robbing us of much of our human potential.

Similarly, excessive regulation of free speech rights can demolish transparency and the spread of information in other parts of civic life. Just as all embodiments of the press must remain free, so too should all manifestations of political speech. While we may not easily say that campaign finance reform leads to *obvious* losses of individual liberties, it certainly impedes our collective ability to successfully monitor and replace our representatives. And as mentioned early in this essay, this function is essential to the maintenance and endurance of our democracy.

Always a political undercurrent, campaign finance reform has become a central point of contention in the last few decades. Congress passed the Federal Election Campaign Act (FECA) in 1971, a piece of legislation that demanded open and widespread divulgence of political contributions and ostensibly ensured that the public would know the sources of funding for all candidates for federal office. But subsequent government actions in this realm should trouble us. Not long after FECA, Congress established the Federal Election Commission and passed additional legislation that curtailed campaign spending by setting legal limits on individual campaign contributions. Though these actions were taken in the interest of preventing corruption, they sparked a trend of regulation that has long since begun to encroach on some of our supposedly unalienable rights. In limiting campaign contributions, Congress is effectively infringing upon one of the chief tenets of the First Amendment, the right to petition the government, thereby impeding our ability to use our means to support and champion causes in which we believe.

A more recent example of government curtailment of political speech can be found in the Bipartisan Campaign Reform Act (also called the

McCain-Feingold Act), enacted into law in 2002. Like most federal legislation, its tedious verbiage and minutiae are difficult to unpack, but the thrust of the law lies in limiting contributions to political parties ("soft money") and restricting advertisements paid for by third parties in support of or against candidates. Again, the goals appear noble on the surface, and the regulations were hailed as a necessary step to allow an even playing field for all candidates. But the realities that arise from such legislation are worrisome. In a truly free nation, why shouldn't political parties be able to fund the candidates whose positions have earned them party endorsements? Why shouldn't individuals and private entities be able to support people who embody their values to whatever degree they wish? In limiting these rights, the government risks rendering a large portion of the First Amendment worthless and undermining the very democratic principles it is designed to protect. It is a slippery slope, as overbearing regulation and subjectively established limits on contributions and spending artificially weaken some candidacies while inflating the perceived popularity of others. It is vital that our government preserve our founding principles, the same principles that protect our right to promote causes which reflect our personal values.

It should also be noted that many results of the McCain-Feingold Act have been precisely the opposite of its intended effects. We continue to see the halls of Congress dominated by multimillionaires, as wealthy candidates are courted for their ability to self-finance campaigns and avoid the contribution limits imposed by the legislation. The power of incumbency remains as strong as ever. And the ban on unlimited soft money contributions was circumvented by the establishment of tax-exempt 527 organizations. Thus, in addition to such legislation's infringement on our free speech rights, it has also proven ineffective at achieving its goal of leveling the electoral playing field.

So what, then, is the government's appropriate role in maintaining free speech? Some argue, and rightly so, that it should simply be to step back and stay out of the way. This represents the appropriate restriction of government actions vis-à-vis free speech. But in addition to demanding that the government not infringe on our First Amendment rights, we should also demand that the government take specific positive action, when necessary, to protect these rights from being infringed upon by others.

Such action is perhaps most obvious in our government's allowance and protection of the right to public demonstration. Public assemblies and protests have fueled large-scale civil rights movements and played a major role in our most important societal advancements. While their immense force and scope might appear to some as threats to the governmental establishment, these are precisely the kind of peaceful and productive actions that our government is obligated to protect. In all cases, it is the right of people to assemble peaceably (guaranteed in the First Amendment) that forces the government to work on our behalf, address our public grievances, and preserve our most cherished freedoms.

A defining characteristic of protests and public demonstrations is their inherent opposition to established power and the status quo. Unfortunately, this very often results in violence. The Bill of Rights explicitly addresses the government's duty in this case. It says that Congress shall make no law that infringes on the rights of free speech, religion, press, and assemblies. In other words, the government should not adopt legislation that curtails any of these expressions of liberty. But implicit in this duty is the corresponding obligation to preserve these liberties by protecting them from others who would take them away.

The Montgomery Bus Boycott, one of the most notable events of the Civil Rights Movement, illustrates the power of public protest. Pushing for desegregation of public transportation, the boycotts brought figures like Rosa Parks and Martin Luther King, Jr. into the national consciousness. The boycotts ultimately led to a federal court's desegregating Montgomery's buses in 1956, a direct result of peaceful rallying. Later, 1963's March on Washington, where King delivered his lauded "I Have A Dream" speech, further publicized the nation's need for racial equality and led to continued advancements in civil liberties. These demonstrations exhibit the need for our citizenry to be allowed to protest peacefully and for the government to take heed if and when it does.

It seems fitting to conclude with the Civil Rights Movement because King's words prove prophetic in light of this discussion. Though he spoke specifically about desegregation, King also touched on the need for the

American citizenry to not be content with seeing its needs go unmet. He reminded us all to "refuse to believe that there are insufficient funds in the great vaults of opportunity of this nation," a lesson we would do well to heed when thinking about how to safeguard the freedom of our speech in the coming years. King's words reflect the central idea of the conservative mindset, that we must vigorously protect the abundant opportunity which allows each American ultimately to determine his own political, moral, economic, and social fates.

Conservatism's utility is immediate, ineluctable, and applicable across aisles and ages. For proof, consider that even John F. Kennedy and his family, staunch political opponents of Barry Goldwater, recognize the value in his conservative assertions. Robert F. Kennedy, Jr., in his afterword to Goldwater's book, writes: "for Goldwater the purpose of government was to foster societies where human potential could flourish. Conservatism, he explains in [his] book, is the art of achieving the maximum amount of freedom for individuals that is consistent with the maintenance of the social order."[7] Nothing serves to ensure our individual freedom and the maintenance of social order more than the freedom of our speech. It must be preserved at all costs, now and forever.

Christian Camerota is pursuing his Masters degree in Journalism and has worked for a variety of publications, including the San Francisco Chronicle and National Geographic Adventure Magazine. After earning an undergraduate degree in English Literature, he worked for a time in finance before launching his writing career. He was born in Italy, has lived and traveled throughout the United States, Southeast Asia, and Europe, and is fluent in both Spanish and Italian. He currently resides in New York City and works for an online hyperlocal news organization called Patch.

III. DISARMED IS DANGEROUS:
A Fresh Take on the Second Amendment
by Richard Lorenc

Do you feel safe at home? How about at work or at school or on vacation? If your answer is yes, then ask yourself why.

In the United States, we live in a generally safe society. We don't worry about stepping onto landmines or being struck by bombs falling from the sky. In fact, Americans feel so safe that we donate our time and money to efforts aimed at making faraway places safer for people who haven't had the opportunity to develop a free and prosperous society like our own.

The people we see suffering on PBS exposés and late-night "Save the Children" infomercials aren't just without food or shelter. Worse than that, they've been forced to place their very lives in the hands of brutal governments or rogue warlords who promise protection from hostile armies, gangs, and murderers.

But this protection comes at a price. In an effort to protect people, governments often demand that citizens surrender the means with which they can protect themselves – namely, their guns. They arbitrarily implement prohibitive levels of regulation or outright bans on gun ownership, with criminal charges facing any who fail to comply. In places marred by war, being charged with the crime of unauthorized gun possession can mean not only defenselessness, but the possibility of life in prison. Or worse.

Even in the United States, where the right to bear arms sits prominently in our country's most basic law, there are frequent calls to disarm the population in the name of public safety. Proponents of such measures claim that they will decrease theft, gang activity, and murder while resulting in a more harmonious society. They dismiss the right to bear arms as a relic of a bygone era, and refuse to recognize the individual's fundamental right to bear arms for any reason, including self-defense, sport, collection, or sustenance.

But of all these reasons for private gun ownership, it is for individual self-defense that the right to bear arms is most important. Here, as elsewhere, disarmament advocates ask why private citizens need guns if there is a capable police force at the ready. They claim that government forces will always be able to defend the rights of innocents threatened by violence in an effective and timely manner. But although the resources with which we have endowed the government have certainly rendered our police force capable of controlling criminal trends and mitigating widespread insecurity, it is both naïve and dangerous to consider the government your first and only line of protection when your home is invaded or someone attacks you on the street.

Instituting laws that disarm private individuals against their will while permitting arms to only a select few government agents is to completely take from people the ability to defend themselves. Disarming everyone but government – and the criminals who, by definition, do not obey the law – neutralizes your ability to mount an effective defense when you, your family, or your property is threatened.

Despite the important role that the right to bear arms has played in our success as a free people, many now blame it for some of the tough problems that we continue to face. However, allowing the government to take our guns in response to the criminal actions of a few will not only fail to cure society's violence problems, but will also amplify them by removing the strongest deterrent to criminal activity available to individuals. Such an action would make victims of free men and would most certainly open the door for the erosion of all of our other liberties.

If this sounds like hyperbole, consider the experience of another free society, one with which ours shares much in common – Great Britain. There, severe restrictions on the right to bear arms have led to government efforts to curb the use of other "weapons," including the most basic of kitchen tools – the knife. While private gun ownership in Britain is essentially illegal, violence continues to rise, and in 2008 the UK Home Office announced the Tackling Knives Action Programme to reduce the incidence of knife crime by setting rules on ownership.

It is true that knives, like guns, are dangerous in the wrong hands, but so is rope. So are cell phones that can be used to detonate bombs, and computers that can be employed to organize terrorist plots. The logic used to justify gun control legislation could be applied to legitimize government control of any private property whatsoever. It is in this way that we can see how allowing the erosion of *any* of our liberties opens the door for the erosion of *all* of our liberties.

While some argue that the right to bear arms is dangerous, it is not nearly as dangerous as living under a government where that right goes unrecognized. Only a government that guarantees the individual's right to bear arms can respond to the changing needs of its people without overstepping its bounds and devolving into tyranny.

The American Founders understood well the unbreakable links between self-defense, representative government, and a free society. They fought a war against a superior enemy with the privately owned muskets and pistols of a citizens' army. When they won a battle, they acquired additional weapons from the bodies of British soldiers and built an arsenal that eventually forced the tyrannical government of King George III to accept American independence.

The Founders crafted a constitution to limit the power of government and protect the rights of the individual. They added ten original amendments to the Constitution to make explicit many of the rights that the new nation's government would protect, including the right to bear arms. James Madison is given credit for developing the Bill of Rights, but he didn't do it alone. Many others contributed to the intellectual and moral justification for guaranteeing individuals the right to bear arms. The Founders considered this right so fundamental that it appears in the Bill of Rights second only to the right to free expression.

Alexander Hamilton explained in the Federalist No. 28 why the "original right to self-defense" is so sacred:

> *If the representatives of the people betray their constituents, there is then no resource left but in the exertion of that original right of self-defense which is paramount to all positive forms of government... In a single state, if the persons intrusted with supreme power become usurpers, the*

different parcels, subdivisions, or districts of which it consists, having no distinct government in each, can take no regular measures for defense. The citizens must rush tumultuously to arms, without concert, without system, without resource; except in their courage and despair.

And he alluded to the experience of the original American patriots who enjoyed no protection of their rights by law:

The usurpers, clothed with the forms of legal authority, can too often crush the opposition in embryo.

To prevent the authority of usurpers of all stripes — whether in the independent states or the young, national government — the Founders codified the right to bear arms in the Second Amendment to the US Constitution:

A well regulated Militia, being necessary to the security of a free State, the right of the People to keep and bear Arms, shall not be infringed.

The Second Amendment is an explicit, direct, and straightforward guarantee that individual American citizens have the right to keep and bear arms — if they so choose — to defend both themselves and their free society. The text of the amendment articulates this clearly; the Founders' writings establish the amendment's intellectual justification; and the history of our Revolution speaks to the necessity for government to recognize and protect this right.

Yet many Americans consider the Second Amendment to mean something else entirely. And even some who acknowledge the right to bear arms consider it outdated and unnecessary in modern society. After all, our society is pretty stable. We don't experience coups like other nations, and we don't have hostile armies amassing troops at our borders. The police are pretty responsive (unless you're in certain neighborhoods), and there are more federal agents than ever checking each of us before we board an airplane.

Yes, all of this is true, but why do those realities lead us to believe there are no longer legitimate reasons for individuals to bear arms?

The right to bear arms is a vital check on government power, perhaps the most important check of all. This is not only the belief of conservatives and libertarians, but the experience of any group of people that has been victimized by abuses of official power. Native Americans were driven from their homelands throughout our country's history, mostly by armies backed by the authority of government. Their bows and arrows were no match for the government's muskets and rifles. African-Americans were enslaved for generations through force and power of law, and were frequently abused by police and other authorities following their emancipation. In fact, the first law on the books in colonial Virginia prohibited blacks from owning guns. Even gay and lesbian Americans have witnessed abuses of official and unofficial power, causing some to respond by forming groups like the Pink Pistols to advocate armed self-defense. Their slogan is "Armed gays don't get bashed."

A lot has changed since the government-backed slavery and genocide that darkened the history of the eighteenth and nineteenth centuries in America, but humanity has remained the same. Despite our progress, jealousy, envy, and bad judgment still lead some to do bad things, whether such impulses manifest themselves in a burglary or a military invasion. The brandishing of arms is often the only recourse that law-abiding men and women have for safety in the face of such threats.

There are many reasons why some are confused and even frightened by the right to bear arms. Some see it as encouraging a violent or chaotic society. Others feel the Second Amendment is an anachronism. In either case, they argue that society neither needs nor should allow an armed citizenry.

Their fundamental error lies in a misunderstanding of the concept of a right. Conservatives and libertarians define rights in a narrow context: a right is something an individual has by virtue of being human. That is, human beings are the only entities that can have rights and, even then, rights belong to each human being individually. Importantly, rights are exercised by individuals, and are not given or ascribed by any person or group, especially government. Rights are also voluntary in that individuals may choose whether to either exercise them or ignore them outright.

This also means an individual cannot have a right that infringes upon or diminishes the rights of another. Benefits such as education, shelter, and a job necessarily require resources from elsewhere, and thus cannot be guaranteed or protected without restricting another's right to the property of his mind or hands.

This is a far cry from the way many use and understand the word "right." Some would like us to believe the list of rights evolves as society changes. This list today, they say, should expand to include rights to free education, shelter, a minimum wage, healthcare, and even wireless Internet access or entertaining reading material. But whereas the rights to bear arms and free expression require nothing of the government except a promise of protection, the "right" to wireless Internet access entails significant government involvement and a coercive redirection of private resources. Benefits such as this cannot be exercised like a choice to speak one's mind or to own a gun. Thus, material benefits clearly do not meet the basic standards of a right.

Expanding the concept of a right to cover contemporary desires represents a cheapening of what a right truly is. This is because in order to achieve that expansion, the natural and timeless rights of humans must be necessarily subordinated to the power of government.

Alas, one of the manifestations of the expansion trend has been the development of the idea of "collective rights." Some have come to understand the right to bear arms as a collective right, as in the right of a society to protect itself with an army or militia. This belief ignores the fact that a society cannot exist without the individuals who comprise it and that only individuals can fulfill the responsibilities that come with rights. An individual may choose to exercise his right to bear arms, but he must also face the consequences.

The right to bear arms, then – as well as every other right – is strictly individual. After all, only an individual can engage in *self*-defense.

The faulty concept of collective rights brings up an important part of any discussion about the Second Amendment – its mention of "a well-regulated militia." Some claim this reference preempts any individual right to bear arms outside of an official militia organization. However, an accurate and honest understanding of what a right actually is shows this interpretation to be false.

The militia reference stems from the Founders' recognition of the need for free and independent states to have the means to defend themselves from foreign attack. In extreme circumstances when the freedom of Americans is threatened – as in the case of the Revolution – the success of such militias may hinge on the availability of privately owned weapons. To this day, states maintain militias in the form of the National Guard, with the governor of each state serving as commander-in-chief. The existence of these militias in no way diminishes the individual's right to bear arms.

Another reason that many understand the Second Amendment to guarantee something other than an individual right is semantic. Opponents of the right to bear arms have replaced the very phrase itself in the contemporary debate with two words: "gun rights."

Forgetting that guns do not themselves have rights, ask most Americans what comes to mind when they hear the term gun rights, and it's likely you'll hear three letters: NRA. The National Rifle Association was formed in 1871 to teach individuals the proper way to use firearms, and it has grown into what many consider the single most effective conservative political pressure group. Its mission is to defend the individual's right to bear arms.

NRA members come from all backgrounds: sportsmen, hunters, collectors, and other regular citizens. The group's four million members are a cross section of America. But despite its political successes, the NRA has an image problem. Many see a loud, lewd, gun-toting man from rural America as the typical NRA member. This does little to broaden appeal for the cause.

Insufficient marketing makes the NRA's message inaccessible to those who might otherwise understand the importance of the freedom and right to bear arms if it were explained to them differently.

Any pro-Second Amendment rights marketing campaign should emphasize three main points:

1. **Good people have guns.**

> For the grandmother who lives alone, a gun on the nightstand could be the difference between attempted robbery and murder. Good, law-abiding people own guns for sport or protection, and they are careful to know how to use them. Ask a

gun-owner with children where she keeps her firearms and you'll likely be shown a safe in a locked room. In 2006, there were 642 reported cases of unintentional deaths by firearms, which is 0.0036 percent of all deaths that year.[1] Compare that to the 40,000 accidental deaths each year on our highways or the nearly 200,000 deaths attributed to medical errors.

2.   Bad people don't obey the law.

Opponents of the right to bear arms claim more and greater disarmament laws will prevent would-be criminals from obtaining the means to commit violent crimes. But a determined criminal will get a gun no matter what, legal or not. Criminals are criminals because of what they do, not what they have. An area with strict gun control laws would be a gangster's paradise because he knows that his victims will have no way to defend themselves.

In London, where gun control is unreasonably strict and a war on knives is in progress, the chances of being mugged are six times greater than in New York City.[2] And in 2009, official statistics rank Britain first in the developed world in violent crimes – 2,034 incidents per 100,000 people. That same report shows the United States with a violence rate of 466 incidents per 100,000 people.[3]

3.   Government should not have the monopoly on guns.

Imagine how short the Revolutionary War would have been had the British succeeded in controlling all the gunpowder in the colonies. Now recall the evil (and government-authorized) acts committed at the end of a gun to the Native Americans, African-Americans, and other minority peoples in the United States. Post-Civil War southern whites passed gun control laws to limit freed slaves' access to self-defense. Government and its agents cannot and should not be the sole armed force in a free society.

A free society can both respect the rights of its people *and* be safe. This should not only be the conservative or libertarian view of the right to bear arms, but also the opinion of self-described liberals and progressives.

Unfortunately, some politicians see violence in our society and continue to blame it on the rights and freedoms that individuals enjoy. They implement waiting periods, background checks, registries, gun buybacks, and laws that dictate how one may carry a firearm. They then move a step further and conduct searches of private homes in neighborhoods plagued by crime or ravaged by natural disaster – snatching the means to exercise rights away from the individuals who need them the most. In the aftermath of Hurricane Katrina's destruction of New Orleans, members of the National Guard were ordered to confiscate all guns belonging to non-government agents. This is a telling insight into how our government intends to deal with the vulnerable citizens in society it has failed – by making them dependent.

In 2009, Congressman Bobby Rush of Illinois introduced the Blair Holt Firearm Licensing and Record of Sale Act of 2009. In an appeal to raw emotion, this bill was cleverly named after a 16-year-old victim of gun crime. Among its stated purposes, the bill would attempt to "protect the public against the unreasonable risk of injury and death associated with the unrecorded sale or transfer of qualifying firearms to criminals and youth."[4] To accomplish this, the bill would direct the Attorney General to create and maintain a federal record-of-sale system for firearms. In other words, it would create a registry of gun owners, and would impose harsh criminal penalties – including jail time – on sellers who neglect to inform the government if a gun-owner were to relocate.

Beyond infringing upon the right to bear arms, this disarmament legislation would also violate the rights protected by the Fourth Amendment's guarantee against unreasonable search and seizure. The bill allows the Attorney General to authorize government agents to "enter any place where firearms or firearm products are manufactured, stored, or held for distribution in commerce and inspect those areas where the products are manufactured, stored, or held."

In essence, the bill would allow the government to know by whom all privately held firearms are owned and where they are located at any time. If this information were to fall into the wrong hands (not unlikely, considering past government failures to safeguard Social Security numbers and other sensitive data), it would leave those who own guns – as well as those who don't – vulnerable to a criminal's nefarious designs. Moreover, it would blunt the deterrent effect that an armed citizenry has on the prospects of even greater governmental tyranny.

Another example of misguided disarmament efforts can be seen in the Assault Weapons Ban, which was passed in 1994 and expired in 2004. Dismissing the fact that the original ban on "assault weapons" only pertained to firearms and not to knives, crowbars, or fists, the ban qualified illegal firearms subjectively through their cosmetic features. Basically, if it looked menacing, it must be made illegal.

Disarmament advocates are seeking to revive this ill-advised law in 2009 to tackle the menace of Mexican drug cartels. But common sense tells us that criminals ignore such laws and procure weapons through black market means. A 2003 study by the Centers for Disease Control and Prevention concluded there is little proof that the original ban led to a decrease in violent crime. The report states, "The Task Force found insufficient evidence to determine the effectiveness of any of the firearms laws or combinations of laws reviewed on violent outcomes."[5]

A new ban would further restrict peaceful individuals from owning firearms without any meaningful impact on the stated problem. These acts not only violate our rights, but also the highest law that our elected officials have sworn to protect – the Constitution. Challenges to these laws often make it to court, but most fail to check the unauthorized government power that implemented them. This is one example of how widespread the misunderstanding of the concept of a right has become, particularly among judges. If this lack of proper constitutional knowledge in the legal field is not addressed, misunderstandings will inevitably persist.

Not only are many current government attempts to provide for a safer society unconstitutional, but they also focus too much on general disarmament instead of punishment for crimes committed. A punitive approach would be more effective at reducing violent crime while remaining in concert with our founding principles. Assigning harsher criminal sentences for crimes committed with guns would be one method of limiting gun violence. Tightening parole qualifications for people convicted of murder and rape is another tactic. Focusing our energies on criminals – rather than infringing upon the rights of law-abiding citizens – is most effective at addressing violence in society because it recognizes that guns are not the problem. Rather, the problem is what bad people do with the guns that they will undoubtedly obtain whether such possession is legal or not.

The law is a blunt instrument, by definition affecting most the people who live within its bounds. Disarmament ultimately betrays the people its proponents claim to want to protect – responsible members of society. In the end, we won't solve problems by banning guns and concentrating power, but rather by trusting individuals to direct their lives as they see fit and respect the rights of their fellow human beings. This is the essence of freedom.

In America, we recognize the sacrifices of the brave men and women in our armed forces by celebrating national holidays filled with parades and feasts and fireworks. Shouldn't we also celebrate their service to our country abroad by defending our most precious freedoms at home? We hold our rights to free speech and freedom of religion to be sacred. But without the right to bear arms and the ability to defend our other basic rights with power, *all* of our freedoms lie subject to the whims of any common criminal or corrupt government official.

Do you trust the government to *always* be there to protect your rights, or would you prefer to have the ability to defend yourself from people who might wish to destroy your life, harm your loved ones, or take your property?

Fortunately, because the Second Amendment protects your individual right to bear arms, you have a choice.

Richard Lorenc is the Director of Communications for Lorenc+Yoo Design, an Atlanta-based exhibit, signage, and museum design firm. He previously served as Director of Outreach for the Illinois Policy Institute, a free market public policy think tank. There he launched the Institute's Liberty Leaders volunteer activist program and the Milton Friedman Internship program. He has written and spoken on topics such as school choice, new media, and civic engagement. A native of Atlanta and a graduate of Emory University, he resides in Chicago, where he is chairman of the Chicago chapter of America's Future Foundation.

IV. FREE TO BELIEVE:
A Secularist's Defense of Religious Liberty
by Andrew Sung

I have not been to church in over a decade. I believe in God and consider myself Catholic. The Catholic Church, on the other hand, does not recognize me. Though I was baptized as an infant, I never attended Sunday School or Confraternity of Christian Doctrine (CCD). Therefore, I never received my first Holy Communion or Confirmation. My church experiences consisted of driving an hour into Pittsburgh with my family and sitting through an hour of mass conducted in Korean, which I could not understand. Around fourth or fifth grade, sports games on weekends took precedence over church, and that was just fine with me. Religion was never an integral part of my life and by no means could I be mistaken for a religious zealot.

While I have never actively practiced religion, it is troubling to see the movement in this country toward a brand of secularization that promotes overt hostility toward religious institutions. Pop culture and many in the political sphere have begun to demonize and ridicule religious practices in an effort to remove the influence of religion from public life. People of faith are often depicted as ignorant, intolerant, and behind the times on issues such as gay marriage, abortion, and stem cell research. As a result, it is generally understood among mainstream American culture that in order for the United States to progress, we must continue to fortify a metaphorical wall between church and state. In other words, it is fine for one to practice religion or express religious beliefs, so long as it is done behind the closed doors of one's church or home.

It is generally believed that the opposition to complete secularization spearheaded by conservatives is a movement only of the "Bible Belt" wing

41

of the Republican Party. It is true that the Republican Party has been associated more closely than others with devout Christians. However, there is a broader, more fundamental argument against complete secularization, and it has nothing to do with attempting to impose certain religious beliefs on the American people.

The conservative's embrace of religious freedom is rooted in an understanding of the values upon which this nation was founded and it represents an effort to preserve those principles. We believe that the government's most important responsibility is to preserve and protect the private property and individual liberties of its citizens. Among those liberties deemed to be most sacred is the right for people to practice the religion of their choice (or none at all) without fear of persecution by the government. So long as one's religious practices do not violate the liberties of another, anyone should be able to practice his faith in either a private or a public setting.

This is our definition of religious liberty and it provides a clear line of demarcation between the acceptable and unacceptable practice of religion in American society. Children's voluntary recital of prayers in public school, the President of the United States' references to God in a national address, and the use of federal funds for faith-based groups that aim to aid those less fortunate are all permitted because they do not infringe upon the unalienable rights of fellow Americans. Religiously motivated terrorist attacks, abortion clinic bombings, or faith-based intimidation practices should never be allowed because they infringe fundamentally on the rights of others. In more technical terms, our approach rests on a literal constitutional interpretation of the constraints on religious influence in public life. This perspective is rooted in the intent of America's Founders. It represents the best approach for our contemporary society because it secures for America the many benefits of religion without subjecting us to the failings that sometimes attend it.

During his first trip to Europe as President, Barack Obama declared that the United States is not a Christian nation. This is correct in that the US is not a Christian theocracy, does not have a nationally sanctioned religion, and allows its citizens to openly practice whichever religion they choose. This is all quite obvious and none of us would argue that our nation should move toward adopting Christianity as its national religion. But while President Obama's statement is obvious in the political sense, even the most ardent proponent of secularization would be hard-pressed to deny that this country was founded on Judeo-Christian ideals and that Christianity has played a crucial part in public life throughout our nation's history. Our Founding Fathers were deeply religious. They invoked God numerous times in our founding documents. Our currency bears the phrase "In God We Trust." Members of Congress recite an oath of office that ends with "So help me God." And US Presidents of both major parties frequently close public remarks with the phrase "God Bless America." God is alive and well in America's public sphere.

Secularists and poorly informed political commentators often invoke the First Amendment to support their contention that religion should be banished from public view. But to make this argument based on constitutional interpretation reveals a basic misunderstanding of both what the First Amendment *actually says* and what it was *originally intended to mean*. Unfortunately, in many cases, the media has grossly misinformed the general public by replacing the Founders' sound logic with platitudes and slogans. With respect to hot-button cultural issues such as gay marriage and abortion, social progressives and secularists alike sloppily invoke the First Amendment by arguing for a fundamental separation between church and state. Sadly, much of the American public has not bothered to question this reasoning by discerning the Founders' intent for the First Amendment.

The United States Constitution explicitly makes reference to religion only twice in its entire text. Article VI reads that government officials shall be bound by an oath to support the Constitution, "but no religious Test shall ever be required as a Qualification to an Office or Public Trust under the United States." The other reference, of course, appears in the often misquoted and misinterpreted Establishment and Free Exercise Clause of the First Amendment. This clause reads, "Congress shall make no law respecting an establishment of religion, or prohibiting the free exercise thereof." Nowhere in the text of the Constitution do we find any mention of a separation between church and state.

The Establishment Clause of the First Amendment, in plain words, prohibits Congress from recognizing a nationally sanctioned church or religion. The Free Exercise Clause simply protects citizens in practicing whichever faith they choose without government interference. The actual text of the First Amendment and the original intent of its authors make no mention of separating religion from public life, nor does it provide guidelines for government to favor irreligion over religion. Sometime over the last several decades, however, the general public's interpretation of the First Amendment has deviated significantly from the original meaning, as secularists have invoked the Establishment Clause to justify their opposition to controversial cultural issues such as prayer in public schools or government funding for religious institutions. Conservatives, on the other hand, have continued to apply the original intent of the First Amendment to today's cultural issues, and for the most part are more accepting of religious influence in public life so long as basic liberties are not being violated.

This literal reading of the Constitution forms the basis of conservatism's defense of religious liberty. We recognize that the power of our constitution lies not just in the document's text, but also the *reasons* that the Founders wrote it this way. The Establishment and Free Exercise Clauses were intended to protect religion and the rights of religious (and non-religious) individuals in particular from the coercive power of government. While it would have been easy for the Founders to assume that future generations would protect these freedoms as a matter of course by recognizing the rights to life, liberty, and the pursuit of happiness in the Declaration of Independence, they went a step further. America's Founders had witnessed firsthand the oppressive hand of government's guiding the spiritual life of a nation in the form of the state-sanctioned Church of England. In fact, many of America's new citizens had fled Europe in search of genuine religious freedom. To ensure that America would forever remain a bastion of religious liberty, the Framers incorporated explicit limits on the government's power to direct the spiritual affairs of the nation by including the Establishment and Free Exercise Clauses in the Bill of Rights.

But over the years, the intent of the Founders has been undermined in an attempt to prevent people from being exposed to religious ideas at all. The cost of this misinterpretation has been an erosion of the right of each American to practice his religion as he sees fit. Conversely, our interpretation affirms the rights of man by allowing all religious activity that does not infringe on another person's unalienable rights. Those who oppose our interpretation fundamentally weaken the American experiment by subordinating the rights to liberty and the pursuit of happiness, of which religious practice is undoubtedly a part.

So where do secularists and social progressives get the idea of a separation between church and state when arguing that it is unconstitutional, for instance, to display the Ten Commandments on government property? After all, as noted above, the text of the First Amendment makes no mention of separating church from state and it certainly outlines no requirement to eliminate religion from public life.

Perhaps the most valid claim for secularists comes from one of the Founding Fathers, Thomas Jefferson, a staunch proponent of secularism. Often referenced is his letter to the Danbury Baptist Association, where he speaks of a "wall of separation between church and State" as the purpose of the Establishment Clause. The Founders were obviously very careful to protect religious freedoms and to ensure that the government could not arbitrarily assign divine sanction to its actions. But Jefferson's idea of a rigid wall separating religion from government is somewhat curious, as this is the same man who invoked the Creator in the Declaration of Independence – a document he penned, which established the very foundation of the United States of America. Furthermore, why does Jefferson's presumed wall between church and state not prohibit government officials from openly expressing their faith so as not to demonstrate favor of one religion over another? This point is difficult for secularists to reconcile, as it was no secret that others among our Founders were devoutly religious. In addition, many US presidents have openly displayed religious faith. In political campaigns, candidates for public office invariably face many questions regarding both individual faith and public positions on religious issues. The fact that these are legitimate concerns for any political candidate debunks the secularist argument that the role of religion is diminishing in the United States.

Over the last sixty years, the Supreme Court has ruled on a number of cases dealing with the correct interpretation of the Establishment and Free Exercise Clause. During that time, the Court's position on this issue has moved decidedly toward the secularists' camp. A common practical manifestation of this theoretical debate has been that of religious influence in the public school system. The focus of this debate has ranged from the constitutionality of government funding for parochial schools, to whether prayer or moments of silence violate the First Amendment. For the most part, the Supreme Court has moved in favor of fortifying Jefferson's "wall of separation."

In *Engle v. Vitale (1962)*, the Court ruled that it was unconstitutional for states to institute an official prayer to be recited in public schools, as this amounted to government's promoting an official religion. In delivering the majority opinion, Justice Hugo Black referenced Jefferson's "wall of separation," much to the dismay of literal constitutional scholars. Almost ten years later, continuing on the secular trend in *Lemon v. Kurtzman (1971)*, the Supreme Court ruled that a Pennsylvania law allowing parochial schools direct aid and access to public funds was unconstitutional. It was in this case that the three-pronged "Lemon Test" was conceived, which was meant to serve as a checklist for appropriate government involvement with religion. The "Lemon Test" stated that government action must have a secular legislative purpose, it must neither advance nor inhibit religion, and it must not result in excessive entanglement in religion.

The march toward complete separation between church and state continued into the 1980s, when the Supreme Court ruled in *Wallace v. Jaffree (1985)* that an Alabama law authorizing one minute of silent meditation or voluntary prayer was unconstitutional. Using the "Lemon Test" as his basis for reasoning, Justice John P. Stevens delivered the majority opinion. In concurring, Justice Sandra Day O'Connor took a more moderate view. She was not willing to use the "Lemon Test" as the definitive code for the proper interpretation of the Establishment and Free Exercise Clauses. Rather, she sought to define religious freedom within the context of the First Amendment in an effort to determine whether voluntary prayer or meditation was unconstitutional.

> *Religious liberty protected by the Establishment Clause is infringed when the government makes adherence to religion relevant to a person's standing in the political community. Direct government action endorsing religion or a particular religious practice is invalid under*

this approach because it 'sends a message to nonadherents that they are outsiders, not full members of the political community, and an accompanying message to adherents that they are insiders, favored members of the political community.'

Justice O'Connor was careful to acknowledge that some degree of government intermingling with religion was inevitable, as many practical laws could be interpreted with the backdrop of religious undertones. Erring too far on the side of complete separation would be detrimental to society, she argued, as "the State could not criminalize murder for fear that it would thereby promote the Biblical command against killing." While Justice O'Connor reasoned that silent meditation or prayer was inherently different from vocal mandatory prayer, she ultimately concluded that the Alabama statute held the purpose of endorsing prayer in public school, which she reasoned was in direct violation of the Establishment Clause.

Fortunately for conservatives, future Chief Justice William Rehnquist was unwilling to accept the constitutional legitimacy of either Jefferson's "wall of separation" or the "Lemon Test." In his dissenting opinion in *Wallace v. Jaffree*, Justice Rehnquist delivered one of the most articulate and reasoned interpretations of the First Amendment ever given. First, he debunked the growing notion that Thomas Jefferson's letter to the Danbury Baptists was a legitimate foundation for constitutional doctrine. As Rehnquist notes, Mr. Jefferson was in France when the Bill of Rights was written, and thus had no basis on which to speak to the intent of the assembly that passed the First Amendment. Moreover, his letter to the Danbury Baptists was written over a decade after the Bill of Rights was passed by Congress and, therefore, at best represented a personal view that very well may have evolved significantly over ten years' time. It was in fact James Madison who was most instrumental in crafting the Bill of Rights. Madison's original language around the Establishment Clause made no mention of Jefferson's "wall of separation." Madison simply wanted to ensure that no national religion would be established. In his opinion, Rehnquist continues,

It seems indisputable from these glimpses of Madison's thinking, as reflected by actions on the floor of the House in 1789, that he saw

the amendment as designed to prohibit the establishment or a national religion, and perhaps to prevent discrimination among sects. He did not see it as requiring neutrality on the part of the government between religion and irreligion.

Rehnquist pointed out the inconsistencies of the metaphorical "wall of separation," and demonstrated that the Court had for decades incorrectly applied this concept to represent the original intent of the drafters of the Bill of Rights. He argued, "The 'wall of separation between church and State' is a metaphor based on bad history, a metaphor which has proved useless as a guide to judging. It should be frankly and explicitly abandoned." Rehnquist continued by questioning the legitimacy of the "Lemon Test," as it had no historical grounding in the drafting of the First Amendment, and it was simply created to form a checklist for First Amendment cases. In short, the "Lemon Test" was simply the way for a liberal court to impose their view of what the law should be rather than interpreting what the Constitution actually says.

Ultimately, Rehnquist brilliantly articulated the Originalist school of thought, that the First Amendment can only be interpreted as it was intended by the Framers. To ignore their original intent is to ignore the lasting influence of the document itself.

The true meaning of the Establishment Clause can only be seen in its history. As drafters of our Bill of Rights, the Framers inscribed the principles that control today. Any deviation from their intentions frustrates the permanence of that Charter and will only lead to the type of unprincipled decision-making that has plagued our Establishment Clause cases since Everson.

The Framers intended the Establishment Clause to prohibit the designation of any church as a 'national' one. The Clause was also designed to stop the Federal Government from asserting a preference for one religious denomination or sect over others ... As its history abundantly shows, however, nothing in the Establishment Clause requires government to be strictly neutral between religion and irreligion, nor does that

Clause prohibit Congress or the States from pursuing legitimate secular ends through nondiscriminatory sectarian means.

Unfortunately, like many other policy issues, the conservative approach does not always fit nicely onto bumper stickers. Communicating the Originalist school of thought on the First Amendment can often be a losing battle. In today's era of media sound bites, a suggestion to read analytical commentary on the First Amendment or Justice Rehnquist's dissenting opinion in *Wallace* is likely to fall on deaf ears. Secularists and progressives who advocate a minimalist approach to religion in public life tend to reason that the government cannot, but more importantly, *should not* interact in any way with religious institutions.

Conservatives can continue making an argument rooted in constitutional interpretation until they are blue in the face. But the message that will ultimately resonate with the American public must explain why our interpretation of religious liberty is a good thing for contemporary society. Most Americans generally care more about a policy's practical results than its adherence to the original intent of a constitutional amendment. This puts the thoughtful, conservative argument at a disadvantage. While extremely weak in its constitutional grounding, the secular argument can certainly be compelling in the practical sense, especially given the country's recent trend toward socially progressive politics. After all, we are a nation of increasing ethnic, cultural, and religious diversity. As such, messages with religious undertones resonate with a shrinking proportion of Americans.

The main problem with the secular approach is that it categorically rejects any sort of positive religious influence in order to avoid religious controversies altogether. Banning public religion robs society of the immense good that religion and religious individuals do simply because of the shortcomings of a few. All institutions and ideologies run the risk of breeding fanatical adherents. The environmental movement, anti-globalization groups, and a whole range of political philosophies have given rise to strands that have violently broken the laws of this country. Yet there is no talk of banishing their ideas from the public sphere, and it is right that there is not. Embracing our rights-based concept of religious liberty precludes the only danger that religion poses to society: the risk that it will inspire radical followers to harm the life, liberty, or property of other citizens. Any such action is already illegal and we recognize that there is no socially acceptable religious defense for these actions. By allowing all other religiously motivated actions and statements, we maintain the many blessings that public religion brings to our nation.

Any prosperous society, to include the United States, needs some sort of a moral code to guide it. This code need not be comprised of Christian teachings and by no means is religion the sole means of establishing a moral foundation. But, while morality is in the eye of the beholder, there are a set of core values, generally believed by most Americans to be moral absolutes that serve as the foundation for a peaceful and prosperous society. Respect for human life, a God-given right to liberty, and strong compassion for those less fortunate are key pillars that make this country the most economically, morally, and culturally rich civilization in the history of mankind. Teachings from religious institutions, for the most part, only help to fortify these values.

Moreover, this moral code must exist in order to provide a framework for society's public servants, and indeed to enable the rule of law itself. Religion serves as a check against government influence. Two of the greatest movements in American history to protect individual liberties, the Abolitionist Movement and the Civil Rights Movement, were spearheaded by religious leaders. These leaders advanced our society by invoking a natural, God-given right to liberty. In the legal sense, the original form of the Constitution provided specific provisions to limit the liberties of African-Americans. But in the moral sense, the Constitution failed and a code higher than constitutional authority was invoked to bring our laws in concert with our values. While the Declaration of Independence does not serve as a legal document of precedence over the Constitution, often quoted is Thomas Jefferson's perfectly worded phrase, that all men are "endowed by their Creator with certain unalienable Rights, that among these are Life, Liberty, and the pursuit of Happiness." Americans need not agree that this Creator is the Christian God, but it is absolutely essential that the document invokes a power higher than any arbitrary dictator or corrupt set of bureaucrats. These rights are unalienable because no political process could possibly supersede the law of humanity, that men have an intrinsic right to liberty. Our concept of religious liberty in the public sphere is essential to the conception of unalienable rights and, therefore, to the very idea of America, itself.

Secularists often point to extremist theocracies in the Middle East as a caution against allowing religion into public life. In their eyes, such excesses prove that religion should be a private matter. But this argument ignores the critical difference between the role of religion in Middle Eastern theocracies and in the United States. Our society allows religion to serve as a tool for the common good and declares illegal any manifestations of religion that infringe on the rights of others. The United States does not use religion as a tool to sanction brutally violent acts such as suicide bombings or mass civilian killings. In fact, the United States does not "use" religion at all. The elevation of a particular religion by the government is fundamentally different than permitting any religion to be practiced by peaceful adherents.

We clearly delineate what are appropriate and what are inappropriate acts with respect to religion. With the protection of liberty as the most sacred American value, we use religion as a means to promote peaceful and productive resolutions. Community churches often serve as a vehicle through which to bolster moral values and to help those less fortunate. The White House under George W. Bush increased aid for faith-based initiatives, and while many found this to be an inappropriate intermingling between the government and religion, there is no denying that the intentions and the actions of these groups yield a very positive influence.

A look at other cultures provides an instructive glimpse into the immense benefits of our conception of religious liberty. One is hard pressed to find another society on the face of the planet where such a plurality of religions exists freely and peacefully. There are very few Jews and Muslims working side by side in the Middle East. Christianity is tightly regulated in China. Even Europe is often plagued by virulent anti-Semitic or religiously fueled violence. America is unique in that its embrace of religious liberty underwritten by a firm commitment to the secular rule of law has allowed the peaceful practice of all brands of religion to thrive. In fact, it is precisely this combination that allows America to face an event like

9/11 – a horrific attack carried out in the name of a religion – without wholesale condemnation of the Muslim faith or devolution into vigilante justice.

Our history is uniquely devoid of any large scale religious persecution, a fact made possible not by our society's rejection of peaceful public religion but by its embrace. As such, we have benefited from the civic virtue that religion promotes while avoiding the worst of its excesses. The intent of the Founders has defined the relationship between religion and the state for nearly the entirety of America's existence. Now, as this societal framework is increasingly threatened, it has become vitally important to defend it. We must also acknowledge that our remarkable society exists at least partially because of our historical acceptance of a rights-based conception of religious liberty.

While religious faith has been the source of much strife throughout the history of mankind, this country has been able to strike a strong balance between politics and religion. We have been able to do so because the values espoused by the plethora of religions represented in American society correspond to the principles that form the philosophical core of our country. Religion continues to strengthen America because these very principles are essential ingredients for a peaceful, prosperous society predicated on mutual respect and a common level of human dignity. Throughout our history, Christianity has helped weave the strong moral fabric of this country: a nation that promotes tolerance, respect for human life, and caring for those less fortunate. These are basic teachings that serve the common good and to relegate them outside of the public arena is not a demonstration of government neutrality. Rather, it is a blatant show of government favoritism for secularism over religion. It is not necessary that Christianity play this role in the future, but it is also not the government's place to prevent it from doing so. The choice should be left to free citizens.

Not only do religious organizations stand for sound principles that are in concert with our most fundamental American and human values, but they are an integral part of our communities. Being an inactive religious participant, there are certainly aspects of religion that make me uncomfortable, and it is understandable that these same sentiments are shared many others. But incorporating religion in public life is not a dangerous proposition. It provides moral direction to our nation, which ultimately makes us stronger. It creates a higher code of natural human rights that is impervious to assaults from even the cruelest of dictators or most corrupt of bureaucrats. Religious freedom provides a critical check against the prospect of tyranny. To weaken its influence would inevitably weaken our most sacred liberties.

Andrew Sung is currently a credit derivatives trader for a global investment bank. He has worked for four years in the securities industry. Andrew attended Phillips Exeter Academy and graduated from Princeton University in 2005, where he received an AB in Economics.

V. LOCKING THE BEDROOM DOOR:
Government, Sexuality, and Society
by Melissa Anne Hayes

Welcome to the twenty-first century! Today you can browse any medium of communication and be greeted by millions of images of sexuality in every form. Sexuality in contemporary society has surpassed that of the free love 1960s, the era of shedding personal inhibitions. Technology has given us the power to instantly observe any number of people who choose to publicly exercise their sexual rights. You can even receive your very own daily dose with hardly any work at all – it is as easy as texting HOT to 12345! The descendant of free love is abundant sexuality and the increasing acceptance of its display. Why then, when sexuality is so readily available, are our rights based on sexuality – among the most personal rights we have – still restricted by a government that was constituted to *protect* our individual freedoms?

Before you scoff at the notion that even in our hyper-sexed society government continues to restrict our sexual rights, consider the following:

> *It's Friday night, and Jesse and Kelly are getting ready to go to dinner with another couple. Both couples are in their mid-40s and they have been friends since college. They get together every month to try out new restaurants, see movies, and go to baseball games.*
>
> *Although Jesse and Kelly have children, Ashley and Jamie do not. Jesse and Kelly own their own home together, while Ashley and Jamie do not.*
>
> *Each partnership has been filled with challenges and blessings. Although they share many things in common, one fact separates these two relationships: the government does not treat the couples equally under the law.*

Jesse is a male who married the love of his life, Kelly, who is a female. They file their income taxes jointly and have a joint bank account. Jesse and Kelly could see each other in the hospital in the unfortunate circumstance of a medical emergency, but Ashley and Jamie do not have the same rights.

Because the government judges the merits – or morality – of one of these relationships, the government does not view each couple equally or afford the same rights and responsibilities to both. Why? Because Ashley and Jamie are in a homosexual relationship.

Our conservatism holds the rights to life, liberty, and the pursuit of happiness as inviolable. As part of those unalienable rights, it grants what many of us consider our most important right: the right to own property. This right includes the products of our own minds and hands. But in its most basic form, it includes the right to our minds and hands themselves. Since we own our bodies, we can act as we wish in a private, consensual situation, including sexually. While this claim may seem unpalatable to many conservatives, to deny it is to deny the fundamental rights that we each possess by virtue of being human. On moral grounds, the lack of sexually inhibitive norms in the law might seem to reflect a very liberal perspective. However, few policies are more conservative than freedom of action and the concept of property rights. The sexual expression of those property rights is just one way Americans exercise their freedom, whether morally or not.

In a free country, consensual sexual behavior must be a matter of personal discretion and is ultimately an individual's own decision. This should be the case regardless of the nature of the behavior and who condones or does not condone it. Our conservatism proclaims that decisions should be made by the people affected. In regards to sex, the person affected is one's own self. If consensual sex is a crime, who, then, is the victim? Though there is none, the government restricts your right to your own body by outlawing practices like prostitution. Our government is narrowing the freedoms it promised us every time it censors television it considers to be indecent and every time it restricts sexual rights between two consenting adults. When Americans look the other way simply because we agree or even just sympathize with the legislated morality, we give in to a body of power that will never return those rights to us of its own accord. We willingly grant the power to control our bodies to an entity without consideration of how it might see fit to control our (very personal) property in the future.

To some, legislating personal morality seems necessary to ensure we remain a morally upstanding society. But this argument is dangerously shortsighted. For instance, the religious right supports legislation that furthers its agenda to define marriage as an institution solely between a man and a woman. It also typically agrees that government should endorse public prayer in schools. Religious voters pursue this agenda because they believe traditional marriage and school prayer are components of a morally upstanding life. We can safely assume that these same voters would not support legalizing prostitution because such an act contradicts the moral standards to which they subscribe. But how will they react when their moral standards represent a small minority viewpoint? Consider that Islam is the fastest growing religion in the world; that the Muslim population in the US is expanding rapidly; and that fundamentalist interpretations of Islamic doctrine are becoming increasingly widespread within the global Muslim community. Imagine how morality would be legislated differently by a Muslim majority in America. If we grant government the power to apply today's popular moral imperatives to issues such as gay marriage and prostitution, the same power might be wielded to dictate Shari'ah law in the future. More realistically (or perhaps only more near-term), home schooling could be outlawed because a majority comes to consider it immoral to shelter a child from the world in such a way.

The religious right has already seen this power begin to turn against it in the form of illegitimate government prohibitions. For example, some school systems restrict voluntary or student-led prayer even when it is not mandatory for students who do not want to participate. Yet advocacy for morally based governance remains strong. Many liberals believe the government should recognize marriage between homosexuals, and many conservatives oppose the government's restricting freedom of religion. The component common to each position is the proposed enshrining in law of a particular set of moral standards. The previous examples highlight the dangerous nature of such a mode of thinking regardless of the side of the political spectrum from which the arguments originate. Though the illustrations of how this government power can snowball into an uncontrollable force might sound extreme, this effect is precisely the nature of expanding government powers. We cannot give our government the power of moral coercion simply because we agree with the morals. If we do, we give our government the legitimate power to control us by imposing moral standards with which we do not agree.

The majority of American citizens are fortunate enough not to have experienced government restriction of their individual rights to the point of individual persecution. We do not have to fear governmentally sanctioned judgment of our actions on an everyday basis. Save for taxation, most Americans go about living their daily lives peacefully without necessarily worrying about the impacts of overbearing government regulations. We do not have to fear being officially targeted because of our religious beliefs or harassed by the government because of our race. But even if we're not constantly affected, does that mean that we are free enough not to be concerned? Absolutely not.

Although we have constitutional amendments prohibiting preferential treatment due to sexual orientation, the United States' government has slowly expanded its power and continues to do so daily at the expense of the populace's equal rights. For the tens of millions of Americans who are apathetic, this ever expanding governance goes unnoticed. But what does this mean personally for every American? Should it matter to the majority of us if a state creates an amendment restricting the rights of the minority by banning gay marriage? Should we care if the Supreme Court rules that certain images created and viewed by consenting adults are obscene? Regardless of the relevance to our everyday lives of the specific issues, the principles involved impact our entire society. These actions should matter to anyone who values freedom of speech, any person who enjoys religious freedom, or any American who exercises the right to bear arms. A government that expands its power by restricting the rights of individuals based on sexual preference can expand powers and restrict rights over anyone for any reason. To argue the contrary requires a misguided hope that the government's prerogatives will forever reflect your own. Morality is subjective, but a government that restricts sexual rights based on what it considers to be an objective moral opinion is not a government that respects the individual rights of its citizens.

Morality is a never ending debate precisely because it cannot be measured. It is completely subjective, yet in any moral argument, each side seems to claim an objective perspective. But the issue of sexual morality and the unfortunate role of government restriction of freedom do not lie in the subjectivity versus objectivity debate. Government should not have a role in sexual rights. Governing sexuality in society restricts the very individual freedoms that our constitution protects. The problem with censorship, for instance, is that so often the underlying message is that sex, outside of one particular controlled relationship, is morally reprehensible. This is a perfectly acceptable belief, but it is just that: a belief. Again, the argument brings us back to the fundamental point that government must not legislate a belief system. When citizens promote an agenda of sexual repression, they are embracing a culture of restriction.

Many people, conservative and liberal, fail to understand that it is possible to live within a society that values the preservation of traditional family values while at the same time minimizing government involvement in sexual rights. Respecting the rights of others does not require that individuals governed by the same body condone the acts of one another. It only means that they respect one another's right to live under the law. We cannot claim to be a country that values liberty if we do not respect the individual's right to determine his or her own moral code. Life experiences, religion, and parenting are just a few among many factors that contribute to the formation of moral opinions. These opinions in turn determine our individual conceptions of morally appropriate lifestyles. As long as they don't infringe upon the unalienable rights of others, we must respect the rights of every person to hold different moral opinions. Allowing our government to determine our moral code is just the sort of government intervention our Founding Fathers feared.

A relevant discussion of morality and sexuality must also address the very prominent public question of homosexual marriage. Some might legitimately ask why the debate over homosexual marriage even takes place within the public arena. Breaking down the term "homosexual marriage" to its constituent parts provides an important clue. If sexuality is inherently of a private nature, then there is no reason for homosexuality (the first half of the term) to play a role in the political debate. Thus, we can infer that society's acceptance of some governmental role in the institution of marriage (the second half) overshadows the private nature of sexuality and forms the basis for the public homosexual marriage debate. But perhaps it is time we question the appropriateness of the government's role in marriage itself.

Why do we never question the mandatory process of obtaining a permit for marriage? Marriage only affects the liberties of two consenting adults. Yet when these same two consenting adults want to have children, no one objects to the lack of governmental sanction required for procreation. Conservative thought would imply that mutual agreement by two adults to do what affects no one else should require no permission from a body of government. The act of procreation most certainly affects the life of a child. But to argue that a permit should be required to have children is ludicrous. In the same way that government restrictions regarding procreation represent an absolute restriction of our individual freedoms, opponents of same-sex marriage find themselves arguing for an even more fundamental restriction of individual rights based on sexual preference.

Foes of same-sex marriage cite many reasons for their opposition, such as the devaluation of the sanctity of their union that would result if homosexuals were allowed to marry. With divorce rates in the United States exceeding fifty percent, it seems as though measuring the sanctity of your own marriage based on that of other marriages would be a flawed approach. But even if we pay no attention to the Vegas marriages that are annulled and forget America's sky-high divorce rate, the issue of homosexual marriage is even more fundamental. One cannot measure the value of one's own marriage based on individual perception of other marriages. For marriages based on religious doctrine, the marriage takes place between two people and is witnessed by their god. It is from this characteristic that the sanctity of the union derives its value, not from any government permit. Recognition of this fact by the majority of Americans who marry in churches and synagogues should be reason enough for them to be utterly unconcerned with the sexual preferences of the people who are granted marriage licenses by the state.

However, even this discussion of equal treatment misses the more critical and fundamental point. We hold that the governmental authority to sanction relationships leads to an unacceptable preferential treatment for married couples. Intellectual honesty requires conservatives to recognize that this is true whether the married couple in question is same-sex or not. It is anathema for a government that proclaims to provide its citizenry equal protection under the law to grant different pay, benefits, taxation status, or rights to a particular class of people based on a subjectively selected characteristic such as marital status. Just as the government does not force anyone into marriage, those governed who enjoy the right to marry should not feel the need to defend the institution through the construct of a legal relationship. That is, they deserve neither governmental recognition nor privileges based solely on the fact that they have entered into a committed relationship between two consenting people. Ultimately, sexual relationships and the contractual agreement that is marriage should affect only the people involved in the relationship. Because of this, the proper role of government is to extricate itself from the institution completely.

If you disagree with this proposition, ask yourself, "Why should marital status be chosen over any other arbitrary characteristic as the basis for preferential treatment by the government?" For those for whom an appropriate answer to this question alludes to the government's role in promoting particular values, I encourage you to return to the earlier discussion on the legislation of morality. Marriage – regardless of what religious tradition it follows – is a relationship of a very personal and private nature. This is only eroded by the government's recognition or registration of it. Most people would also recognize the intensely private nature of almost all committed romantic relationships, regardless of the sexuality or marital status of the two people involved. The government's involvement in these romantic relationships is unfounded, arbitrary, and should be abdicated.

What does the practical application of the government's legal recognition of marriage look like? It takes the form of different tax burdens for individuals whose circumstances are identical save for marital status. It allows for unmarried governmental employees to receive reduced compensation for the same job compared with married co-workers. It manifests itself in the payment of Social Security benefits to one person's committed partner but not another's, because the second couple chose not to consummate their relationship in the courts. And it ultimately takes the form of granting moral sanction to one lifestyle while withholding it from another. This is the precise problem that we run into in the more hotly contested but less fundamental gay marriage debate. The practical application of government's involvement in the bedroom is always denial of some of its citizens' constitutional right to equal protection under the law. The only way to reconcile the marriage debate with the existence of mankind's unalienable rights is to take government completely out of the marriage equation.

Just as we have the right to create our own moral codes as individuals, private enterprises should also have the right to advance their agendas and corresponding belief systems as they wish. Without infringing on the fundamental rights of others, businesses and organizations that wish to exist within a certain moral code should not be forced to abide by legislation that prevents them from adhering to that code. If a church determines the standards for recognizing a marriage, the government has no right to intervene to enforce a progressive, politically correct agenda. In cases like this, the argument that one form of marriage is devalued by the existence of another is legitimate. In a free society, the standards for measuring such value must be allowed to exist within the confines of private institutions. Qualifications and standards within a religion are perfectly acceptable for the people within that religion because each of us has the freedom to select or reject membership in any religion.

In the private sector, companies and organizations, whether secular or based on a religious set of values, should be able to individually determine appropriate codes of behavior and lifestyle if they wish to do so. If recognizing homosexual relationships contradicts the intrinsic values of a private organization, forced abrogation of these values by the government denies the very freedoms that the government was established to protect. Allowing governmental intervention into private sector moral codes is as patently unjust as allowing the government to force a particular code onto each of us as individuals. Employment and organizational membership are voluntary. As long as enforcing a set of values does not infringe upon the life, liberty, or property rights of others, we have the right as individuals and associations to do so.

Although our Constitution is meant to protect equal freedom for all, Americans too often blindly accept government-sponsored injustice. Because we allow government to slowly encroach upon our sexual rights and regulate our relationships, we do not all live equally under the law. We live in a society where we accept sex advertised on every corner under the guise of free speech, yet we balk at the idea of "liberty and justice for all" in the bedroom. Some citizens accept what has essentially become government-endorsed persecution of homosexuals in America, yet they circle the wagons when the Ten Commandments are taken out of our courthouses or when values-based private organizations are made to cater to the homosexual minority. The knife of governmentally-sanctioned morality cuts both ways. When we base government policy on morality, the moral standards of the most well connected and well established inevitably hold sway. Fortunately, we have recourse in America. The concept of governmentally prescribed morality runs into a brick wall in the form of the Founding Fathers' promise to the citizens of this country – equality under the law. In other words, government must not make or interpret laws based on private morality. In light of our Founders' promise, it is clear that moral governance is morally wrong. And it's insulting to the people living under the law.

Imagine a truly free society that does not legislate the sexual rights of its citizens.

It's Friday night, and Jesse and Kelly are getting ready to go to dinner with another couple. Both couples are in their mid-40s and have been friends since college. They get together every month to try out new restaurants, see movies, and go to baseball games.

Jesse and Kelly have children, as do Ashley and Jamie. Jesse and Kelly own their own home, as do Ashley and Jamie.

Each partnership has been filled with challenges and blessings. But there's one thing that they share in common: the government treats each couple equally under the law.

Each individual files his or her own income taxes but both couples have contracted for joint bank accounts. Just as Jesse and Kelly could see each other in the hospital in the unfortunate circumstance of a medical emergency, Ashley and Jamie have the same rights because they previously established this as their wish.

The government makes no effort to judge the merits – or morality – of either relationship, and as such promises not to restrict the rights or the responsibilities of any of its citizens.

The society in which this scenario plays out is inherently just and represents the practical application of the most vital American values. While the contemporary debate over same-sex marriage is the most prominent element of the larger discussion on sexuality and society, it remains just one element. Reaching a resolution to this controversial issue requires a fundamental shift in the way in which we view the relationship between sexuality and government. Our conservatism's adherence to the core values upon which America was founded facilitates the development of this new means of considering issues of sexuality.

The essence of our principled approach to sexuality and society rests in the fact that we live in a changing world. Moral beliefs regarding sexuality can and must be developed by each individual member of society and must not be promoted by government. Government support for any set of sexual values inherently represents the subjugation of others, and as such violates the rights of free men. Our conservatism recognizes that virtue, the free choice to consistently live a morally upstanding life, is only possible in a society where a moral code is neither coerced nor imposed upon individuals by their government. The development of one's own moral standards is a critical and supremely personal process. It most certainly does not take a village, but if the entire village consented...

Melissa Anne Hayes graduated cum laude with a BBA in Music Business from Belmont University in Nashville, TN. She currently serves as the President of the Nashville chapter of Liberty on the Rocks, a national organization of liberty-minded individuals who gather to discuss free market- and individual liberty-based solutions to today's problems. An entrepreneur by nature, Melissa sells clothing under the brand, "Libertarians Make Better Lovers." She worked for three years as a personal assistant to country music star Lee Ann Womack and currently lives in Nashville.

VI. EXTENDING A HAND:
Promoting Volunteerism in America
by Brett Gibson

"Of all tyrannies, a tyranny exercised for the good of its victims may be the most oppressive. It may be better to live under robber barons than under omnipotent moral busybodies. The robber baron's cruelty may sometimes sleep, his cupidity may at some point be satiated; but those who torment us for our own good will torment us without end, for they do so with the approval of their own conscience."

- C.S. Lewis

America is a country with a proud legacy of public service. Throughout history, each time that our citizens' unalienable rights have been threatened by foreign enemies, the ranks of our nation's military have swelled with volunteers ready to die serving in their defense. Domestically, too, our teachers and our police officers are just some of the many who dedicate their lives to service of their communities. Meanwhile, in times of challenge or hardship, Americans have consistently banded together – voluntarily forming associations and institutions that offer our fellow countrymen a hand up, rather than a handout. Volunteerism and community service are engines of America's democracy. Our country was built by men and women who paid the cost of freedom with service in war and peacetime through sacrifices of time, talent, and treasure.

A society that values the rights of life, liberty, and the pursuit of happiness recognizes that its government must provide those critical public services that defend these rights as unalienable. However, that same society must also recognize that most other brands of charitable service properly take the form of individuals' personal choices and represent decisions about how to use individual resources to help others. When government imposes mandatory charitable service, managed by bureaucracy, individual rights are threatened and the impact of local, impassioned, community service is weakened. This essay is intended to provide a warning of the dangers of federalizing community service and to provide alternatives for increasing volunteerism nationwide.

There is a constitutional distinction between the services that are properly provided by the American government and those whose provision is best left to private individuals and institutions. According to our founding documents, governments have a fundamental responsibility to secure their citizens' rights to life, liberty, and the pursuit of happiness. In fact, our Declaration of Independence identifies the protection of these rights as *the* reason for a government's creation. Thus, our government has an obligation to create organizations that effectively accomplish this function. These institutions are the military (the entire national security apparatus); the police force and the court system (both of which include local and federal responsibilities); public schools (a local function, augmented by a variety of private institutions); and a minimal, necessary bureaucracy (a much smaller IRS to collect legitimate tax revenue, and a body of elected officials).

The provision of these services, along with necessary infrastructure creation, constitutes the appropriate role of government in a society. By effectively fielding the institutions that provide them, our government fulfills its obligations to the American people. Extending the government's public service role beyond this mandate is doubly dangerous. Not only does expanding the scope of government's responsibility ensure that it will be less able to focus on its legitimate functions, but also fundamentally threatens individual liberty.

This limited set of governmentally administered public services stands in stark contrast to the expansive social programs present in America today, which many would like to see grown dramatically. Government service programs, other than those mentioned above, overstep the intent of the Constitution by federalizing charity and volunteer efforts in ways that our Founders never intended. A dedication to true liberty requires that governments give up the ability to coerce citizens into choosing particular vocations, even if the intentions behind the coercion are benevolent. Thomas Jefferson understood this when he said, "I would rather be exposed to the inconveniences attending to too much liberty than to those attending too small a degree of it." By mandating volunteerism, the government oversteps its legitimate bounds, and in so doing it erodes the liberty of its people.

Our Founders recognized that a community of free men is a much more capable and accountable steward of resources than any government program ever could be. The private sector develops solutions when innovative Americans strive to help their fellow citizens as a matter of personal choice. The dramatic expansion of government that any national service plan entails only serves to drain resources from private charities. This occurs in the form of overwhelmingly burdensome levels of taxation, resulting in funds being redirected from private charities to much less effective public programs.

The best activists and social entrepreneurs are those who act on free will and passion for a cause, not as employees filling government billets. There is a marked distinction between the quality of work, care, and provision of service from a person who acts based on a calling for social enterprise and a person who is simply collecting a government paycheck. By federalizing community service, private ownership and accountability for performance are lost. An honest look at society shows us that public workers are less motivated and less effective than impassioned service entrepreneurs. The private sector has repeatedly proven itself better at innovating, creating opportunity, and stimulating growth for non-profit and philanthropic organizations. Would you rather your child be taught by a Teach for America teacher – the best and the brightest of the next generation – or a tenured teacher in America's public school system? Would you rather have your residence conceived of and built by Habitat for Humanity volunteers or the bureaucrats who made possible Chicago's infamous Cabrini Green Public Housing Project? Time and time again, we are shown that the choice between public or private provision of charitable services determines whether these programs succeed or fail.

Volunteer service is an individual decision that should not be mandated or enforced as a rite of passage for American citizens. Indeed, such a system is entirely contrary to the very definition of volunteerism. Freedom is not true freedom if we are only free – or if we are coerced – to choose the outcome that the government sees as appropriate.

The worst outcome for our country's poor and sick would be for the federal government to claim more responsibility for their care by developing a universal program to deliver volunteers. Yet that is exactly what it intends to do. For example, the Kennedy Serve America Act of 2009 seeks to grow AmeriCorps from 75,000 participants to over 250,000. AmeriCorps has the laudable goal of coordinating worldwide service opportunities for American volunteers. Despite being steeped in good intentions, the bill would make AmeriCorps the 17th largest employer in the world.[1] The result will be a huge government entity, a breeding ground for the same incompetence that the Federal Emergency Management Agency (FEMA) displayed when it mobilized to respond to Hurricane Katrina in September 2005.

Indeed, America's federal government has provided countless examples of its inability to manage charitable programs efficiently or effectively. In recent memory, food stamp programs and public housing have firmly established that fraud, waste, and abuse are the unavoidable byproducts of a federal bureaucracy. Welfare reform of the 1990s was driven by the massive waste and fraud that occurred in government agencies responsible for issuing food stamps.[2] Reform was needed because of the failure of even strict government controls to stop participants and administrators from exploiting the system to gain unearned benefits. Public housing was rife with crime in the 1980s and 1990s because under-qualified workers were placed in charge of development, supervision, and security of government-provided housing.[3] This resulted in the opposite of the desired effect as inner-city crime and poverty rose after the government housing was erected.

Even more recent history has shown that federal solutions to local problems are woefully ineffective. Most notably, FEMA failed miserably to provide relief to the people of New Orleans after Hurricane Katrina. As a member of the Army National Guard, I served in New Orleans as part of the relief effort. Once on the ground, I immediately realized that FEMA was disorganized, clumsy, and communicated poorly between the various federal agencies and local authorities. FEMA illustrated exactly why federal solutions for local problems do not work.

While my unit provided security for a destroyed section of coastland, FEMA displayed its most telling example of incompetence. Thousands of city residents were without electricity, running water, and basic human necessities. Meanwhile, FEMA employees occupied a nearby convention center and constructed mobile showers, modular kitchens, and beds. Sadly, these amenities were only allowed to FEMA agencies and staff, and not even made available to the neediest local residents. Each night after serving dinner to its staff, FEMA's garbage cans filled with hundreds of pounds of uneaten food while local shelters struggled to meet the overwhelming needs of New Orleans' starving people. By way of contrast, the most effective responders in New Orleans were local organizations with close ties to the needs of the people. Faith-based organizations, churches, and community centers proved adaptive and resourceful. Shelters formed in synagogue sanctuaries, YMCAs, and local soup kitchens while donations and volunteers flooded in from across the country to help the victims. Today, local organizations and citizen-led, bottom-up service projects are still leading the way in the revitalization of New Orleans.

The government intends to use the national service plan not just to help the unfortunate, but also as a tool to teach values to young Americans: patriotism, hard work, and shared sacrifice. These are certainly positive values that provide some of the strongest strands in our American fabric, but we once again find the government overstepping its legitimate bounds. Nevermind that we already have well-established government organizations – the military, the police force, the fire department, the public schools – that are hiring and where young Americans can choose to develop these values. These organizations foster specific values not as their primary purpose, but because those values are the most effective way to achieve their legitimate mandates. In contrast, national service plans are often justified solely on the basis of their being a good vehicle to teach values to America's youth. Once people accept that the government has a valid interest in teaching values simply for values' sake, the door to tyranny is opened. In the past, our government has been complacent with and even used its power to ingrain the acceptance of what it determined to be "good values." Do segregation and prohibition ring any bells? Is this really the track record that we want from an institution charged with teaching morality?

Allowing the state to instill values in our young people seems benign, even benevolent, when the government is instilling values in which we believe. However, accepting such a role for government as legitimate also implies that we accept the government's ability to change the values that are being taught and to instill in our society values that we do not share. For instance, when the government teaches values today, those values are generally grounded in moral relativism. This doctrine of the complete tolerance and acceptance of all perspectives is a dangerous belief system and one that the majority of Americans do not share. Yet, it is tacitly taught in our classrooms, government employee training courses, and federal programs of all stripes. It would doubtlessly infuse the federal provision of charitable services. Instead of granting a hand up and teaching personal responsibility, our government would grant the status of "victim" to the unfortunate and give them a handout. This will inevitably be the nature of the values taught to young Americans pushed into service by the government.

Moreover, government control of the values of its populace is a fundamental characteristic of all totalitarian states. Once we accept the government's claim to do this, we begin the process of throwing away our freedom. It is the role of family to teach values. It is the role of churches and synagogues, not government, to teach beliefs and morals. This has always been the case in America and has formed the cornerstone of civic virtue in our country. When the family, the church, and the community group take the lead in fostering values, both faith-based and secular associations of free men are formed to help others and strengthen our democracy. These associations are formed based upon the values that those private institutions inculcate in the populace. Alexis de Tocqueville called these social agencies "little democracies" and he became supremely aware that they could only exist in a place like America, where the conditions were set for people to act freely, independent of a dictating hand of government. We must let the engine of social entrepreneurs and associations work. In order to allow that to happen, government must extricate itself from the provision of charitable services.

We have seen that when federal powers inherit the responsibility to determine local needs and deploy resources to respond to them, the needs go unmet or are met inefficiently by a lethargic bureaucracy. Luckily, there is an alternative. The people who are best able to offer help to Americans in need are those who are closest to the needy. The PTA, Boy Scouts, and faith-based organizations are small, accountable, and closely tied to the communities they serve. While government programs have come and gone, these institutions have endured. The success of these organizations shows that social needs are best met locally. Local community service and charity organizations are nimble and geared toward developing solutions, achieving results, and providing effective aid to their fellow Americans. Without actually solving the problems they were designed to tackle, these organizations would cease to exist. Moreover, these organizations are run lean by budgetary necessity – which ensures they are efficient in the provision of services. Neither of these statements can be made about government programs. Efforts to make community service a national commodity will dilute the effect of citizen-led, locally impactful programs. Our communities are incubators for ideas and initiatives where one man can identify a need and design the organization to address it. Replacing individual, human initiative with the government's regulations and dictates can only interfere with the process by diverting resources and stifling individual innovation.

Many people worry that if the government does not provide relief to America's unfortunate that no one will. This concern is unfounded. A smaller government pruned of its inefficient social programs requires fewer taxes, leaving more money in the hands of individuals to fund private charities. This dynamic will redirect social capital from public programs to non-profits and other charities, allowing these more effective and efficient organizations to deploy more resources. Recent calls to reduce or eliminate charitable tax deductions would have the opposite effect. As such, they should scare the heck out of those Americans who are dependent upon the generosity of others. Such a policy would do little more than severely diminish philanthropic incentives and reduce effective assistance to those who need it most.

Philanthropists give most freely and generously when they are allowed to choose where and how to give their money. Additionally, these dollars are spent much more effectively. Empirical studies support this logic. The Department of the Treasury's 2003 Financial Report of the United States Government includes a short section entitled, "Unreconciled Transactions Affecting the Change in Net Position," which explains that these unreconciled transactions totaled $24.5 billion in 2003. These are funds for which auditors cannot account. The government knows that $25 billion was spent by someone, somewhere, on something; but no one knows who spent it, where it was spent, or on what it was spent. Blaming these unreconciled transactions on the failure of federal agencies to report their expenditures properly, the Treasury report concluded that locating the funds is a "priority."[4] To put this number in perspective, the entire Manhattan Project to develop the atomic bomb cost just under $25 billion in 2008 dollars.[5] In 2003 alone, the federal government essentially lost this amount of money. Such negligence would never be tolerated at a private charity!

A more effective way to promote community service is to do away with ineffective government programs and use the cost savings to lower individual and corporate taxes. This would allow individuals and entrepreneurs to decide how to spend their charitable money – holding the charities they choose to support accountable for the use of those funds. Such a policy has been demonstrated to result not just in more effective use of resources, but also in increased support for private charities. In states where taxes and regulation are lowest, charitable giving is highest. This provides social innovators and entrepreneurs the access to capital that they need to build organizations to meet society's most pressing needs. Kevin Burke's 2009 study comparing states' charitable giving rates established the disparity in charitable donations between conservative and liberal states. In 1996, 2000, and 2004, charitable giving was highest in states with the highest percentage of conservative legislators – areas characterized by lower taxes, less regulation, and less litigation.[6] This further establishes that limited government and fewer bureaucrats translate into more generosity, philanthropy, and efficiency in charitable service provision.

The most effective view of charity is of a man putting his hand into his own pocket to give to someone that he knows to be in need. Contrast this with the liberal view of charity: the government's putting *its* hand in *your* pocket to give to someone *it* decides is in need (a determination too often based on political calculations). The attempt by the current administration and Congress to drastically expand government public service programs is simply another way to enhance their power by keeping citizens reliant on handouts and stifling the innovation and progress that are the hallmarks of private charity. Why allow an individual citizen to give $500 to the local food bank when you can tax everyone and earmark them $500,000? Such an approach to governance results in massive inefficiency and is the definition of tyranny.

There are better avenues for increasing volunteerism and philanthropy than through expanding government-run, compulsory service. Grassroots and civic organizations should take the place of government and take the lead on a national scale to meet community needs and solve problems. Church soup kitchens, community food drives, and Little League baseball: these are the manifestations of a free man's conscience driving charitable activities. In the absence of large-scale government social programs, faith-based groups will be even more active than they already are. Already, more Americans volunteer through church organizations than any other institutions. Faith-based organizations are more trusted, quicker to respond, and closer to the needs of the people they serve than other types of charitable groups. It is in the nature of these organizations to be leaner, lower cost, and more innovative precisely because they can't count on a line item in the next federal budget. When Hurricane Katrina devastated New Orleans, Louisiana and parts of Mississippi, Christian churches responded quicker than any other groups in service to their fellow men.[7] By freeing up tax revenue that currently funds expansive, inefficient, and unaccountable federal programs, faith and community-based organizations will find themselves awash in funds that they can immediately put to work for the benefit of the needy.

But this dynamic is not limited to religious service organizations. Public-private partnerships and education-based service models provide yet another example of the innovative solutions developed by the private sector. They spotlight the vast potential for social entrepreneurs to improve America. Bentley College introduced a program called "Give a Year" in 2007 where students participate in a program called "City Year" to complete a year of service underwritten by Fortune 500 companies. Rosabeth Moss Kanter, a Harvard Business School professor, said,

Major companies increasingly seek leaders who are visionary problem-solvers and who embrace social responsibility as a critical component of

73

business strategy. The innovative 'Give a Year' partnership between Bentley and City Year is a path breaking way to develop great leaders for the future. This powerful combination of higher education with an inspiring year of civic engagement and national service is sure to produce a talent pool of skilled business leaders who will be in high demand at America's leading companies. This has the potential to fundamentally change the way business sees its role in the world.[8]

All told, there are many options for harnessing individual goodwill and charity to meet growing demands of the poor and sick in our country and abroad. When the onus for taking care of our nation's underprivileged is once again put on the backs of their neighbors, citizens will bind together to find and fund solutions that work.

Finally, reestablishing the focus of government from solving *all* of our problems to solving *some* of them will dramatically improve its ability to execute its core mandates. A federal government charged with a limited set of responsibilities – national defense, law enforcement, diplomacy, and infrastructure development, among the most prominent – will necessarily be better at those tasks simply by virtue of increased focus. As voters, we will be much more able to hold our federal government accountable for its actions if it acts within the framework of this limited mandate. State and local governments, too, will redouble efforts on their legitimate functions and develop best practices for police action, litigation, and educating our children rather than seizing and squandering resources that the private sector could better marshal and deploy.

There must be a bright line test to evaluate the scope of public service in America. Government should not expand its role into the provision of extra-Constitutional public services where it does more harm than good. Rather, it should focus its efforts and resources on maintaining and improving the institutions that preserve and expand our individual liberties. In the absence of government, a robust private sector will provide the social services for which it is far better suited than government – through churches, affinity groups, and other private associations and local initiatives. Because individuals have proven themselves time and again to be the best stewards of resources, limited and sensible levels of regulation and taxation will clear the way for free enterprise to find solutions for social challenges. A government that stays out of the way is a government that is truly doing its part for America's underprivileged. As government expands its reach, teaching values and confiscating individuals' resources for a nebulous "common good," individual liberty is lost, private charity is crippled, and the neediest among us pay the steepest price. It is a price we cannot afford to make them pay any longer.

Brett Gibson is currently a student at Harvard Business School. Prior to matriculating, he served as political assistant to Virginia Governor Bob McDonnell. Brett completed his undergraduate degree at the University of Virginia in finance and American politics. Prior to the campaign, Brett achieved the rank of Captain in the US Army Reserve and was a member of the elite Army Rangers, serving in both Iraq and Afghanistan. He has also worked in real estate for the global private equity firm, The Carlyle Group, and in financial services for Deloitte Consulting.

VII. TRUE MULTICULTURALISM:
Shattering the Walls that Divide Americans
by John Amble

When you finish this sentence, take a moment before reading further, imagine you and I are meeting for the first time, and consider how you would respond if I asked you to tell me about yourself.

Have you come up with an answer? This question is posed to each of us frequently throughout our lives. Would you tell me where you grew up? Perhaps you would share with me what you do for a living. You might tell me where you went to school, list a few of your hobbies, or show me a photo of your family. I'm not certain of what my exact response would be, but it would likely consist of these or similar components. I do know how I would not respond, however. I would not tell you that I'm a white, heterosexual, Christian male of northern European descent. Though all accurately describe me, these characteristics alone do not define me.

Yet every day, government policy is made based upon these few attributes of the American people. Evidently, this information alone equips the government to implement far-reaching programs that shape our society. Many of these initiatives promise to treat individual Americans differently based upon a list of factors so short that I just typed them on a single line. My application to college was weighed differently than it would have been had I been a racial minority. The government requires that I obtain a license in order to marry and, in nearly every state, will only grant me one because I am straight. My property rights may be violated if I attempt to worship with others on private property without prior zoning approval by the government. And my federal scholarship options when applying to graduate school were limited to a fraction of what they would have been had I claimed a different ethnic descent. But why?

The subject of multiculturalism in America is a sensitive one. A discussion of the proper role of government with respect to the rights of minority groups – be they defined in terms of race, ethnicity, gender, religion, sexuality, or any other characteristic – is inherently difficult. Equally difficult is a commitment to effectively learning from our unique history by seeking out the lessons of America's successes while acknowledging and addressing our tragic errors. But the difficulty of these tasks is only equaled by their importance. This discussion is necessary in order to ensure America remains a nation in which everybody has an equal opportunity to succeed, regardless of any single characteristic of our individual identities.

Ours is a nation of immigrants. My own family arrived from Norway and Sweden just more than a century ago. Inquire about the respective heritages of the students sitting in almost any classroom in the United States, and you might fill an atlas of the world. This is a phenomenon unique to our nation. Our ancestors first sought the promise of an American life five centuries ago, and we've continued to come ever since. Throughout our history, people from all corners of the globe have risked everything for a chance at the American dream. That there is no similar French dream, or Costa Rican dream, or Russian dream, or Kenyan dream is indicative of two important facts. First, our culture sets us apart as a nation where opportunity abounds for all who make America their home. The opportunities available surpass that of *every other nation in the world*. Secondly, an American who moves to Mexico does not become Mexican (the same holds true for American emigrants to any other country). But a Mexican who comes to America and embraces our culture can freely choose to become an American, thereby opening the door to the promise of the American dream.

The stories of immigrants have combined over generations to form our national culture. We must continue to fully appreciate this culture if we wish to remain a nation where opportunity flourishes. The dream of improving one's lot and providing a quality life for one's family does not exist here only on the periphery, as it does even in many other Western nations. This dream is supremely attainable, with evidence of this fact accumulating daily in the newfound prosperity and happiness of our most recent immigrants. But what makes this dream so much more achievable here than anywhere else?

A myriad of factors combine to make the American dream tremendously realistic, but it is critical that we identify a few of the most important of them. Since the earliest days of immigration in America, widespread adoption of the English language has facilitated communication and co-operation, allowing America's newest arrivals – from Chilean farmers to Chinese factory workers – to identify and accomplish common goals. Our free markets guarantee that the son of an impoverished laborer need not languish in a society where he is forced into his father's field. The rule of law promises that the rights of every man and woman are protected with equal vigor. And a culture that rewards hard work ensures that from the moment he steps foot on American soil, an immigrant may reap the fruits of his own labor.

These ideals remain the bedrock on which dreams are built. With them in mind, we can create a picture of the society that America should strive to achieve. Our government should foster a diverse meritocracy blind to the color of one's skin, the categorization of one's gender, the nature of one's religious beliefs, or the orientation of one's sexuality. Such a society must be enhanced by an effort to foster those elements of our culture that set us apart from every other nation in the world, while simultaneously promoting a notion of equality that guarantees to treat all individuals fairly and justly. Any policy that subjectively places individuals into categories based on any of the characteristics listed above undermines the very richness of our nation's diversity.

It is this very diversity which is in many ways responsible for our success – as individuals, communities, and as a nation. This success is made possible when free men and women come together in a spirit of fairness and cooperation. Such blending can only occur where all individuals embrace a common culture. The subjugation of American culture to the innumerable subcultures that exist within our country today inevitably breeds isolationism. This in turn mitigates the plentiful benefits available to Americans of all backgrounds when we truly foster an environment of unity.

Today we see countless groups who choose to define themselves by a single characteristic, creating a de facto atmosphere of segregation. Among the most successful of these groups are cultural minorities, whose status as such provides a powerful psychological asset in a debate which takes place in a system that unnaturally elevates our differences. But the lessons of history show that the majority is also supremely capable of employing government advantage to the detriment of others. Whether majority or minority, the critical fact we must recognize is that these groups may be defined by any trait. Unfortunately, an honest discussion of multiculturalism, equality, and government action is too often derailed by spurious charges of racism, most frequently by groups whose existence is threatened by such an honest discussion. Acceptance of such charges does a disservice to the millions of Americans who are discriminated against based on any characteristic other than race, and who only want to be treated fairly.

Though free association is a fundamental right which must be protected, forming such associations solely to achieve favored status from our government contradicts the very spirit of America. The influence that these interest groups wield over government policy is contrary to the common interests of American society. Under our Constitution, Congress allocates funds for federal programs. Despite its seeming belief to the contrary, the resources at Congress' disposal are in fact limited. As such, competition for federally sanctioned advantage is characterized by its zero-sum nature. Any benefit given to one individual or group will inherently be paired with a reduction of opportunity for another. When the government arbitrarily designates one man as naturally more deserving of employment, an education, or housing, based on any measure other than merit, the cost may very well be the elimination of another man's chance to achieve the American dream. It is inevitable, then, that negative feelings will spread throughout society, emanating from any one group and directed toward its opponent in the contest for official government advantage. These feelings are the natural product of a system that encourages its people to seek division rather than celebrate the common culture which promises to bring us together.

Thus, the voluntary isolationism of various subgroups within the United States is at odds with the blind meritocracy that should serve as the ultimate objective of both our government and our people. Government acquiescence to the demands of self-segregated interest groups pushes us further from this goal, making ours less and less a nation of equals and creating a perverted tendency to deny our fundamental American culture. Such acquiescence may take many forms, but the policy manifestations and their negative impacts can clearly be seen by taking a look at education, housing, and employment.

In our education system, a twisted sense of multiculturalism first manifests itself in a curriculum that discounts our American heritage. In our public schools, a trend toward inculcating in students a sense of moral and cultural relativism can be clearly discerned. As such practices have become more and more common, attacks on teachers and schools who dare to teach a respect for American history, culture, and traditions have become increasingly accepted. Indeed, to even acknowledge in the classroom the existence of a distinct, American identity is virtually taboo. In 2009, an American History teacher in Kansas was dismissed from his job, claiming he was told by his assistant principal that his school-affiliated website, which included links to the US Army website and other military and historical sites, was "too patriotic."[1] The school district was later forced to acknowledge a grievous injustice and reverse its decision.

Teachers need not coercively instill in students a particular set of values; indeed, this would represent an infringement on the fundamental right of all individuals to develop our own set of beliefs and moral code. But formulation of a personal set of values requires a firm understanding of our nation's culture and history, a task with which America's teachers are charged. In 2002, justifying his threat to veto a bill that would reintroduce the Pledge of Allegiance into Minnesota's classrooms, then Governor Jesse Ventura stated, "Patriotism is voluntary. It is a feeling of loyalty and allegiance that is the result of knowledge and belief. No law will make a citizen a patriot."[2] While true, consider the sources of patriotism – broadly defined as pride in one's nation and culture – that the former governor references: knowledge and belief. While the beliefs of our children are rightly formed as a result of parental and religious influence, should we not expect that knowledge, the other source of patriotism that Ventura cited, be acquired in the classroom? Is imparting knowledge not the principal mandate of our education system? Unfortunately, Governor Ventura's belief that an understanding of and respect for our American identity must be banished from the classroom is shared by many of our nation's political leaders.

The ramifications of the minimization of American culture in our education system are serious. In 2008 and 2009, as many as twenty young

Somali men left their homes in Minneapolis and travelled to Somalia.[3] It is believed that the men joined al-Shabaab, a militant organization reportedly allied with al-Qaida. Some of the Somali-Americans were killed in the months following their arrival, including one who blew himself up during a wave of suicide attacks orchestrated by the group (the first ever attributed to an American citizen). Most of these young men were infants or toddlers when their families first sought refuge in the US from the lawlessness and brutality that plagued East Africa in the 1990s. Though raised in the United States and educated in American schools, this group evidently felt a greater kinship with fundamentalist terrorists half a world away than with the nation that provided them with a safe haven from the nightmares of perpetual war. Our status as such a haven is important, and we must strive to remain a beacon of hope in a broken world. But along with this open-arms reception, we must promote assimilation into our culture, opening the door to opportunity for all who come to our country. Our public schools provide the best means to do so.

The argument that teachers should foster in their students an understanding of American history and traditions is anything but controversial. In 1999, a study by the nonpartisan, nonprofit group Public Agenda revealed that parents of all demographic groups overwhelmingly support the view that schools should teach traditional ideals and stories of what it means to be an American.[4] The study further found that more than nine in ten foreign-born parents believe that the US is a better country than most others – a sentiment echoed by white and Hispanic parents. More than eight in ten African-American parents agreed. Yet ten years after the study was published, the government pushes to further restrict curricula that reflect this widespread attitude, enforcing ever more severe subjugation of American culture in the classroom.

After completing more than a decade of this culturally diluted education, the fate of a student's application to a public university may rest on the racial identification he is asked to provide. In 2003, the US Supreme Court ruled permissible a race-conscious application concept employed by the University of Michigan Law School to select admitted students.[5] That the court ruled against the more standardized advantage given to racial minority applicants in the university's undergraduate points-based system only demonstrates the subjectivity intrinsic in determining suitability to pursue higher education based on race. Whether you are white, black, Hispanic, or of any other racial background, is this the criteria upon which you wish to be offered the opportunity to follow your dreams? Sadly, we cannot be surprised that many students accept such a system after spending their formative years in schools that too often refuse to teach the essential elements of American culture, chief among them the belief that all men and women truly are equal, and should be treated as such.

Preferential treatment in federal housing policy has similarly worrisome effects. In 1999, the Clinton Administration pressured Fannie Mae, the massive, government-subsidized underwriter of mortgages, to ease credit requirements for home loans. The move was hailed as an opportunity to increase home ownership among groups who have historically been less likely to secure approval for loans, primarily minority and low-income borrowers. Reducing barriers to this elemental aspect of the American dream for the widest array of individuals and families is a supremely important goal. But doing so in a way that undermines our foundational principles, including equality of opportunity and free access to unfettered markets, represents an abrogation of the government's most basic obligations. Influencing the housing market by creating artificial prices may open doors to some, but because our economy contains a finite supply of money available to be borrowed, it necessarily closes the door to others. Seen in this light, is such a program truly consistent with the spirit of fairness which undergirds American culture?

Programs that treat people differently based upon subjectively defined characteristics such as race, gender, or any other also have dangerous repercussions that extend throughout our society. When the program detailed above was implemented, our economy remained strong, propelled by the technological innovations that pushed prosperity and market returns to sky-high levels in the 1990s. But a slight economic downturn could yield catastrophic consequences, potentially prompting an exorbitantly expensive government intervention to cover economic losses in the housing market, similar to that required by the savings and loan "thrift industry" in the 1980s. Indeed, when the policy was first introduced, Peter Wallison of the American Enterprise Institute worried of the artificially eased credit requirements that "from the perspective of many people, including me, this is another thrift industry growing up around us. If they fail, the government will have to step up and bail them out the way it stepped up and bailed out the thrift industry."[6] Having witnessed the economic downturn of 2007-2009 and the plethora of government bailouts that ensued, Wallison's foresight seems prophetic. Unfortunately, the desire to artificially incentivize economic outcomes based purely on social factors blinded our policymakers, ultimately leaving both our economic prosperity and the very principle of fairness as its victims.

The most widely publicized example of governmentally enforced unequal treatment is found in federal affirmative action employment policies. First coined in 1961 by President Kennedy, the term "affirmative action" applies to government policies which require that race, ethnicity, and gender play a role in hiring practices. They originated as a temporary measure to erase the inequalities created by the centuries of discrimination that form an inexcusable dark spot on our nation's history. Such policies are not unique to the US. The employment of mechanisms intended to introduce equality into societies where it has previously not existed can be found in all corners of the globe. In Iraq, for instance, quotas have been imposed to guarantee legislative seats to women, Shia Muslims, and Kurds, groups who have been persecuted in the country for generations. But few Iraqis would argue that the quotas are an ideal permanent solution. Most hope that they will serve only as a bridge that will allow them to reach the type of society in which equality prevails and the quotas themselves are unnecessary.

The same mentality should shape our thinking in America. We should strive to create a meritocratic community of individuals who need not be defined by a single characteristic. Many justify affirmative action policies by citing the great strides we have made toward equality since their initial enactment. Given this, is it not appropriate to ask if the very progress we have made has rendered these policies outdated? Their continued existence only serves to acknowledge and thereby perpetuate the lines of division that continue to segregate our society. It is time to take the next step in eliminating these ugly walls, finally removing the blemish of discrimination from the landscape of our society forever.

These examples of inappropriate and exclusive government action should be instructive to anyone who seeks a vision of appropriate application of governmental authority. The goal toward which such authority should be focused is the development and maintenance of a society in which all individuals are afforded equal opportunity to pursue their dreams and reap the benefits of their work. Current policies that magnify our differences cannot go on indefinitely, even those that are least controversial. In the words of Martin Luther King, Jr., "True peace is not merely the absence of tension: it is the presence of justice." In other words, Americans' tacit acceptance of government-sanctioned preferential treatment for one group over another will not yield a spirit of cooperation and tolerance. But a just society will. The society that elevates merit over any arbitrary characteristic will. The society where individuals are not judged by the color of their skin, or their gender, or sexual preference, ethnic background, or religion, will. The philosophy that calls for a blind meritocracy exists as the intellectual descendent of our nation's heroic civil rights leaders, while many of those who claim such a lineage foment the very lines of division that King and others devoted their lives to eliminating. So what would be the hallmarks of the blind meritocracy that we seek?

First, equality before the law would guarantee that all men and women are held by society to precisely the same standards of behavior, and treatment of those who fail to achieve this standard is identical across the demographic spectrum. Any law that guarantees different treatment for different individuals is inherently unjust, as is any application of an otherwise just law which results in unequal treatment. Equality before the law served as a bedrock principle upon which our nation was founded. The failure of our founders to extend universally the protection provided by this principle allowed for the continued existence of the inexcusable institution of slavery. But we must not attribute this shameful aspect of our history to a failure of the principle of equality before the law, but rather to the failure of men to adequately implement it. This should only strengthen our resolve to guarantee that it is extended to all Americans. We should again heed the wisdom of Dr. King: "The failures of the past must not be an excuse for the inaction of the present and the future."

Second, our society should be characterized by our commitment to ensure equality of opportunity, rather than equality of outcome. Any movement toward the latter necessarily diminishes the role of the former, thereby undermining the chances for some to achieve the American dream. The earlier discussion of the zero-sum nature of governmentally sanctioned advantage lends itself to this notion. Those who call for preferential treatment fail to recognize that by extending unearned benefit to any group based on subjectively chosen attributes, the government inevitably places other groups at an undeserved and unjust disadvantage. Furthermore, such policies foster an amplified consciousness of our differences, inevitably leading to even greater organization along artificial lines. Thus, they serve only to foment segregation in American society.

There are those who argue that seeking equality of outcome is a necessary short-term step that must be taken in response to past harms done to particular groups. Benefits given to racial minorities based on past discrimination are often supported with this argument, as is advantage provided to women because of the historically unfavorable status they have held in the workplace. But while past discrimination suffered by any group is absolutely wrong, be it the result of official government policy or informal societal prejudice, organizing along demographic lines to seek redress is not the answer. Consider the case of Japanese-Americans, who were subject to rampant discrimination for decades and even placed into internment camps during World War II. As of the most recent census, per capita income of this group in 1999 was $30,075, while that of the nation as a whole was $21,587.[7] This is true despite the fact that there has been no large scale Japanese-American interest group activity along the lines of other racial or ethnic minority organizations. Rather, such success has been the result of widespread assimilation into American culture by the vast majority of Americans of Japanese descent.

All Americans should recognize unequivocally that our nation's guiding principles dictate a universal respect for human rights. But what does it mean for a government to promise to protect the fundamental human rights of its people? In America, it should be entirely unacceptable for prejudicial treatment to occur based on race, creed, ethnicity, gender, sexuality, or religion. Discrimination against a Hispanic, a woman, or a

Muslim is not wrong because the victim is Hispanic, female, or Muslim. It is wrong because he or she is human.

A commitment to ensuring complete equality of opportunity is the only way to achieve the true meritocratic community of free men and women that we seek. Such a community inherently fosters an atmosphere of cooperation. Where in the world can you expect to see an Indian and a Pakistani working together to solve common problems? Not in India, and not in Pakistan. Where might you find an Orthodox Jew and a devout Muslim seeking common ground to resolve differences that reach back more than a thousand years? Not in the Middle East. These are literally phenomena unique to Western culture, and even more so to the United States. We must cultivate those aspects of American culture that make such cooperation possible.

If America's promise of equality of opportunity encourages cultural comingling on a scale not seen anywhere else in the world, it also facilitates the learning about people who may have different backgrounds than our own. Every one of us has much we can learn from others. Our lives are made richer by sharing our experiences with each other. Only in a society whose government does not differentiate between black and white, Hispanic and Asian, male and female, or Christian and Muslim, can we truly take advantage of the opportunity to learn from each other's unique experiences.

This is the society for which we should strive. In this society, men and women compete fairly for jobs and promotions in the workplace. College applicants are accepted by virtue of their merit, and not degraded by policies which use skin color to determine suitability to pursue higher education. Freedom of religion truly reigns supreme and nobody is prevented from worshiping or displaying the symbols of his chosen religion. New arrivals to our nation are encouraged to learn the English language, which serves as a key that will unlock the door to the American dream. The rule of law is applied fairly and evenly, ensuring that shameful discrepancies in criminal prosecution and sentencing cannot exist. Each person's hard work is of value to society, with such value rewarded in the free market. And American history, traditions, and heritage are taught in our public schools, promising that those values which combine to form American culture guide our society's development for generations to come.

Both Americans and guests in our country should feel free to live their lives as they see fit. But for the good of our nation, as well as the individuals and communities of which it is comprised, we cannot afford to subjugate our culture to any others. There is room for men and women of literally every background within the structure of traditions, values, and principles that together form American culture. A meritocratic society that is truly blind to subjectively defined divisions will be one of free association, where the rule of law guarantees our fundamental rights. At any moment in such a society, any individual might succeed in his quest to fulfill the American dream.

John Amble is a graduate student in the War Studies Department at King's College London. In 2008, he served in Baghdad, Iraq as commander of a tactical psychological operations detachment, where he was awarded the Bronze Star Medal for exceptionally meritorious service. He subsequently served as an intelligence officer at the Defense Intelligence Agency. His extensive military training includes resident professional courses at the US Army Intelligence Center and the JFK Special Warfare Center. Prior to his military service, he worked as a financial consultant for a variety of political campaigns in the Midwest. John is a graduate of the University of Minnesota.

VIII. VOICES OF THE DAMNED:
A Rights-based Analysis of Abortion in America
by Robert Wheeler

"We hold these truths to be self-evident, that all men are created equal, that they are endowed by their creator with certain unalienable rights, that among these are Life, Liberty, and the Pursuit of Happiness."
  - Thomas Jefferson in the Preamble to the Declaration of Independence

Each of you reading this book that was born after 1973 was a choice. Neither your exploits nor achievements nor your perceived level of individual autonomy can change the fact that you exist by virtue of two gifts. The first of these gifts was the gift of life given to you by your parents when they chose to have sex. The second of these gifts was your mother's conscious decision to carry you to term; in so doing she granted you a chance to live that life. Regardless of the circumstances surrounding your conception, your mother made that second decision and had she not, you would no longer exist. Despite the fact that in the womb you embodied all of the potential that you have exercised to this point in your life and all that you have become, you were still a choice. And a different choice would have yielded a different world – one in which you did not exist to hold this book in your hands.

It is your mother's right to this second choice that cannot be justified. Each year in the United States, more than 1,000,000 women make a different decision than your mother did. Fully 22% of all pregnancies (excluding miscarriages) in the United States are terminated by a mother's election to have an abortion.[1] This statistic bears witness to a blatant contravention of the values so eloquently expressed in America's founding documents. Your right to life is not a right given to you by your mother. Our nation was founded on the premise that each individual has the unalienable rights of life, liberty, and the pursuit of happiness. More importantly, these rights do not simply become rights by virtue of birth; rather, we are endowed with these rights by our creator, at the moment of *creation*. The form of the creator invoked by the Founders is irrelevant to the public debate, but what is relevant is that our country at its very founding acknowledged that by virtue of being created, of being conceived, the unborn child has a right to live. It is not a right that is alienable – even by the child's mother.

Our conservatism embraces a special brand of pro-choice sentiment. We believe in a woman's ability to make decisions about her own body and to prevent unwanted pregnancies. Many conservatives disagree with the use of contraceptives on moral grounds. However, this is not a morality that the government has any business legislating or enforcing upon the population as a whole. This is because the use of contraceptive devices does not infringe upon the rights of any other individual. However, we also acknowledge the reality of birth control and other methods of contraception: occasionally they fail. In light of this fact, we make one simple statement that is irrefutable under all circumstances. The decision to engage in sexual intercourse is inherently the acceptance of the possibility of becoming pregnant.

This, then, is the heart of the conservative's pro-choice position. From a societal perspective, the decision to have sex is not just the decision to engage in a single act of pleasure. It also must be the decision to accept all of the responsibility embodied in that act. In much the same way as buying a house is implicitly the decision to accept responsibility for the future mortgage payments, the decision to have sex is a decision that has implications for the future. These implications are inextricable from the act itself.

This point cannot be stressed enough. The majority of conservatives are pro-choice people: we simply believe that the choice to which an individual has the right is the decision to have sex or not rather than the decision to abort or not. We ask that all acknowledge this fact: that sex, no matter how well planned, can result in pregnancy. Given this prior knowledge, we believe that it is an unjust intrusion on the unborn child's rights to life, liberty, and the pursuit of happiness to arbitrarily snuff out his or her life by an abortion that is the choice of a mother who knew that pregnancy could result from her *free choice* to have sex.

It is from this position that we affirm the obligation of our government to protect the lives of the unborn by restricting access to abortion only to those situations in which the mother's life is in danger or in cases of rape or incest. In cases where the mother's life is in danger, the mother's right to life and the unborn child's right to life have competing claims for governmental protection. We believe it should be the mother's responsibility to weigh the life of the unborn child versus her own and to decide the appropriate course of action. This is a wrenching personal choice that we wish upon no one, but for anyone else to make such a decision for her would be to deny most the most basic rights and responsibilities she possesses by virtue of her humanity.

When the tragedies of rape or incest hit a woman, her decision to engage in sexual activity is stripped from her. She does not become pregnant by virtue of a choice that she made but rather, pregnancy is a burden forced unwillingly upon her. Each woman's moral code requires different actions from her if she is the victim of rape or incest. Again, in this instance, we believe that because the choice to have sex was taken from her, society should allow her the option to terminate the pregnancy. These are the only exceptions we acknowledge as acceptable and we do so because of the legitimacy of the claims competing with the right to life of the unborn child.

Our detractors pose many arguments for widespread access to abortion that appeal to our sense of empathy for the women who find themselves in the position of carrying a child they did not plan on conceiving. These arguments often tug at our heart strings and we truly do sympathize with the daunting challenges of being pregnant, unprepared, and often alone, without the resources that many others have to care for a child. It is for this reason that millions upon millions of dollars pour into charities each year to support young mothers-to-be without the resources to support themselves. It is for this reason that adoptions exist and countless couples across the country wait to give unwanted children loving homes.

Although pregnancy can be viewed as an inconvenience, it is an inconvenience that is foreseeable. When children are taught about sex, the first thing that they learn is that it is the act from which babies come. We steadfastly reject the notion that the inconvenience incurred from a mother's informed choice outweighs the unalienable right to life of the child she bears by virtue of that choice.

We first note that the vast, vast majority of abortions performed in the United States are performed for reasons that can be broadly categorized as "matters of convenience." In an aggregated study of 27 nations, women seeking abortion services generally cited the following reasons for their decisions: the desire to delay or end childbearing, concern over work or education, issues of financial or relationship stability, and perceived immaturity.[2] A 2004 survey of American women at abortion clinics yielded similar results.[3] Again, we understand that the concerns these women have regarding their newly uncertain futures are serious. We just do not believe that they constitute a valid justification for infringing upon the child's right to life.

There is a place in the public debate to discuss the support that should be given to women who find themselves in the unenviable position of an unplanned pregnancy. Furthermore, we believe that many support services exist in the private sector that can make the burden of bearing the child to term not painless, but easier. However, the province of this essay is to clearly establish that on-demand abortion is antithetical to the ideas and ideals upon which America was built. In so doing, we seek to reframe the question of unplanned pregnancies. The question prospective mothers now ask themselves is, "Should I get an abortion?" The question that they should ask themselves is, "What support is available for me throughout this pregnancy and do I want to raise the child or give it up for adoption?"

Abortion proponents often postulate hypothetical (or extremely unique but true) situations that at face value cannot easily be answered by our position of restricting abortion to all cases except for the previously outlined ones. Generally, these situations are some variation on the mother's or child's health being at risk or some variant of the rape/incest argument in which the mother truly did not have a choice in becoming pregnant.

The first response that we as conservatives make to these challenges is that they are extremely rare. In the survey quoted earlier, concerns about the mother's health were cited in just 12% of cases as a reason to pursue an abortion in the United States. Furthermore, just 1% of women seeking an abortion in America were pregnant by virtue of rape and only .5% had pregnancies that were the result of incest.[4] The fact remains that the majority of abortions are performed as a matter of convenience. However, even if that were not the case, abortion prohibitions are currently applied in an extremely backwards manner.

An abortion is a horrendous act. As with other horrendous acts of violence, it should be condemned in general and specific circumstances delineated where it, as a necessary evil, must be allowed. In the vast majority of cases, the taking of a life is illegal, yet allowances are made when such an action is in self-defense. In the same way, abortion should not be allowed in general to ensure access for the minority with a legitimate claim to it. As a society, we should err on the side of the unborn's unalienable rights.

Another faction of abortion supporters has begun advancing an even more insidious justification for the practice. The argument has come in many forms – that the parents of aborted babies cannot afford to raise them properly; that certain birth defects or genetic conditions render the child expendable; that the babies most often aborted are from a seedier element of society and are highly susceptible to commit crimes in the future. Here, the justification for abortion is not necessarily the primacy of a woman's right to control her reproductive system. Rather the argument is that these children, due to their circumstances, are unfit to live.

This line of reasoning is underwritten by a belief that these weaker elements impose too high of a cost on society to justify their existence. It is argued that if, through elective abortions, we can shed some of the excess baggage then society on the whole will be better off. To be fair, these arguments are generally posed as "added benefits" of abortion rather than reasons to promote it. However, that line is a blurry one. The idea that some members of society are expendable and thus not worthy of the governmental protections afforded to more "fit" members has underwritten the most heinous acts of organized slaughter in human history. Perhaps this is why our national conscience is slow to awaken. If we acknowledge the barbarism of abortion and relegate it as an archaic practice of a bygone age, then we must also admit societal guilt of an infanticide that dwarfs the holocaust in the number of lives extinguished. Over 45 million babies have perished at the hands of abortion doctors since the *Roe v. Wade* decision in the United States. This number speaks for itself.

Rather than focusing on the miscreants that abortion has prevented from entering society, I find myself thinking of the beauty, intelligence, creative power, and solutions that we have forgone in the form of people snuffed out of existence before they had the chance to take their first breaths. How many future doctors, lawyers, scientists, researchers, entrepreneurs, fathers, and mothers have we aborted? How many truly great men and women have we killed? How many world-altering discoveries have we sacrificed on the altar of convenience? These are the societal consequences of abortion upon which I reflect.

I find myself marveling at our current President, a transcendent figure who has already profoundly shaped the history of our country. An African American, abandoned by his father and raised in his youth by a single mother, Barack Obama belonged to a cohort group that faces one of the statistically highest chances of being aborted. He was born in 1961, before the liberalization of Hawaii's abortion laws and before the US Supreme Court's *Roe v. Wade* decision – his mother did not have the legal right to abort him. It is right that she did not.

To some, my argument that we are all endowed by our creator with the unalienable right to life will ring hollow. They will say that conception is not the moment when we attain such a right, but rather we achieve it when we become "a person." We can address this argument even if we ignore the fact that the Declaration of Independence, which Abraham Lincoln identified as a lens through which the Constitution should be interpreted, essentially demands the right to life be afforded to even the most newly created of our brothers and sisters. We address it with a simple thought experiment that asks: When does life begin?

We begin at the moment of birth and work retroactively, moving backwards in time at one-second increments and we ask, "Is killing this infant justifiable at this time?" The only two true, bright lines one will discover in performing this test are conception and birth. All other decision points are completely subjective. Utilizing trimesters, weeks of pregnancy and specific developmental milestones to gauge personhood is simply arbitrary – we have no idea when a fetus becomes a person (outside of the *philosophical* guidance given us by the Declaration to which we should defer). Does a heartbeat imply that a fetus is a person? Does the lack of one imply that a fetus is not? In many ways the newborn is just as much of a non-person as the newly conceived – yet we afford the infant's life legal protection. The only truly unique milestones in the thought experiment are birth and conception. To those who would argue that one second prior to birth a baby should be able to be aborted, I applaud your intellectual consistency but lament your morality. That leaves simply conception: the moment at which a fetus embodies all of the potential that it will achieve if not actively destroyed.

Finally, there will be those who say that it is a pipedream to hope to stop abortion. Abortion has always been with us, they will argue. They will say that if abortion on demand were illegal, those abortions would still happen but they would happen in back alleys and public bathrooms rather than in sanitized medical facilities. To them I would ask: what is it about sanitized medical facilities that make civilized people accept evil? Hitler's gas chambers and eugenics experiments were also carried out as sanitary processes and accepted by ordinary Germans – butchers, bakers, and bankers alike, even medical professionals. That did not make them right.

Doubtlessly the number of abortions would decrease by an order of magnitude if abortion on demand were made illegal. The effect of this change would be immediate and dramatic – of this we can be certain. However, even if such an effect were not achieved, it does not mean that the societal stance is not worth taking. We do not throw away the criminal codes dealing with murder because they fail to stop all murders and we do not throw away our laws against racketeering because Capone was able to best them. Abortion should be illegal because in the vast majority of circumstances it is profoundly wrong. Our society should proclaim this and our government should uphold its obligation to protect the lives of those endowed with the right to life but whose circumstances place their lives in jeopardy. Violations of mankind's unalienable rights *should* be relegated to the back alley. And then they should be driven from there as well.

The unborn are unique in our society's concept of the protection of life and liberty. They are unique in much the same way that African Americans were unique in the era of slavery. Talk of trimesters and debates over when a fetus becomes a person are as arbitrary and absurd as the discussions that yielded our young nation's three-fifths compromise or the "separate but equal" provisions of Jim Crow. The institutional barriers of legalized persecution, systemic illiteracy, lack of access to education, and denial of the status of "a person" are what made it so difficult for African Americans to shed the bonds of chattel slavery and to gain true equality before the law.

Our courts recognized and supported the institution of slavery – much like the courts of today defend a woman's right to abort. The slave masters of the day claimed their right to property outweighed the African American's right to liberty – much like the pro-abortion crowd subjugates the child's right to life to the mother's comfort. By and large, slaves had no means to plead their case and as a few miraculously transcended their conditions, this country slowly began to hear their stories and slowly began the process of positive change. America began the process of granting the status of "personhood" to those who were people all along.

Sadly, the institutional barriers faced by African Americans in chattel slavery pale in comparison to the barriers aborted children face in telling their stories. None of us will ever meet an abortion victim. We will never see the inherent personhood that makes an aborted child as worthy of life as the person whose mother chooses to give birth – no aborted baby can plead his brethren's case to power the way that Frederick Douglass did to Abraham Lincoln. Neither can the aborted babies take their story to the masses in the way that William Lloyd Garrison's *Liberator* allowed African Americans to do. No Underground Railroad exists for victims of abortion – there is no Harriet Tubman in an abortion clinic.

And perhaps in this respect, the plight of the unborn is even more hopeless than that of a slave in bondage: because the victim is wholly without voice and cannot resist. This is why it is imperative to look at your friends and family and to ask yourself whether their lives should have been a choice. Let them stand as a testament to the potential of the aborted babies who cannot testify on their own behalves. Every abortion victim *could* have someday been a friend or a neighbor, a sibling or a spouse. Abortion kills people who otherwise would have lived – about this there can be no argument.

One may rightfully ask: what then is the hopeful vision that springs from this conservative position on abortion? I envision a society where the rights of man guaranteed in our Declaration of Independence are given the honor they deserve. The right to life is not bestowed by a government nor is it bestowed by a mother. Rather, it is intrinsically tied to our conception – to our creation. The simple fact that our government allows abortion does not make it right and does not mean that it has the *legitimate* power to do so. The fact that mothers are given the choice to abort or not does not mean that they have a *legitimate* claim to that choice.

An unalienable right is one that cannot be taken away no matter what actions outside powers take. If you murder me, I still have the right to life. You do not take away my right to life, you simply take away my life. My right to life still exists as the force that compels the government to take legal action against you. We are guilty of taking away the lives of millions of unborn children, but it is their right to life that remains, that compels us to take a stand, and that will eventually require the termination of on-demand abortion itself. A better society recognizes this truth.

We offer the vision of a society in which human beings are respected and given the dignity they deserve, particularly the women in our society. In such a society, men and women are not simply animals, unaccountable for the results of their decisions and the impact of those decisions on other human beings. Rather, the consequences of decisions are inextricably linked to the decisions themselves. It is a society where people are treated with enough dignity and respect to *expect* of them the ability to make a decision and to require that they take responsibility for the results.

In such a society, women are truly empowered. The right to on-demand abortion does not empower but rather dehumanizes women. It treats them as children, unable to make complex decisions, and gives them as reprieve against poor decisions the ability to infringe upon the rights of others without consequence. Infringing upon the rights of others without consequence is not empowerment. It is enablement.

In a better society, women are empowered enough to make decisions about their bodies without violating the rights of the innocent. It is a society in which the burden and responsibilities of parenthood are shared between a mother and a father and in which they are treated as deserving of those responsibilities. In short, we can create an America where people are treated like people and not imbeciles. We can create a country where decision makers are expected to make decisions and accept the consequences of those decisions and where the right to life is truly unalienable. It is a society that grants the dignity of personhood rather than the stain of victimization to women and men facing unplanned pregnancies and to their unborn children as well. It is a moral society.

We offer this treatise against abortion to further the public debate on the issue and in hopes of forcing America the country to live up to America the ideal – the America that we were promised at our nation's founding. We do not invoke a deity because we recognize that while religious belief is fundamental to the formation of the individual's conscience and action, governmental policy cannot be formulated in response to a particular faith. It must be based in reason. And the reasoning that drives governmental action must be internally consistent. This is why we make this argument: to ask America to once again own up to its failure to secure its populace's unalienable rights. We ask America to do what it does better than any other nation on the face of the planet: to right its own wrongs. In so doing, this country can move yet another step closer to truly making manifest the ideals it so proudly proclaims.

Robert Wheeler attended Harvard University where he graduated cum laude with a degree in Applied Math and Economics. After Harvard, Robert joined the US Army where he served as an officer responsible for integrating Air Force, Navy, Marine Corps, and Army Air Defense assets. His assignments took him across America and to South Korea, Italy, and Puerto Rico. Robert recently separated from the military and is attending Harvard Business School where he is a member of the Class of 2011.

IX. LIBERTY AND STEWARDSHIP:
Going Green the American Way

by Devin Foley

When asked whether I like to camp, I generally respond with, "Not really." I see it as betraying all of humanity past by not taking every chance I can to embrace the joy that is modern life: freedom from the elements. It is incredibly satisfying to be warm inside my home while watching through the window as a blizzard rages. I like mattresses, electricity, refrigeration, lawns, running water, modern sanitation, and the multitude of other contemporary conveniences.

"Don't you like to experience nature?" is usually the follow up question. "Well, sure," I say. "I enjoy it most by driving with the windows down on a Sunday through the country." In response, I am usually told in disgust that this does not qualify as truly experiencing nature. To many people, I am the embodiment of everything wrong with modern America.

But am I? What is this silly desire to "experience nature" that preoccupies modern Americans? Does buying $1,000 worth of equipment, packing up your Subaru, and heading off to a state park for a week *really* constitute a nature experience? The reality is that nature is mean and nasty. Humanity has experienced nature for millennia. That cruel mistress heaped floods, drought, disease, shifting climates, inclement weather, and various other trials and tribulations upon us. We died in droves.

The colonists at Jamestown had a *real* nature experience in 1607. Brian Fagan describes the scene in his book, *The Little Ice Age:*

> *"... at Jamestown, the colonists had the bad luck to arrive at the height of the driest seven-year period in 770 years. Of the original 104 colonists who came in 1607, only 38 were still alive a year later.*

99

No fewer than 4,800 of the 6,000 settlers who arrived between 1607 and 1625 perished, many of them of malnutrition in the early years of the settlement. Like their predecessors at Roanoke, the colonists were expected to live off the land and off trade and tribute from the Indians, a way of life that made them exceptionally vulnerable during unusually dry years. They also suffered from water shortages when the drought drastically reduced river levels. Jamestown's archives make frequent references to the foul drinking water and the illnesses caused by consuming it..."[1]

That is nature. And the suffering experienced by those colonists is utterly incomprehensible to Americans today.

Only with the rise of industrialization, widespread private property ownership, and the proliferation of technology has man largely been able to free himself from the brutality of nature. Improvements in property rights allowed for the development of farming technology, which in turn allowed for greater efficiency and more food. More food meant more people able to focus on improving farming as well as developing other new technologies. New technologies and even more food eventually freed up others to increase scientific and ecological knowledge. As this process continues, man has been able to weather the nastiness nature throws at us.

And yet with all of this advancement and the increased comfort it has brought, are we proud of our progress? No. It seems that we are not just incredibly resilient and innovative, we are also neurotic. For thousands of years, we strived to overcome the challenges of our surroundings. And now that an ever-increasing segment of the world's population has achieved the dream of humanity past, we feel guilty about our success.

The American mythology casts an image of Native Americans sharing a pristine, natural America in a sustainable balance with surrounding life forms. This image is often juxtaposed with a picture of evil European colonizers armed with muskets, swords, and disease, who upset the natural order as they plundered resources, built cities on the remains of clear-cut forests, and plowed the continent's unspoiled grasslands. Modern environmentalism would have us see the comparison of Native American vs. European colonizer as natural vs. unnatural.

Today, the messengers of the environmental movement warn of impending global doom if we continue our unnatural, industrialized ways. After decades of environmental activism spreading its message and stoking the flames of fear, a new revolution is afoot. In this revolution, we are likened to locusts, rapidly depleting the earth of its resources, polluting the waters and air, killing off other species, and generally threatening to destroy the planet. This revolution's message is quite clear: live green or die.

Against this green juggernaut, what are those of the "live free or die" persuasion to do? Is it time to scrap the goal of limited government based on the ideas of life, liberty, and property in order to embrace a new era of international green governance that will return us to a state of harmony with nature? Hardly.

Separating Ecology from Environmentalism

Clean water and air, preservation of natural resources, sustainable development, and other ecological issues were a central concern to individuals, businesses, and governments long before the birth of the contemporary environmental movement. These issues are best categorized under the modern term ecology, the study of organisms' (including man's) interactions with their environment. To its benefit, the modern environmental movement has muddled the meaning of the terms ecology and environmentalism to the point that the public believes the two are synonymous.

For those of us who like clean air and water but still believe in the fundamental American principles of private property and limited government, our first goal should be to cleave ecology from environmentalism in the public mind. For mankind to continue to flourish, we must differentiate the science of ecology from the philosophically-driven worldview of environmentalism.

The earliest seeds of the philosophy of environmentalism in America took root well before the country's landscape was dominated by electricity, skyscrapers, cars, or suburbia. The movement originated as a negative reaction to America's rapid transformation by European colonizers and later became the ideological home for critics of industrialization. Asia, Europe, and parts of Africa required thousands of years to transition from prehistoric living to industrialized civilizations. America compressed the same transition into a few centuries and now stands at the forefront of the earth's technological progress. Should we be surprised that some Americans reacted negatively to the transformation? Not really. The early environmentalists saw the irreversible change taking place and mourned the loss of the wilderness. In their view, Americans had set themselves in opposition to nature. These fledgling environmentalists developed their own ethos, which has evolved over the last century and a half.

It is with the environmentalist ethos that liberty-minded individuals should be concerned. Simply put, today's radical environmentalism is incompatible with a free society based on the principles of life, liberty, and property. That environmentalists have succeeded in portraying the radical nature of their movement as mainstream only magnifies the threat posed by their philosophy to our foundational principles. Broadly speaking, environmentalists view the world as a web of interconnected lives in which we are all one through common energy. Michael Crichton describes the religious nature of environmentalism best:

> *What you see is a perfect 21st-century mapping of traditional Judeo-Christian dogma and myths. For example, there is an initial Eden, a Paradise, a state of innocence and unity in nature; there is a fall from grace into a state of pollution as a result of eating from the tree of knowledge, and, as a result of our actions, there is a judgment day coming. We all are energy sinners, doomed to die, unless we seek deliverance, which now is called sustainability. Sustainability is salvation in the church of the environment, just as organic food is its Communion.*[2]

Viewing the world through the paradigm of this green ethos, environmentalists seek to return mankind to a more natural, sustainable condition. They elevate this aim to such a lofty position that the violation or annihilation of individual freedoms is deemed an acceptable cost.

Many factions within the environmentalist movement assert that the prehistoric hunter-gatherers lived in harmony with the environment, that today's urban environments are unnatural at best, and that we should attempt to return to a state of harmony with the environment. And just what does a society based on a hunter-gatherer lifestyle living in harmony with the environment look like? Frederic Bender, who teaches philosophy at University of Colorado, gives us his version:

> *Neither poverty nor its vices can arise when an entire society has a common stake in the Earth and what it offers. Land can neither be sold nor inherited; goods are produced co-operatively and for collective use; and private ownership, if present at all, is confined to personal and household goods. Although this may seem like a utopian fantasy to us, such was the norm for ninety-five percent of the time anatomically modern Homo sapiens have existed. Moreover, accumulation of property leads inexorably to ecological unsustainability. From the evolutionary perspective, capitalism is a deviant economic system and agrarian, urban, and industrial societies culturally deviant. The culture of extinction has forgotten to keep the ratio of population to resources low, to underutilize nature's affordances deliberately and to eschew maximum effort in favour of enjoyment. Hunter-gatherers' supposed poverty, it turns out, is a deliberate, rational quality-of-life choice.*[3]

Recreating America in this way would require, at the very least, a radical change in the structure of our government and society, not to mention the slaughter of hundreds of millions of people. Professor Bender doesn't seem to see a problem with that. Some might say, "Well, that's just some professor." Thirty years ago, they would have said the same about John Holdren, the current Director of the United States' Office of Science & Technology Policy (OSTP). The OSTP's mission is to "serve as a source of scientific and technological analysis and judgment for the President with respect to major policies, plans, and programs of the Federal Government." In 1978, Holdren coauthored the textbook *Ecoscience: Population, Resources, Environment* in which forced abortions, involuntary sterilization, mandatory limits on family size, world government, and other measures were considered as possible methods of curbing population growth by year 2000.[4] While Holdren has distanced himself from the textbook since becoming director of the OSTP, the mere fact that someone who once advanced such extremist views is now in such a high position of government should give pause to the liberty-minded. Make no mistake: When living in harmony with the Earth becomes the highest goal of those in charge of the government, freedom will be the very first thing eliminated. Such an ethos would all but guarantee despotism and a horrific loss of human lives.

When pushing back against the environmentalist ethos, conservative and liberty-minded individuals must acknowledge the laudable objectives of preserving clean air and clean water and conserving "the environment." To pursue these goals without sacrificing the principles upon which America was founded, however, we must fully sever environmentalism from ecology in the public's mind. We must present a cohesive counter-ethos and reestablish an accurate lexicon by correctly defining terms such as natural, environment, and sustainable. Environmentalists promulgate nebulous meanings for these terms, effectively using them to obscure a radical agenda with which Americans should be supremely worried. Additionally, we must show how man will be better served and how the environment can and will be protected and preserved in an ecology-conscious world built on property rights and freedom. As a result of the environmentalists' nearly unbridled march forward in spreading their message and ethos, the liberty-minded have a very difficult fight ahead.

The United States Constitution and the Declaration of Independence provide the central ideas on which our government and society rest. Chief among them is the fundamental belief that government is instituted to secure to men the rights of life, liberty, and property. This concept of government is based on an ethos that men are natural, independent, and unique creatures, neither animal nor god; that human nature is at once capable of good and evil; that men are rational, emotional, and fallible; and that men take ownership of their work. But can this ethos continue to carry us forward? Absolutely.

Life, Liberty, Property, and Ecology

Human building and development, like that of beavers or ants, is natural. There is value and beauty to behold in what man develops, as well as that which he leaves untouched. Each man acquires property by mixing his labor with the surrounding environment. We view private property as an individual right because it is the product of an individual's labor. As such, no man, government, or business has the right to take or destroy another's property or property held in common without considerable justification and proper compensation.

It is true that environmental change results from some human (and non-human) activity. However, in many cases, the change is not destruction, but rather a transformation of the environment. It is important to remember that nothing in the environment is static. Whether man is involved or not, change is always taking place in nature. Climate transformation regularly threatens the survival of plants, animals, humans, and even civilizations. Environmental destruction by individuals, groups, businesses, governments, and various species of wildlife compounds climatic-based transformation by adding to the dangers posed to humans and non-humans. Environmental destruction can best be seen in water pollution, air pollution, and unsustainable consumption of natural resources. It is often a byproduct of the work necessary to overcome environmental transformation and the elements. The acts of destruction to private and common property should be studied (ecology) and should be kept in check through a system based on limited government and the principles of life, liberty, and property. A system of common law exists and is capable of addressing these concerns, but it has not always been used to achieve this end.

Now, let us explore how these ideas can guide our society in addressing the environmental challenges of water pollution, air pollution, natural resources and sustainability, and climate change.

Water Pollution

Water pollution has been problematic for mankind ever since we transcended our early status as hunters and gatherers. Archeological accounts show that 4,500 years ago the Indus and Minoan civilizations had advanced public utilities with in-house latrines and plumbing, sewage and drainage pipes, and other sanitary measures designed to keep drinking water clean.[5] Even more surprising is that this level of advancement wasn't limited to the upper echelons of society, but was in some cases available to the majority of urban dwellers. These early civilizations understood the danger of man-made water pollution as a result of unsanitary disposal of sewer and refuse.

Located in present day Illinois, the vast Native American city of Cahokia peaked from A.D. 1050 to 1200. The city covered six square miles and was occupied by 10,000 to 20,000 people.[6] Unlike the Indus and Minoans, Cahokia showed no sign of waste management systems or clean water delivery. The resulting water pollution likely caused the population to be ravaged by dysentery and tuberculosis at epidemic proportions.[7]

In America, the Native Americans weren't the only urban dwellers to have problems with water pollution. Since European settlers first arrived in America, many individuals and local governments have recognized that water pollution stemming from poor sanitation was to blame for rising levels of typhoid, cholera, infant mortality, and other serious health concerns. New types of water pollution coincided with the dawn of industrialization. Like individuals and local governments had been doing for centuries, industry began to dump its waste into the waterways. Farming, too, contributed to water pollution as pesticide and fertilizer run-off added to the dirty mix.

With the exception of the Cahokians, all of these American examples are cited as evidence of the failure of our system of limited government and property rights to protect the health of the people and the surrounding environment. The reality is that laws did exist to control water pollution within these societies, but they were largely unenforced and property rights were often not upheld. In other words, government failed to "secure to men the rights to life, liberty, and property." In turn, the public largely accepted the argument that a limited government could not protect the water, which paved the way for the federal government to substantially increase its control over water with the Clean Water Act in 1972.

After decades of industrial and other waste being pumped into the Cuyahoga River, it caught on fire in 1969. The affair served as the catalyst for the Clean Water Act (CWA) that gave the Environmental Protection Agency and the Army Corps of Engineers the broad mandate "to restore and maintain the chemical, physical, and biological integrity of the Nation's waters."[8] Few recall that existing laws, such as the 1948 Water Pollution Control Act, prohibited the dumping of industrial waste into the Cuyahoga River well before 1969. Few also remember that the river burned in 1868, 1883, 1887, 1912, 1922, 1936, 1941, 1948, and 1952.[9] Short memories allowed for heretofore unseen powers to be granted to the government under the auspices of environmental protection.

The CWA did play a major role in codifying the public's demand for clean water. However, the simple fact remains that it was only necessary because the laws that existed prior to it were not enforced and because both private and common property were not staunchly defended by the courts. It was not a *lack* of government but a *failure* of government that created the conditions for the CWA. Ironically, a massive increase in government power was deemed to be the appropriate response. Had previous laws been enforced, innovative solutions to water pollution would have developed as companies and local governments would have been forced to find new ways to eliminate waste without dumping dangerous substances into the waters. Instead, American leadership decided to create a regulatory behemoth with substantial leeway to infringe upon the freedom and property rights of average Americans.

Admittedly, water quality has improved since the passage of CWA. But that improvement is not a result of the CWA legislation. Rather, popular opinion has forced government to actually enforce laws prohibiting pollution of the waterways. In fact, despite the massive power that the CWA granted to the federal government, we still do not know the quality of the majority of water bodies across America. Surveying America's waters was mandated by the law nearly forty years ago, yet as of the EPA's 2004 reporting cycle, the condition of only 16% of Americas' streams and rivers, only 39% of lakes, and only 29% of bays and estuaries were known.[10] We are spending money, abdicating our freedoms, and giving enormous powers over privately owned property to government bureaucracies in an attempt to correct a problem we have yet to fully identify.

Meanwhile, the environmentalists are unsatisfied with the level of government control they have achieved. They claim that, because all water is connected, the federal government must also regulate any land that water touches. Taking water regulation to this extreme would represent a de facto elimination of private property rights.

Numerous examples exist of individuals' losing their property without compensation, being forced into bankruptcy, or even being jailed as a result of the CWA and an overreaching bureaucracy. In 2006, it took the Supreme Court to rescue a citizen from the CWA in *Rapanos v. United States*. John Rapanos had chosen to fill portions of his property with dirt in order to build. But federal regulators considered the area to be a wetland, despite the twenty mile distance between the property and any navigable water. The ruling was contested for twelve years in the courts and Rapanos at times faced over a million dollars in fines as well as jail time, until the Supreme Court made its decision in his favor. Recognizing the absurdity of restricting individual liberties based on the idea that all water is connected, Justice Scalia referenced the movie *Casablanca* in his opinion:

> *We are indebted to the Sonoran court for a famous exchange, from the movie Casablanca (Warner Bros. 1942), which portrays most vividly the absurdity of finding the desert filled with waters: " 'Captain Renault {Claude Rains}: "What in heaven's name brought you to Casablanca?" " 'Rick {Humphrey Bogart}: "My health. I came to Casablanca for the waters." " 'Captain Renault: "The waters? What waters? We're in the desert." " 'Rick: "I was misinformed.' " 408 F. 3d, at 1117.*[11]

This is what vast sums of money and the forfeiture of our liberties have bought us: government entities bent on expanding their power at all costs, regardless of the ludicrous justification that such expansion requires. The CWA stands in stark contrast to the common law approach preferred by limited government types. The act is a top-down, command-and-control structure, which gives immense power to a few federal bureaucracies. Roger Meiners and Bruce Yandle of the Independent Institute contrast the current system to a common law approach:

> *Under the CWA, water pollution is defined mechanically and by a politically controlled process. The regulation is akin to a federal agency being mandated by Congress to study technology, tell companies how to build products, and certify products as safe. Under such a scheme, companies that complied could not be sued when products were defective and injured people because the government declared the products legally safe. Few would assert that a command-and-control production and*

liability regime would yield better results than when individuals exercise their rights in a free market.

This does not mean that the common law always produces the most economically efficient or "just" results. The principled nature of the common law lies in its evolutionary and competitive nature — individuals enforcing their rights. The decisions of independent judges, responding to independent cases filed by private parties seeking to protect their common law rights, are far more likely to produce sensible principles than are legislative bodies that produce rules greatly influenced by special interests, or rules that may reflect a crisis of the moment but make little sense for the long term.

As well-intentioned as the CWA is, its many problems necessitate a new look at how individuals, companies, localities, states, and the federal government can deal with water pollution. The overreach and abuses by the EPA and the Army Corps of Engineers simply cannot be allowed to continue. A system of defending property rights under common law, mixed with reasonable preventative laws, can carry us forward to an even cleaner future.

Air Pollution

Like water pollution, air pollution is not a new problem. As soon as fire was discovered, man started polluting the air. Mummified remains from the Paleolithic era (cavemen) reveal blackened lungs from breathing smoke inside caves.[12] Today, similar problems are seen in developing countries, where many people live in shanties and a constantly burning fire is required for both heat and cooking. Lung disease and premature death commonly result from this indoor air pollution.

Thousands of years ago, air pollution from smoke intensified as populations grew and societies began to urbanize. Reports of the problem can be found from ancient civilizations in Rome, Greece, the Fertile Crescent, and China. Ancient industries further contributed to air pollution. According to a study from 1994, ice core samples from Greenland reveal a rise in global atmospheric air pollution as a result of lead smelting in the Roman

Empire. The lead pollution was so significant that it remained unmatched until the Industrial Revolution.[13] While many would have us believe that only modern life, and particularly American life, is destructive to the surrounding environment, this is simply not true.

The challenges of dealing with air pollution are even greater than those posed by water pollution. Air flows around the world and is shared by all humans. Modern satellite imagery shows huge plumes of air pollution blowing from China out over the Pacific Ocean. From an ecological perspective, air pollution should be considered at four different levels: individual/indoor, local/regional, national, and global. While America has contributed greatly to air pollution in the past, our country is improving tremendously in each of these categories.

Because of improvements in energy technology, Americans' indoor quality of living is outstanding. Yes, scientists are finding evermore pollutants to track, but can Americans say their homes are filled with smoke from heating and cooking? Excluding cigarette smokers and workers in certain industrial settings, our lungs are pink. From the perspective of a liberty-minded ethos, this is great news. While there are various regulations on chimneys and wood-burning stoves, the main drivers of clean indoor air were property owners and entrepreneurs. Private innovation has made clean sources of energy and cooking progressively less expensive. This reality combined with increasing per capita wealth to greatly expand Americans' demand for domestic clean-burning technology. Today, it would be unthinkable for a new house to be built without a clean-energy furnace and clean-burning ovens, *regardless of government mandate*. It is an uncompromising expectation that has arisen as a result of the technological advances made widely available by private industry.

Moving outside the home, liberty-minded individuals must confront head on the very real problems of regional- and national-level air pollution. I grew up in the mountains of San Diego where, as a result of wind patterns, we had fairly clean air. Trips up to Orange County and LA were always an ecological experience because of the poor air quality. My eyes would water after only a day in the smog. Just like one campfire burning, a single car running without a catalytic converter will have such a miniscule impact on air quality that it can easily escape our concern. On the other hand, one million cars or one million campfires will combine to pollute at a level that cannot be overlooked. Throw in a few thousand factories releasing pollutants into the atmosphere and air pollution is an even more serious concern.

In large urban settings, it is not easy to determine who or what is responsible for environmental and property damages. As a result, our society was forced to take action to prevent continued and further damage done by air pollution to the property of individuals (including the individual's health), businesses, and governments. The Clean Air Act was passed in 1970. It gave the EPA the job of cleaning up America's air. But like the Clean Water Act, it was a classic command-and-control, top-down law that focused on punishment and bureaucratic regulations rather than on incentivizing cleaner air and harnessing the innovative solutions brought about by the private market.

While proponents of limited government are not likely to be fans of the Clean Air Act's methods, it has at least helped to achieve a culture change similar to that of the Clean Water Act. Pollution still occurs, but America's air is much, much cleaner. Between 1980 and 2005, we saw a 96% reduction in the amount of lead in the American atmosphere, carbon monoxide decreased by 74%, and sulfur dioxide content has been diminished by 63%.[14] We have made great strides.

The problem with a command-and-control approach to air pollution is that it is too likely to be driven by inflexible technology mandates rather than sensible, objective standards. An example of the type of expensive and wasteful technology mandate that such a system creates is the EPA's requirement for all coal-based power plants to use the same type of coal scrubbers, which "scrub" certain pollutants from the plant's exhaust as power is generated. Claiming the scrubbers were necessary during the Carter Administration, the EPA required power plants in the western US to use the same expensive coal scrubbers to reduce sulfur emissions as eastern coal-based power plants. However, western power plants use low-sulfur coal and have little or no need to employ the same scrubbers. The command-and-control approach relies on technology developed by bureaucrats and implemented across the board to solve critical problems without respect to local conditions – misallocating resources that could be better used elsewhere.

More effective strategies exist to reduce air pollution that leverage, rather than hamstring, the power of markets. One strategy would be to set a limit on the amount of pollution that can be emitted, and then to allow each independent company to figure out the most efficient way of meeting that goal. Starting in 1995, it is argued that the EPA successfully employed this strategy to curb SO_2 emissions, a much more intelligent approach than that embodied in the earlier, one-size-fits-all scrubber plan. An even better strategy is to simply create a pollution tax, where the tax charged is roughly equal to the "cost" of the pollution to society. Polluters are able to adjust operations and innovate to reduce their tax burdens. Additionally, taxes can be targeted at specific pollutants – ensuring that each pollutant is treated appropriately.

Both scenarios require government oversight, but in an entirely different manner. The bureaucratic command-and-control approach that currently dominates is extremely costly and highly susceptible to manipulation by lobbyists and special interest groups seeking to benefit particular industries, or even specific companies. They are often extremely successful in using governmental mandates to achieve advantages for their technologies in the marketplace. By moving away from command-and-control to a fair, standards-based approach, entrepreneurs can develop less expensive and more effective approaches to the air pollution problem. Our society's approach should ensure that all solutions compete on a level playing field and that the best is eventually chosen. The result is a solution that is both effective *and* just.

As mentioned earlier, satellite images reveal a plume of pollution extending from China out over the Pacific Ocean. International air pollution is not limited only to China. Recall, too, that evidence exists of Rome's lead pollution far from the Roman Empire. To be fair, any urban area will likely be a source of pollution. Where urban areas are near national borders, international agreements between the parties polluting and the parties affected should provide the means of addressing the challenge.

As we move into the twenty-first century, we must reevaluate both the Clean Air Act and our broader ecological goals. If clean air is the goal, then "clean" emissions should be lauded, particularly if they are achieved by market mechanisms which are consistent with the American principles of freedom of choice and equality of opportunity. It is time to move away from the expensive, bureaucratic methods of pollution reduction mandated in a bygone era. Technology continues to evolve at a lightning pace and the private market can leverage those advancements to improve our air quality – as long as it is allowed to do so. Is there any reason not to take full advantage of the powerful minds of our scientific and business communities to create enduring solutions to the problem of pollution? Finally, we should seek frank answers to an important question: how clean should the air be? At the air quality levels in most regions around the country, is truly significant ecological harm being done? And is the burdensome price tag of incrementally pushing for zero-emissions worth its cost?

Natural Resources & Sustainable Development

Like the other ecological issues confronting the United States, natural resource destruction and sustainable development are not new challenges. History is filled with examples of successful and unsuccessful resource management. In light of the historical record, the United States is doing remarkably well.

Wood provides an excellent example of resource destruction and the power of private property rights to ensure sustainable development. As a key source of energy for heating and cooking, as well as a raw material for building homes and ships, wood was one of the earliest natural resources to be recognized for its value to humans. It has also been terribly abused. Historically, forests have often been considered part of the local and regional commons (or have been the property of the ruling government), and thus have been poorly defended across the ages. Sadly, even prior to the Industrial Revolution, many forests were destroyed around the world. Long before modernity, Lebanon's vast tracts of cedar trees were reduced, Easter Island was subject to wholesale clear-cutting, and Iberian forests were razed for shipbuilding.

Thankfully, knowledge of resource management has increased tremendously over the last few centuries. Throughout history, more often than not, natural resource destruction took place either at the hands of governments or when resources were owned in common. Consider the absolute environmental carnage that took place in the Soviet Union under the banner of communism. In America, our system of private property and individual freedom, combined with ever increasing and widespread knowledge of resource management, has resulted in well-protected natural resources.

It is in the best interest of the forest owner to renew the forest. It undoubtedly benefits the fish hatchery to make sure that there are enough fish to breed new fish. No one worries about the elimination of cows, apple trees, chickens, pine trees, rainbow trout, or corn. The owners of these resources protect them and continuously renew them.

Many environmentalists' goal of preserving nature and natural resources isn't necessarily a bad one. It is when they push for government regulations that deprive private property owners of their land or individuals of their freedom that Americans should object. Rather than using the brute force of government, some conservationists have begun buying large tracts of forest, wetlands, prairies, and other habitats undeveloped by man in order to preserve them. As of 2003, the Nature Conservancy had $3 billion in assets, much of it land.[15]

Free marketers have long recognized the truth that property held in private is much more likely to be preserved and protected than property held in common or by government. It is human nature to look out for oneself and one's possessions. It is also human nature to loot and plunder whenever we think we can do so without personal cost. By holding property in private, the owner serves as the very first line of defense against external looting, plundering, and all other forms of destruction. Understanding human nature, the efforts by conservationists and even environmentalists to hold property in private should be celebrated. Meanwhile, efforts by environmentalists to achieve their goals by eliminating, seizing, or blocking the growth of private property should be fought.

Lately, many metropolitan areas have attempted to prevent the expansion of private property under the guise of "Smart Growth." We are often told that our society is paving over farmlands and prairies and clear-cutting forests to make room for sprawling suburbs, and that it all must be stopped. With such a deafening outcry, one would think there's not a bit of "nature" left in America. The reality is that the United States has a tremendous amount of land still available and defined as "undeveloped." In 2002, only 5.5% of land in the contiguous United States was considered developed.[16] While the amount of non-urban land has naturally decreased as the population has expanded, the argument that we are running out of land is unsound at best.

Largely as a result of private property, forests in the United States are well managed, farmland is plentiful, and urban development only takes up a very small percent of all available land. While there is always room for improvement as knowledge and technology increase, one can hardly say that Americans are developing at an unsustainable pace that is destroying the environment. Moreover, the best way to integrate and leverage any improvements that do occur is through a strict adherence to the concept of private property and the free market principles it enables. When resource destruction does take place, history has shown us that the damage most likely will be done to those resources *without* owners, common to us all.

Climate Change

These days, one cannot discuss the environment without addressing climate change. In all of my exposure to the issue, I've learned a simple lesson: don't believe anyone who tells you that global warming is a hoax, and don't believe anyone who claims absolute certainty about global warming's existence, its impacts, or its causes.

The reality is that the earth has been both cooler and warmer in the past. Greenland borehole ice readings support this statement as fact.[17] Historical records show a medieval warm period and a little ice age in the last millennium. Let's not forget *the* Ice Age that thawed many, many millennia ago. To blame current changes in climate around the globe solely on industrialization is downright foolish. History establishes that climatic changes have taken place both gradually and swiftly in the past, all before industrialization.

As students of history, though, we should be concerned by climate change. At times it has had devastating results. Consider the experience of the colonists at Jamestown described earlier. The importance of cheap and plentiful energy cannot be overstated. We are surviving and thriving as a species because of electricity and the internal combustion engine. If you beg to differ, try to avoid using anything that depends on either for a year and see how well you're doing.

There are two great dangers associated with global warming alarmism. The first concerns our ability to adapt to changing temperatures. Alarmists maintain that climate change is a result of greenhouse gas emissions, and that we therefore need to cut energy consumption immediately and dramatically in order to reduce greenhouse gases. But doing so means that when the climate inevitably changes anyway, our critical ability to adapt will be restricted by the constraints of artificial, self-imposed energy limits. Energy and technological advancement enable us to overcome climate change.

The very real second danger of global warming alarmism is to regard carbon emissions as pollution. Any acceptance of carbon as *the* pollutant responsible for worldwide or regional shifts in climate or incremental weather gives environmentalists carte blanche to push for further regulations limiting actions that emit carbon. Unfortunately, the Supreme Court supported the labeling of carbon emissions as pollution in *Massachusetts v. EPA*. Compromises made by way of carbon taxes or cap-and-trade regulations can and will open up a veritable Pandora's Box of freedom-killing regulations. Additionally, any country which implements carbon reductions unilaterally should brace for the inevitable failure of the measure to impact global carbon levels or reduce global temperatures, and should expect its carbon producing industries to leave for more friendly nations.

For argument's sake, let us say that the demand for everyone to live a carbon-neutral lifestyle gains nationwide momentum. Every breath you and your pet exhale, any barbeque you light, and each car trip you take will be treated as damaging to the earth's climate. Every person's life will be micromanaged and monitored to an extreme degree. For any who might discount such a possibility, consider the 2008 EPA proposal to tax livestock "emissions" as a precursor of what might yet come. It is plain to liberty-minded individuals that such thinking should be dismissed as insanity. Regrettably, it is considered logical by too many in local, state, and federal government.

Environmentalists are using the issue of carbon pollution in order to achieve their overall ideological goals of the elimination of limited government, individual freedom, and property rights. Evidence is building that the models the alarmists depend upon to make their case for carbon pollution are not bearing out in the real world. The Mann Hockey Stick, which helped start the massive spread of global warming ideas, has been thoroughly and irrevocably discredited.[18] Methane gas was predicted to continue to rise at alarming rates, yet it is now decreasing.[19] And despite the $79 billion spent by the US Government since 1989 on global warming research, the claim that carbon emissions are *the* contributor to climate change is still unproven.[20]

Every freedom-loving American needs to push back against the global warming alarmists respectfully, but in earnest. We cannot ignore the historical fact that climate is always changing. It has been hotter and it has been colder and will continue to be both, with or without our efforts. The best way forward for humanity is to continue to make energy more affordable and more plentiful.

Concluding Thoughts

Stewardship of the environment cannot be left to the environmentalists. Americans care about the condition of their water and air, as well they should. Many enjoy camping in our plentiful state and national parks, while those of us who would rather not face the elements like to know that we could find an undeveloped corner of the world if we ever changed our minds. If conservatives and free marketers hope to preserve and promote limited government and the principles of life, liberty, and property, we must find ways to incorporate those ideas into talk of clean air, clean water, and preserving nature. Additionally, we must aim to actively separate ecology from environmentalism at every opportunity. Education and creative advocacy will be the best tools to achieve those ends.

As Americans, we should also be proud of what we have accomplished as a people. In just a few centuries, we have largely conquered the elements and greatly diminished the severity of pollution and natural resource depletion that have devastated humanity for ages. Throughout human history, individual liberty, limited government, and private property have repeatedly proven to offer solutions that are environmentally friendly, while also serving as the catalyst for advancements in knowledge and prosperity. It is time to tell this story and to illustrate to the public that a free society based on the rule of law and defense of property rights is the best system to take us forward to a cleaner and more prosperous tomorrow.

Devin Foley was born and raised in Southern California. Since graduating from Hillsdale College in 2001, he has worked at the Center of the American Experiment, a non-profit, public policy think tank. In 2009, he helped found Intellectual Takeout, a non-profit institution aimed at inspiring the next generation of Americans. He currently serves as the organization's president. Devin and his wife Nicole reside in Stillwater, Minnesota, with their three children.

X. POWERING AMERICA:
Enduring Solutions to the Energy Problem
by Robert Wheeler

Any principled discussion of energy policy must be rooted in the government's two obligations to its citizenry: allowing individual liberty to flourish while protecting the people's unalienable rights. On one hand, the individual's choice to use energy has no practical effect on the rights of any other citizen. Today, even the energy consumption of the most massive corporations has a negligible impact on any individual citizen's quality of life. The environmental impact of my car can be compared to the impact of my dumping a glass of water into the ocean: technically it affects the sea level but for all practical purposes my contribution is meaningless. On the other hand, the aggregate effect of all energy users does impact our environment and, by extension, the lives of Americans. Properly framing the energy debate requires us to weigh the individual's right to utilize energy, remembering that his particular effect on his fellow citizens is negligible, against the necessity to protect Americans from the harmful effects of the country's aggregate energy usage.

The energy discussion also has very real national security implications. Ensuring domestic development of the energy sources required to fuel our nation's war-fighting apparatus is a legitimate governmental concern. This is especially true in light of the fact that well over 60% of America's oil, the lifeblood of our expeditionary military and our transportation industry, is imported – generally from nations that are either opposed to American values, politically unstable, or both.[1] Currently, maintaining ties with these bellicose nations is in America's national interest. Thus, the fact that our government nurtures those relationships is a good thing. However, this is only the case in a world where imported oil is America's singular option for military and motor vehicle fuel. Weaning ourselves off of foreign oil will afford us the flexibility to conduct principled foreign policy that advances more critical national interests than simply securing our access to a solitary natural resource. It will also ensure that American policymakers have every option available when dealing with belligerent nations – even belligerent nations with massive petroleum reserves.

These two considerations, the negative effects of energy use on the population as a whole and the national security implications of our energy portfolio, justify a federal energy policy. Pollution is an example of what economists call a negative externality. That is, it is a consequence of the decision to use (most forms of) energy, but one that is borne by society rather than only the energy's user. Thus, the price an individual pays for energy does not reflect that energy's true cost – a cost that includes, in addition to the price of the energy, the cost of that energy's effects. Because pollution produced in one US state is not constrained by the state's borders, the federal government is the most appropriate institution to address it. Additionally, in order to effectively secure the populace's rights to life, liberty, and property from foreign enemies, the federal government has an obligation to address the military's reliance on an energy source that we cannot supply for ourselves. By keeping these two justifications for a federal energy policy in mind, we can develop effective solutions for America's energy problem in both the short- and long-term.

But before we delve into a discussion of solutions, it is important to first recognize how integral energy is to our daily lives and the role that it has played in America's economic ascendance. The various forms of energy consumed by individuals and organizations quite literally power America. Simply put, without cheap and abundant energy sources, of which fossil fuels are the primary ones, Americans would die by the millions. Those of us in the north would freeze to death in the winter and southerners would succumb to heat exhaustion in the summer. We would starve as crops rotted in their fields and refined foods sat in warehouses, unable to be shipped. Technological advancement would screech to a halt as individual struggles for survival replaced the pursuit of a greater future that occurs each day in the halls of America's businesses and educational institutions. Each of us would be unable to escape the carnage because the only means to flee available to us would be our feet – on which we would be even more susceptible to the elements, disease, and famine that surrounded us.

We believe that the question of which fuels will power America in the future is critical. But we firmly reject the notion that the American people or the American way of life can survive while dramatically reducing our energy requirements. Moreover, the US Energy Information Administration anticipates global energy consumption increasing by 44% over the next twenty years. The world's undeveloped nations will see their energy consumption nearly double. Demographic and economic trends will lead to Asia's developing economies supplanting North America as the largest consumers of energy and similar forces will drive demand in Russia, Latin America, the Middle East, and Africa.[2] Energy is not the enemy. In all of its various forms, energy is a powerful asset that enables all of our society's greatest strengths. Meeting world energy demands in the twenty-first century will be a challenge, but the future of energy represents an amazing opportunity for American businesses, workers, and principles to move the globe forward. And more capitalism, not less, is the way to achieve that progress.

As America was emerging from its revolution, the modern steam engine was in its infancy. The next fifty years would witness the transformation of America as the steam engine was improved upon, which allowed it to power the Industrial Revolution. Where, in the past, production of any sort had required intense manual labor, steam engines could now power factory machinery. As the steam engine was further developed, it was made small enough to be utilized in various transportation applications. Steamships and steam-powered locomotives were the result, revolutionizing transportation and allowing goods to be shipped great distances. These early steam engines were relatively inefficient and were primarily powered by coal, which generated significant pollution as it was burned. But the pollution was a small price to pay for the unprecedented improvement in the lives of everyday people that the Industrial Revolution brought. For instance, in 1730 in London, nearly 75% of children born were dead before they reached their fifth birthday. By 1830, that figure had dropped to just above 30%.[3] Wages for laborers also increased dramatically during that time and England's population exploded, doubling twice in the span of a century.[4][5]

A little over 100 years after the Declaration of Independence was penned, Karl Benz was granted a German patent for the internal combustion engine in 1879. Between 1888 and 1893, Benz sold a whopping 25 automobiles powered by his engine using a relatively new fuel: gasoline. Benz and his engine set the stage for the dramatic improvements in transportation that characterized the twentieth century. The internal combustion engine led to the ascendance of petroleum as the energy form of choice for transportation. This revolution in transportation eventually allowed millions of Americans and billions of people worldwide to enjoy the freedom of movement that car ownership made possible. But again, pollution was part of the cost that had to be borne. While more energy efficient and not nearly as dirty as the steam engine that it replaced, the internal combustion engine – even in its modern form – generates greenhouse gas emissions.

In the mid-twentieth century, America entered the fray of breakthrough energy developments. Under the auspices of the Manhattan Project, American scientists exploded the world's first atomic bomb in 1945. This represented the culmination of a multi-billion dollar effort to harness the power of the atom. Although nuclear energy fueled the Cold War arms race with the Soviet Union, it also held the promise of a plentiful and environmentally friendly energy source that we are still attempting to effectively tap today. While nuclear fission represents the cleanest energy source widely currently available, it still poses serious societal concerns regarding the disposal of nuclear waste and the potential for a nuclear meltdown like the one at Pennsylvania's Three Mile Island in 1979. Indeed, this incident is widely cited as the event that turned the American public against nuclear power.

Finally, the early 2000s witnessed runaway increases in oil prices as the forces of global demand and widespread speculation in the oil market created the conditions for a price bubble – pushing the price of a barrel of oil to $150 in the summer of 2008. In concert with the price of oil, gasoline prices steadily rose for five years prior to 2008, and Americans eventually felt the sting of $4.00/gallon gasoline. Politicians on both sides of the aisle clamored for "relief for consumers." Their shameless pandering included populist claims that hardworking Americans were being run through the ringer to pad a corporate "bottom line." Paradoxically, these same politicians were the ones calling for a fundamental shift in America's energy portfolio while demonizing rising fossil fuel prices, which are the surest way to change consumer behavior. And change behavior the prices did. Americans abandoned their SUVs in droves – pushing the American automakers who had bet big on future demand for the gas guzzlers into bankruptcy. Between May of 2007 and May of 2008, Americans decreased their driving by 4.3%, the largest one-year drop since records have been kept.[6] Moreover, rising gasoline prices pushed public transportation use in America to its highest level in 50 years.[7]

This brief history of American energy is not meant to be exhaustive. However, these four vignettes offer powerful insight into how we, as a society, should address our energy problem. They offer us three general principles, which we will outline here and then apply to an analysis of America's energy portfolio.

The first principle that should guide our energy policy is that of free markets. All solutions come from the mind of a man or woman. The free market is the most powerful tool available for organizing human talent, combining it with financial resources, and allowing these well-financed men and women to develop solutions to society's problems. It is no coincidence that the less free a market is – the more rules, regulations, and dictates from Washington that it faces – the less innovative it is. This is in the nature of central planning and it has been borne out by history countless times. Silicon Valley thrives while nearly all of the transportation industries languish.

The root of the free market's success lies in the notion of price – the amount of money required to buy a good or service. The price forms the basis for the revenue received by a producer for his or her product. It was the promise of commercial success that drove James Watt to develop the steam engine that powered the Industrial Revolution. It was the prospect of riches that caused Benz to study for years and toil in his laboratory to finally develop the internal combustion engine and the automobile it spurred. And it will be this same potential for financial gain that will lead to the next advancement in cleaner and more efficient energy. The sums of money earned by innovators past and future pale in comparison to the immense good their discoveries have done and promise to do for the world.

Price is also the value that a consumer must forfeit to obtain a product. As prices increase for one good, opportunities are created for other, more innovative people to develop alternative solutions to a problem and offer them to consumers more cheaply. The higher that prices rise, the more profitable new solutions become. This explains why six of the ten most popular cars in 2006 were Toyota models.[8] The Japanese automaker committed massive amounts of money to research and development of fuel-efficient cars and promoting them in the American market. They did so because they saw the opportunity to steal American consumers away from American automakers as they looked for ways to save at the pump. No governmental dictate forced Americans out of their SUVs – free men's free choices were sufficient.

This is not to say that a completely laissez-faire approach is the way to go in America's energy markets. The negative externalities inherent in some energy sources encourage a particular role for the government in energy pricing. But our federal government should avoid the urge to impose arbitrary limits and restrictions on individuals' and corporations' use of energy. Punitive taxes and arbitrary caps should be off the table. Such actions necessarily blur the conditions of the free market in which consumers and producers interact, inevitably leading to unfair prices and stifled innovation. However, the government should commission an independent review to determine the exact societal costs associated with the use of various types of energy. Then, the government should tax each form of energy at a rate that will allow society to recoup these costs. This externality tax is the only legitimate way to tax energy that is consistent with our nation's foundational principles of individual liberty and property rights. This proposal actually buttresses the free market approach by ensuring that the price of energy reflects both its utility to the consumer as well as its cost to society.

The second principle that our vignettes illustrate is the appropriate role of the government with respect to research and development. Government's role here is entirely dictated by its commitment to protecting its citizens' rights. As the Manhattan Project example so aptly illustrates, governmental coercion can marshal significant talent and resources and bring them to bear in pursuit of a particular objective. There are two problems with this approach, however. The first is that such coercion is only philosophically justified in defense of the principles that our government was established to defend – in support of individual liberty. The second problem is that creating a new Manhattan Project for "twenty-first century energy" is very difficult because the mandate is so broad. Robert Oppenheimer, head of the Manhattan Project, and his colleagues were among the smartest men in the world, were given nearly unlimited resources, were told that the fate of the world hung in the balance, and still only had to solve a single, well-defined problem. Split the atom and weaponize its power: that was their job.

Remaking the future of energy is a much more nebulous task. Every lobbyist in Washington stares greedily at the prize, telling the American people why his client's approach is the right one, all the while just hoping to get the chance to stick his nose in the trough. Less cynically, the truth is that no one knows exactly what the definition of the task is. No one knows which future energy technologies are viable and which are not so there is very little objective means of framing a Manhattan Project for energy security.

We can address both of these concerns by handing the task of research and development over to America's national defense apparatus. Philosophically, developing innovative energy sources to power our military conforms to the correct notion of governmental responsibility – ensuring the life, liberty, and property of its citizens. Pragmatically, the most revolutionary of our groundbreaking technologies were born in the US military. The Internet, atomic energy, the computer, satellites, the space shuttle: all of these world-changing technologies were originally developed by the Defense Department (or its predecessor), framed as matters of national security.

Additionally, the Defense Department already has infrastructure and organizations designed for the particular task of developing and making practical use of "long-shot technologies." We should unleash the brains at MIT's Lincoln Labs and in the Defense Advanced Research Projects Agency (DARPA) on concrete problems such as creating light, rugged, solar cells to power American troops' tents in the desert or developing an energy source capable of powering a Humvee for a week. Solving problems like these and then declassifying the technology is the best way that the government can help the private sector develop and commercialize innovative solutions for our energy future. And the funding for these energy-related defense expenditures should come completely from the externality taxes that the government collects on energy use. This will couple the funding source with the solution that it seeks, offering accountability and ensuring that the project's money dries up once it has addressed the problem for which it, and the tax, was implemented.

The final principle that should inform our government's approach to energy in the twenty-first century is that of standards development. Events such as the Three Mile Island nuclear meltdown establish the necessity of governmental safety regulations regarding the delivery of energy to the marketplace. The federal government should shoulder the responsibility for developing the standards that guide how we deal with energy waste, the safeguards required for the nation's energy infrastructure, and the methods by which we ensure the safe transport of energy in our country. The government's legitimate responsibility in this arena is implicit in its mandate to secure the rights of its people.

Armed with these guiding principles, we have the tools to analyze America's energy portfolio. In so doing, we can develop policy prescriptions that will allow the free market to flourish, providing real solutions while protecting Americans' rights.

Fossil Fuels

Many on the left would have you believe that fossil fuels are evil, that their use has laid waste to the environment, and that continued reliance on them will cripple America's global economic competitiveness. In the face of such vitriolic rhetoric, often the best that conservatives can muster is a dispassionate, "but they're the only option we've got." We must do better.

Fossil fuels are simply one of the greatest gifts ever bestowed upon the human race. Since ancient times, we have harnessed the power of oil, gas, and coal to give us light, motion, and relief from the elements. Fossil fuels are cheap, abundant energy sources that have made possible virtually every major human advancement of the last two hundred years. The lights by which you are reading this book are powered by electricity – probably generated from coal. It was written on a computer and you very likely purchased it over the internet – again, powered by electricity. It was delivered to your local bookstore or directly to your house by a truck that ran on gasoline. And even its physical construction – its mass printing, binding, and layout – was made possible only by the existence of these cheap, plentiful energy sources. Something as simple as reading a book is only possible because man has harnessed the power of fossil fuels. Imagine the impossibility of powering our homes, our businesses, and our future without them.

This is not to say that fossil fuels are perfect or even that they should constitute the largest portion of our energy portfolio in the future (although they will for some time). However, it is important to root a discussion of energy policy in an accurate understanding of the role fossil fuels have played in the development of our world. This understanding dictates a humble and incremental approach toward the energy sources that make our way of life possible. Such an approach relies on a proper application of property rights and the taxation of externalities to make the use of fossil fuels reflect its true cost, while providing a revenue stream for the government to fund its crucial, legitimate functions in the energy realm.

I argued earlier that the federal government should commission a board to determine the actual costs to society of various forms of energy. These quantifiable costs should be borne by energy's users and should take the form of taxes levied on the use of energy. By doing this, prices would accurately reflect energy's true cost and ensure that the free market allocates capital effectively – to the sources of power that are most promising and most cost-effective. Such a role is the appropriate one for government to play in the fossil fuel arena.

This principle has already been applied in the form of gasoline taxes that pay for road maintenance, improvements, and other aspects of the automobile transportation infrastructure. Federal, state, and some local governments levy taxes on gasoline in order to fund investment in the infrastructure that supports automobile transportation. But this revenue is often diverted to pay for unrelated programs, which is an abuse of the system and an unjust use of government's coercive power. However, on principle, this represents the appropriate way for government to fund its legitimate activities: by taxing those who benefit from government action in order to pay for it. The users of a particular product – the roads – pay for their upkeep and the amount they pay is linked to how often they use that product. In this way, driving reflects its true cost as those whose driving impacts the roads also pay for the roads' maintenance. Similarly, we believe that fossil fuel users should pay the true cost of their pollution.

In the past, conclusions about those costs have been driven by sensationalist media that portray humans as parasites, dooming the earth to a slow death by global climate change wholly caused by mankind's use of fossil fuels. However, consensus about the energy implications of global climate change is rapidly deteriorating. Is the earth warming? Maybe. Are humans contributing to the warming? Possibly. What are the costs that global warming will impose on American society? Who knows? And finally, would America's complete abandonment of fossil fuels stop the earth from warming? Definitely not. In a June, 2009 Wall Street Journal article, Kimberly Strassel outlines exactly how the scientific and political consensus about global warming is crumbling. She paints a picture of a scientific community, ruled by orthodoxy, slowly coming to the realization that human activity probably is not the main cause of global warming – if such warming exists at all. Indeed, despite consistently increasing concentrations of carbon dioxide in the atmosphere, global temperatures have plateaued since 2001. Additionally, Strassel notes that many other developed nations are rethinking their governmentally enforced caps on carbon emissions that have proven to be overwhelming hindrances to economic growth based in shaky science.[9]

By pursuing our strategy, rather than capping carbon emissions outright, the government ensures that all economically viable energy use is allowed. Approaching energy policy in this way would force our government to transcend the politics of the issue and determine the true cost of individual Americans' carbon emissions. Energy use would be directly tied to its economic benefits, rather than to the bureaucratic whims of Washington, the hyper-connected environmental movement, or the energy industry's lobbyists. Such an approach to energy policy is true consumer protection.

The price mechanism, rather than controls and dictates from Washington, is the best means to achieve an ideal energy portfolio for America. Remember that Americans did not dramatically alter their driving behavior in 2008 because the government made them. Rather, they chose to do so precisely because fossil fuel prices rose significantly. Companies that catered to this new demand succeeded while those that did not lost vast sums of money.

There are clear economic and personal incentives for utilizing energy effectively and efficiently. These incentives have been at work in America's economy for quite some time. Over the past forty years, the free market has done more for the environment and to ensure affordable energy in our country than any government program could ever hope to do. Between 1970 and 2003, the carbon intensity of America's economy was cut by more than half.[10] That is, every dollar of goods or services produced in America in 1970 required twice as much carbon emissions as it did in 2003. And this figure does not even take into account the rapid improvements that we have seen in the last five years as high fossil fuel prices forced even more dramatic efficiency gains. This stunning achievement is the direct result of millions of individual decisions to cut waste, increase energy efficiency, and invest in America's energy future. It is a testament to the free market's power to deliver goods and services and to do so in the most environmentally friendly way possible.

The incentives that made this achievement possible would only be strengthened by an environmental movement that, rather than lobbying Congress to control the lives of average Americans, utilized its resources to educate the American people. In this way, we have no qualms with the goals of energy independence and decreased use of fossil fuels. But we disagree fundamentally with the methods being utilized today to achieve those ends. In the society we envision, environmentalists will not be able to bind the entire nation to their agenda through the use of political maneuvering and command and control policies. They will compete in the free market of ideas, making their case to individual Americans and changing behavior one decision at a time.

Even in the presence of a cap-and-trade system or other command and control measures, America will be dependent upon fossil fuels, particularly in the transportation sector, for some time. Today's technology allows oil and natural gas to be safely extracted at sea and on land without harming the environment. It is time for the government to grant oil and gas companies access to the land and raw materials that can allow America to achieve a measure of energy independence while alternative energy sources are being developed. To bolster our national security, we must tap the California and Atlantic Coasts as well as Alaska's natural resources to ensure the ability to power our military and our economy in the event that hostile nations try to block our access to fuel. With over two-thirds of our oil imports coming from OPEC countries, and Venezuela and Russia supplying much of the rest, it would seem that developing domestic capacity would be a matter of common sense. Today, we *can* do so while preserving the environment and creating American jobs. We *must* do so to secure our future.

Internationally, energy consumption will increase dramatically over the next twenty years. The majority of this demand will be met by fossil fuels – primarily oil, natural gas, and coal. Major American integrated oil and gas companies like ExxonMobil and Chevron employ world class research and development teams to ensure that those energy needs will be met. American companies are poised to lead the infrastructure development, extract and refine raw materials, and improve energy efficiency across the globe. The result will be millions of Americans employed in high paying jobs. These men and women will work to develop and export the solutions that allow other nations to take a step up the ladder of prosperity, improving the quality of billions of lives. Rather than demonize the companies and employees that make our way of life possible, our government should be embracing this change and the opportunity it presents for America to demonstrate the power of both its economy and its principles to the rest of the world.

Most importantly, our plan gives policymakers a framework for evaluating future calls to restrict Americans' freedom to produce and consume energy based on principles and not politics. An energy externality tax concept will guarantee that all energy sources receive an equal treatment by our government while making sure that the true societal cost of energy use is reflected in its price. Moreover, ensuring that American companies have access to American natural resources gives us the flexibility in foreign affairs that comes with the ability to provide our own energy. Finally, this framework guarantees that the free market can continue to function and provide us with breakthrough energy developments in the future and a steady supply of affordable energy in the interim.

Nuclear Energy

Subject to the constraints of current technology, nuclear power provides the cleanest, most viable source of energy available today. Currently, 20% of America's electricity is produced by nuclear power plants. Contrast that with a nation such as France where 80% of electricity is generated by nuclear power.[11] While Americans have grown accustomed to leading the world in technological development, it appears there exist lessons we have yet to learn from European nations.

Nearly fifty percent of America's electricity use is derived from coal.[12] Achieving 80% electricity generation from nuclear power could completely wipeout our dependence on one of the dirtiest energy sources still in widespread use. A government dedicated to protecting the liberties of its populace can ensure that we do so safely.

Nuclear energy poses twin security concerns regarding its widespread use. The first is that the plants themselves are vulnerable to attack or failure. People imagine a September 11 style attack on a nuclear plant and envision a radioactive Armageddon scenario. Alternatively, America's collective memory still reels from the 1979 meltdown at Three Mile Island and the 1986 disaster at the Chernobyl Nuclear Power Plant in the Soviet Union. The second challenge that nuclear energy poses is the disposal of the used nuclear fuel that remains once energy is produced. Used nuclear fuel takes the form of small, ceramic, uranium pellets that are radioactive. In order for America to effectively use nuclear energy as a long-term, large-scale energy source, nuclear energy producers must have a way to safely dispose of this material.

With regard to the first challenge, the nuclear energy industry and the federal government have done a remarkable job safeguarding America's nuclear facilities. The US Nuclear Regulatory Commission (NRC) is the federal agency responsible for regulating the nuclear industry. Along with industry groups, the NRC ensures that America's nuclear facilities are safe. Comprehensive federal regulation combined with redundant security systems ensure that the processes occurring in nuclear reactors are safe. These processes are overseen by skilled technicians, who are subject to extensive background checks and screenings, and have undergone rigorous training and certification. Over 8,000 specially trained paramilitary officers guard

65 American nuclear sites.[13] Even the September 11-style fears seem to be unfounded as the Electric Power Research Institute conducted an independent study that found the typical nuclear power plant could withstand and protect its fuel from the impact of a Boeing 767 crash.[14] Indeed, America's nuclear power plants are among the most secure facilities in the country.

The second challenge has not been met nearly as effectively. In order to facilitate the use of nuclear energy and in order to protect the American people, Congress voted in 1982 for the Department of Energy (DOE) to build and operate a deep geologic repository to safely store used nuclear fuel for the long term. 1998 was set as a deadline for used fuel to begin being transported from temporary storage in the nuclear plants themselves to the new location. This storage facility was to be set deep underground in a remote area – capable of protecting people and the environment alike from the dangers posed by the radioactivity of used nuclear fuel.

In 1987, the DOE began fifteen years of intensive study of Yucca Mountain, Nevada as a possible location for the repository. During that time, Yucca Mountain came to be referred to as one of the most studied pieces of geology in the world, and as of 2008 over $9 billion had been devoted to the studies.[15] Based upon the findings, President George W. Bush approved the Yucca Mountain site as the location of the repository. But in 2009, President Barack Obama announced plans to scrap the Yucca Mountain repository at the behest of well-connected Nevada politicians. In its place he formed a "blue-ribbon panel" to determine how to proceed with regard to the storage of used nuclear fuel.

All this occurs while a $33 billion fund – composed of taxes paid by users of nuclear power – sits waiting to be put to work on a project that the government promised would be operational over ten years ago.[16] It seems as if, once again, politics trump principle as the government fails to meet the obligations it has to protect the American people.

However, the private sector may just be able to save the government from itself. The Westinghouse AP 1000 nuclear reactor, one of the most advanced in existence, can store its used nuclear fuel indefinitely in water on the reactor's site. Even for the less advanced nuclear plants in the US, the NRC has determined that their used fuel can be stored onsite safely for up to a century. These advancements have bought the government time but do not absolve it from its abject failure to meet even its explicitly acknowledged, self-imposed obligations to the American people.

Despite its failure to develop the deep geologic repository, the nuclear energy industry provides an excellent case study in the appropriate and complementary roles of the government and private sector in the energy industry. For the most part, the government has worked with the industry to develop standards for the care of nuclear material and the safety of nuclear plants. Meeting these standards is the industry's responsibility and is paid for by the producers of nuclear energy. As such, it is ultimately funded by the consumers of nuclear energy. Those who use the energy pay the full cost of its delivery. Even the cost of the deep geologic repository is to be largely borne by consumers through taxes on the use of nuclear energy.

Thus, in nuclear power, we have an abundant, clean energy source that provides an amazing opportunity for America to transform its energy portfolio in the twenty-first century. As we look for ways to implement other game-changing technologies, policymakers would be wise to learn from the successes and shortfalls of the government's approach to nuclear energy. The principles that led to its ascendance as the most viable alternative energy source available today – from conception under the US Department of War (DOD's predecessor), to governmental standards generation, to free market commercialization – should guide us in our approach to comprehensive energy policy in the future.

Renewable Energy

Today we often hear calls for the creation of a new national priority to develop viable alternative energy sources. Proponents argue that we need a "moon shot" to propel America to energy independence, alluding to the Apollo program that fulfilled the goal articulated by JFK of putting an American on the moon within ten years. Often, these programs call for massive curtailment of individual liberties, dramatically increased levels of taxation, and the selection of a politically, not scientifically, chosen energy source to promote.

What proponents of such an energy program fail to realize is that the American government was able to successfully execute earlier programs precisely because it accepted our concept of governmental responsibility.

The Manhattan Project cost just under $25 billion in today's dollars.[17] The entire Apollo program – from initial conception to the uttering of Neil Armstrong's famous words – cost just over $145 billion in 2008 dollars.[18] That's right, for roughly the price tag of ExxonMobil's 2008 tax bill, we beat the Soviets to the moon.[19] We could have nearly funded three Manhattan Projects with the revenue that federal, state, and local governments received from gas taxes alone in 2008.[20][21] And these programs were the product of a government that took seriously the responsibility to secure the freedoms of its citizens from the two greatest threats of the twentieth century – Nazi fascism and Soviet communism. They were successful because they were conducted under the auspices of protecting the individual liberties of everyday Americans, not curtailing them.

Perhaps it takes a discussion such as this one to put the current government's massive fiscal failures in perspective. As the average American's conception of their government has morphed from that of an institution that should address *some* of their problems to one that should solve *all* of their problems, the government's mandate has grown and its focus has evaporated, rendering it a plodding behemoth incapable of effectively achieving even its highest priorities. The entire Apollo program or the Manhattan Project would not even be the biggest line items on a single year's budget today. And for all of its expenditures, our government accomplishes nothing near the significance of these programs' achievements. Such failure is unacceptable and should urge caution to anyone who looks to the government to develop the solutions for the future of renewable energy.

Expansion of government through the creation of vast new bureaucracies that hold command and control powers over individuals' lives and are funded by large tax increases is a recipe for disaster.* Even so, programs such as the Apollo program or the Manhattan Project do allow us to appropriately frame the government's involvement in renewable energy research and development. By reframing the issue of energy taxation as one of taxing negative externalities, we can focus on exactly how that tax revenue should be used. And it should be used in a very particular way to address the societal challenges that lie at the root of the tax.

---

* And yes, Cap-and-Trade is a massive tax increase on every American man, woman, and child.

The private sector has proven extremely capable at incrementally improving energy efficiency given current technologies. There is no need for governmental promotion of these incremental steps as there are ample economic and personal incentives to achieve them. However, the government can aid in the development of game-changing technology that has the possibility to revolutionize the future of renewable energy. This should be the goal of any government program funded by the externality tax revenue. Moreover, the externality tax revenue should be the only source of funds for these programs. These initiatives should be carried out by the Department of Defense, most likely at DARPA. As noted before, DOD has a history of capably developing breakthrough technologies and then declassifying the research to be commercially developed by companies in the free market.

The argument for funneling the money to the Defense Department is not one made out of a desire to cling to ideology. Rather, it is born out of the recognition that the Department of Defense has very real incentives to develop these technologies to empower our troops overseas and offer our civilian policymakers the flexibility that would result from America's emergence as an energy-independent nation. Utilizing our military's research and development arm allows us to approach the problem in the most effective way to solve it. Rather than giving an unaccountable bureaucracy the broad mandate to "cut emissions by 20% in ten years," we can give the best and brightest minds specific guidance for product and technology development. Two such possibilities were mentioned earlier and countless more could be developed, all the while putting our troops at a competitive advantage against our overseas adversaries.

Finally, placing the money under the control of DARPA or a similar organization will avoid much of the politics as usual that dooms the majority of government action to failure. One reason that the Apollo program and the Manhattan Project were such resounding successes is that people understood they were truly vital to national security. As such, anything but the best was unacceptable – from the minds involved to the companies and products that supported the effort. Putting the future of our energy security in the hands of the military can bring this dynamic to the cause – precluding the political favoritism and the woefully inefficient resource allocation decisions to which Congress is so susceptible.

Coupling the energy externality tax with a mandate for the Department of Defense to develop breakthrough renewable energy solutions is a recipe for just and effective governmental action addressing America's energy future. Such an approach is the only one consistent with our foundational values and the most likely means of ensuring a government dedicated to protecting and securing its populace's unalienable rights.

Conclusion

Perhaps the most powerful effect of adopting these policies is to grant decision makers in America's homes and businesses a degree of certainty regarding our government's approach to energy. As we move forward, it is imperative that we frame any discussion of government energy policy in terms of standards development and enforcement to ensure that America's energy is supplied safely throughout the country. Additionally, it is critical that we adopt a principled concept of energy taxation – ensuring that the price of energy reflects its true cost. Finally, we must clearly define a use for the tax revenue that is consistent with the goals of the taxation. As long as energy suppliers comply with the safety standards, they are free to operate as they see fit. Additionally, all energy sources are treated equally – being taxed at a rate that reflects the objective reality of their societal costs. The rules of the game thus established, investors, business owners, and individuals will be confident about how they will be treated by government in the future.

Developing and commercializing a new energy source, building an oil refinery, constructing a nuclear power plant: these are all multi-billion dollar propositions that must operate for decades to be economically viable. But these ventures will never materialize if the government's approach to a particular energy source can change on a whim. No one will build a nuclear power plant if he believes the government will tomorrow decide to subject nuclear energy to new, overly burdensome rules and regulations. No one will construct a refinery if he fears that the government will simply expropriate its profits through "windfall" taxes. And the incentive to develop alternative energy sources is severely dampened if investors and entrepreneurs fear that the government will just tax the new energy source to replace revenue lost from the decreased use of fossil fuels.

By employing this principled approach to energy, we can develop a sense of certainty within those who power America that they will be treated justly and consistently by their government. By promoting the free market and accepting its mandate to protect and defend the individual liberties of its citizens today, our government can pave the way for America's industries to power our nation and the world tomorrow.

Robert Wheeler attended Harvard University where he graduated cum laude with a degree in Applied Math and Economics. After Harvard, Robert joined the US Army where he served as an officer responsible for integrating Air Force, Navy, Marine Corps, and Army Air Defense assets. His assignments took him across America and to South Korea, Italy, and Puerto Rico. Robert recently separated from the military and is attending Harvard Business School where he is a member of the Class of 2011.

XI. LIVE FREE OR DIE:
Principles for a 21st Century Healthcare System
by Adam Oszustowicz

Over 230 years ago, our Founding Fathers put forth a set of guiding principles that has propelled our country to the pinnacle of achievement. These principles remain just as relevant today as when they were first penned. It is our unalienable right as individuals to freely pursue what we want in life. The obligation that this freedom implies is that we must take responsibility for our own lives. We must recognize this fact and craft for the government a role in healthcare that supports and promotes liberty, safety, and the pursuit of happiness. It must fulfill this role by embracing policies that enhance individual independence and empower decision-making, thereby affirming the natural right to self-ownership.

The American Revolution completely altered the world's concept of governance. A young America disposed of the tyranny that had defined its relationship with the British monarchy, and indeed the relationship between the governed and government for ages. Throughout history, societies had been structured so that individuals derived all privileges by virtue of the benevolence of the government. In America, the Declaration of Independence reversed these roles by recognizing that the US Government "deriv[ed] [its] just powers from the consent of the governed."

The Founding Fathers envisioned a limited government where every individual is the king of his own castle and lord over his own body. However, just as one is not actually a king and government does play an important role in a functioning society, neither is an individual the only one stewarding over his body. Although their actions were limited, governments were involved in people's health well before the 1700s. This involvement was primarily confined to broad public health concerns, such as sanitation and disease control. Meanwhile, personal healthcare remained primarily an individual responsibility.

The US Government's role in healthcare has evolved with advancements in medical science and technology, as well as the economics of personal health. For example, improvements in epidemiology – the study of factors affecting the health and illness of populations – led to the creation of The Center for Disease Control (CDC). And in an effort to increase access to healthcare and limit risk of widespread disease, incentives and regulations were enacted to create and expand the availability of health insurance.

This makes clear the particular juxtaposition that characterizes how people approach their health. On one hand, healthcare is highly personal, requiring independence and deeply intertwined with each of our unalienable rights of life, liberty, and the pursuit of happiness. In confronting illness, Americans enjoy great freedom to pursue the best medical opinions and treatments to restore their health. But on the other hand, the costs and complexity of healthcare options require that individuals give up some autonomy to seek assistance and leadership when faced with such decisions. These conflicting passions, independence and the desire to be assisted or led, cannot be removed from the healthcare discussion. Both are fundamentally important to achieving optimal health for individuals and the nation as a whole. In order to effectively reform our healthcare system, we must bring our founding principles to bear while acknowledging these twin desires.

Governmental attempts to satisfy the citizens' desire to be led in healthcare decisions risk creating what Alexis de Tocqueville referred to as an "immense and tutelary state." Tocqueville ominously characterizes this form of government as "a power [that] does not destroy, but [that] prevents existence; it does not tyrannize, but it compresses, enervates, extinguishes, and stupefies a people, till each nation is reduced to nothing better than a flock of timid and industrious animals, of which the government is the shepherd."[1] Whether our society devolves into that soft despotism depends largely on whether government takes the role of nanny or of protector of liberty, empowering people to take responsibility for their own health and happiness.

The guardian state arises under the guise of providing safety, security, and prosperity for all. Government seizes powers that never belonged to it, while grossly intruding on individuals' freedoms. The government justifies these infringements by promising that regulations and laws will free individuals from their concerns, needs, and labors. Essentially, government promises to spare us from the responsibilities of life, guaranteeing each individual an equally safe, secure, and prosperous outcome.

This guardian state is corrupt at its premise. In order to exist, it requires a citizenry and a political class equally dismissive of our founding principles. Citizens must voluntarily forego their most basic rights and abdicate the freedoms and responsibilities implicit in them. Our political leadership must forget that the nation was built on the idea that no one has the right to plan anyone else's life. Within this corrupt state, individuals elect politicians who promise to fulfill their every whim and yield to any decision that politicians deem necessary. Hidden behind the veil of populist rhetoric, politicians propose legislation and programs that benefit the influential and ensure electoral success. Ultimately, the relationship that develops between these two groups strips individuals of independence, allowing government to be guardian and sole arbiter of our health and happiness.

An understanding of the principle of equality is essential to correctly framing the healthcare debate. Our nation's Founders were inspired by Enlightenment era thinkers such as Thomas Hobbes, John Locke, and Jean Jaques Rousseau, who advanced the notion of natural equality through their discussions of natural law and social contract theory. At its core, their interpretation embraces the equal respect, worth, and dignity of all persons. This concept of equality infuses the Declaration of Independence and the Bill of Rights.

Prior to the Enlightenment, the common understanding was that individuals were not equal, which justified a hierarchal relationship among classes.* Society was organized on this foundation and the masses accepted that their lot in life was to serve their leaders. The Enlightenment marked the beginning of the end for theocratic, monarchical, and aristocratic rule

---

* Plato and Aristotle's concept of equal justice and Christianity's idea of all humans being equal before God are notable exceptions. However, they were not implemented to organize society.

in the West and witnessed the replacement of those systems with self-governing, democratic republics.

In common usage, equality means being treated as an equal. However, in the political environment of healthcare reform, equality is about the kind of treatment one receives and, specifically, what is fair and just. These are distributive qualities that require uncompromising adherence to the founding principles; otherwise we risk falling victim to a "sole, tutelary, and all powerful form of government." Tocqueville warns of this risk, arguing that if democracy is accompanied by the citizenry's demand that all be, "more equal and alike," then we risk losing the associations, freedoms, and differences that limit government power.[2]

Behind the differing approaches to healthcare reform are competing philosophical conceptions of equality. Each side answers differently the questions: what is fair and just; what should be equalized; what are the parameters? Only one definition of equality, that which defines it in terms of opportunity, is compatible with the founding principles of life, liberty, and the pursuit of happiness. This concept of equality requires that all members of society are able to live and compete in life on equal terms and enjoy their just deserts. Equality of opportunity presupposes that individuals' prospects in life begin equally, and thereafter the most meritorious rise in status. In the Declaration of Independence, the Founders recognized that government should "*organiz{e} its powers in such a form, as to them {the people} shall seem most likely to effect their Safety and Happiness.*" As such, government has a role in the preservation and promotion of public health as a means of promoting the safety of the American people. Moreover, in the Federalist Papers, Thomas Jefferson discussed the importance of government's preservation of human life within the nation. Based on this, the government has a responsibility to encourage conditions that reduce risks of disease or disability through the promotion of clean and safe living and working conditions and the provision of some protection against infectious diseases. In keeping with our concept of equality of opportunity, the scope of these actions must be to equitably reduce risks for the entire population.

Even with extraordinary attention to public health, disease and disability necessitate that most people will require access to medical care during their lives, especially during their later years. Equality of opportunity places a moral value on healthcare access and requires that financial, geographic, and other discriminatory constraints should play a minimal role in whether individuals receive the healthcare they need.

Healthcare reform centers on addressing this moral value. The Hippocratic Oath articulates how doctors should treat their patients. It states, "I will apply, for the benefit of the sick, all measures which are required." The same standard should guide healthcare reform. But, the oath also requires, "avoiding those twin traps of overtreatment and therapeutic nihilism." This should apply to healthcare reform as well, ensuring that no federal policy oversteps its bounds. While healthcare reform should benefit and focus on people's health, it cannot come at the expense of our founding principles.

Certain government actions have effectively addressed this moral value and at the same time affirmed our founding principles. The Emergency Medical Treatment & Labor Act (EMTALA) is one example. EMTALA ensures public access to emergency services regardless of one's ability to pay at the time. This can be contrasted with the State Children's Health Insurance Plan (SCHIP), which was established to address financial constraints and allow quality medical care to those children from low-income families just above the threshold to qualify for Medicaid. Despite its noble intentions, SCHIP has evolved into a program that assumes guardianship over healthcare matters for the majority of American children, an absolute example of systemic overtreatment. Medicare and Medicaid rest between EMTALA and SCHIP. Both initially sought to address the health concerns of the neediest Americans. Medicaid targets the poor and disabled while Medicare focuses on the elderly. While these programs were intended to address the true needs of the poorest among us, both have grossly overstepped their mandate – while saddling American taxpayers with a massive bill.

We must also recognize that public health programs and federal healthcare policy are not the only variables affecting the health of individuals. Many factors combine to determine the relative health of each person. The National Health Service (NHS) of the United Kingdom carried out a bloc of research known as the Whitehall Studies that showed a significant correlation between higher status and a longer, healthier life. The Whitehall results were consistent with findings from other countries, including those with and without universal coverage. The findings reveal that income and wealth, education level, social inclusion and exclusion, social cohesiveness, and perceived level of autonomy all have a substantial influence on health.[3]

Thus, the fact that increasing access to healthcare will not eliminate all of the preexisting differences and fundamental inequalities between people suggests that the current debate on healthcare reform is misguided at best and dishonest at worst. Even if it were the government's obligation to ensure a certain level of health, universal healthcare coverage is not a guaranteed way to do so. Governmental efforts should be directed to areas that promote health equitably for the entire population, while not usurping our rights as free citizens.

This would represent a certain and reasonable direction for healthcare reform. Any move toward government-planned healthcare would form the beginning of a fundamental transformation in the relationship between the government and the people. Government-planned healthcare would reinstitute a relationship similar to that between a feudal noble and his serfs. Nobel Prize winning economist Friedrich Hayek's book, *The Road to Serfdom*, characterizes this relationship in much the same was as Tocqueville describes the "immense and tutelary" state. In such a system, they both argue, tyranny is the inevitable end state.

Hayek credits the same principles upon which our nation was founded for the great progress in science, technology, and business since the Industrial Revolution. When the freedom to take risks was matched with human ingenuity, people could pursue their occupational desires to create the greatest advancements in human welfare that the planet had ever seen. From the simple worker to the captain of industry, in America there has always been a sense of control over destiny, of the unlimited possibilities that lay ahead, and of freedom from many of life's worries. Naturally, people's desires expanded in accordance with the promises of the time. What had not been solved was seen as a deficiency, thereby pushing planning to the forefront of people's thinking.

Planning to coordinate human efforts is effective and appropriate. Any of us would stockpile supplies of food, water, and medical provisions in the face of an impending storm or plan a defense in the face of a looming threat to our safety. In each case, what determines success from failure is the amount of freedom and autonomy that individuals are given to make plans with their resources. Without the freedom to employ knowledge, initiative, and resources as one sees fit, it is nearly impossible to assess, adapt, and respond to changing circumstances. Likewise, making static plans to address the dynamic field of healthcare is an ineffective way to achieve success.

Competition is fundamental for effective and successful planning of human activities. Competition is the nature of life; in evolutionary terms, it literally explains the very existence of plants and animals. Success in human endeavors lies in making the best use of the driving engine of competition. Nevertheless, competition must occur within a defined framework of rules and regulations. In the same way that baseball cannot be played unless three strikes result in an out, business and public health require rules for competition as well. In other words, successful competition does not prohibit governmental involvement. Government participation is necessary for competition's preservation and nutriment. For instance, Occupational Safety and Health Administration (OSHA) guidelines provide a framework for basic public health and safety. Furthermore, it is essential to acknowledge that as advancements are made, new rules may need to replace the old ones to ensure effective competition.

Competition succeeds in guiding human activities because it is efficient and egalitarian. This is particularly true in America, where the meritorious are rewarded, and where our culture makes even those of us who lose today likely to dust ourselves off and try again tomorrow. This spirit of "getting up and trying again," has led to a large part of humankind's advancement. Most significantly, competition is neither coercive nor arbitrary; there is no visible prod shoehorning people along a defined path. Instead, as Adam Smith observed, the forces of competition operate through an "invisible hand," presenting opportunities and affording people the chance to decide which path to pursue based upon what makes them happiest.

The Founders understood this dynamic and the benefits that it brings. In fact, the previously referenced Whitehall study established that good health is linked to professional autonomy. Individual pursuit of self-interest is the fundamental principle of free market capitalism. Our economy functions best when unlimited numbers of individuals freely pursue their own desires by making plans and executing them. This stands in stark contrast to the statist or collectivist. With hubris and contempt for human nature, the collectivist lords over all, convinced that his own infallibility and genius can create a utopia where no one is left wanting. The collectivist is blinded and ignorant to the fact that, as German poet Friedrich Holderlin put it, "what has always made the state a hell on earth has been precisely that man has tried to make it his heaven."

The proponents of government-planned healthcare believe that through their genius and purity of intention they can deliver the finest healthcare to each citizen. In a swell of populism, they promise to deliver, "the same healthcare Congress receives." Similar utopian promises have been made before, without success. However, their failure was not for a lack of effort. Only the coercive and tyrannical powers of a despotic state can do battle with the natural forces of competition. The first modern central planner and French utopian socialist, Claude Henri de Rouvroy, comte de Saint-Simon (1760-1825), desired that those who did not obey his planning boards would be "treated as cattle." Less corrosive American progressives after World War One called for the central marshalling of man, material, and resources seen during times of war for the purpose of tackling the "ills that confront man."

Simply put, any proposal for government-planned healthcare reform is necessarily anti-competitive, and thus doomed to failure. The Executive Office of The President, Council of Economic Advisers (CEA) report on healthcare argues that national, state and personal budgets cannot sustain the financial burdens of healthcare. Moreover, the CEA states that the steep rise in healthcare costs has and will lead to businesses' dropping healthcare coverage for their employees. It argues that, "perhaps the most visible sign of the need for health care reform is the 46 million Americans currently without health insurance. CEA projections suggest that this number will rise to about 72 million in 2040 in the absence of reform."[4] The solution, according to the CEA, is mandates and controls on what individual American citizens are allowed to spend for healthcare. Secretary of Health and Human Services Kathleen Sebelius asserts that the dire straits of Medicare's budget can only be solved by the government's taking a greater role in the coverage of all Americans, because it is the only way to control costs.

But such proposals undermine the very competition that is a critical element of our economy and essential for effective healthcare delivery. Competition is a morally superior way of allocating resources and goods. It minimizes financial, geographic, and other discriminatory constraints because it responds to supply and demand rather than bureaucratic whims or interest group lobbying. Competition facilitates the exchange of products and services in the marketplace whereas governmental controls dictate what can and cannot be exchanged. Competition between goods or services can drive demand, influence supply, and bring the two into balance through the setting of market-based prices. From this perspective, it is hard to see how government planned healthcare can successfully achieve the generally agreed upon goals of expanding coverage while lowering spending.

Under any universal coverage plan, the government's cost controls will be achieved not through competition but through coercion. Prices will be arbitrarily set, procedures will be rationed, and access to care will be limited. Bureaucrats, not doctors and patients, will determine what treatments you can have.

Proponents of government-planned healthcare disagree and present what they call an "elegant solution" that not only yields economic gains but also advances the delivery, scope, and quality of healthcare. They promise to eliminate waste and inefficiency in medicine, to fully leverage technology, and to improve preventative care in order to decrease the cost and raise the quality of healthcare in the US. While well intentioned, no system of government-run healthcare in the world has been able to achieve these objectives simultaneously. And any attempt to implement these proposed reforms through governmental coercion will fail to address the key shortcomings of America's healthcare system.

Eliminating waste and inefficiency is the holy grail of politics, with many politicians claiming that they hold the keys to this Shangri-La. Waste and inefficiency are matters of perspective. What was economical and efficient in a particular time period, location, or situation may no longer be because circumstances change. Addressing waste and inefficiencies through legislation can only be done by looking to the past to provide dictates for the future. But, conditions change and consequences cannot be completely anticipated, if they can be anticipated at all. Initially, some economic gains may be achieved through legislation but the forces of competition offer the only prudent manner to address waste and inefficiency systemically and in the long-term. The forces of competition drive the entrepreneurial spirit of individuals to resolve waste and inefficiency. Unlike legislation, which is codified once signed into law, competition allows for unlimited number of potential resolutions, all competing in the marketplace, changing and adapting to the latest ideas and technologies, even opening unrealized realms and new avenues for success.

For a simple example, consider the invention of the prescription pad. In the name of efficiency, the government could have mandated that all prescriptions would be written on a prescription pad and taken to the pharmacist by hand. Doing so would have yielded efficiency gains in the short run, but also would have destroyed incentives for finding better ways of delivering prescriptions – as any new system would be illegal. It would have taken significant political clout and lobbying to change the system and allow the current, much more efficient, use of electronic prescriptions. Undoubtedly, the change would have been delayed significantly, implemented poorly, and then codified in law again – hamstringing the next breakthrough in prescription technology. In this way, the promise of eliminating waste and inefficiency is the fool's gold of politics, making shiny promises that disappoint us in the end.

Proponents of government-planned healthcare also highlight the gains that can be achieved by the government's centralized collection and dissemination of information and knowledge in the healthcare field. President Barack Obama stated in a 2009 speech to the American Medical Association (AMA) that, "identifying what works is not about dictating what kind of care should be provided. It's about providing patients and doctors with the information they need to make the best medical decisions." He went on to say that he does not see any reason to dictate the nature of care because when information on best practices is circulated, providers will naturally adopt those methods.[5] The President's claim is that certain expensive procedures have outcomes that are statistically no better than cheaper procedures. He argues that this proves there is a need to educate doctors in best practices. The goal is to standardize practices and reduce costs.

In order to determine these "best practices," the collection of information is essential. This forms the impetus behind recent proposals for government to mandate the use of electronic medical records. Politically, the electronic medical record is being sold as a modern convenience that will eliminate the need to repeat medical histories when seeing a new doctor, as a money saving mechanism that will lower administration costs, and as a safety measure that will reduce medical errors such as allergic reactions to medications. Many hospitals and clinics already use electronic medical records for competitive reasons, primarily as a means of lowering administrative and record keeping costs. Although many doctors consider electronic records helpful in expediting care, they do not necessarily improve the delivery of that care. Moreover, the additional infrastructure and administrative costs associated with implementing and standardizing a nationwide system of electronic medical records make any potential savings realized over a very long period of time.

That the electronic medical record even exists is thanks to the forces of competition, and its acceptance is spreading for the same reason. For instance, use of portable electronic medical records is now proliferating in emergency care situations because practitioners, patients, and healthcare providers have observed that these are the situations where the majority of medical errors can be averted by their use. The government's motive for supporting the electronic medical record is different. Universal use of electronic records would allow the federal government to track your health records, ostensibly in the name of identifying and disseminating best practices. The 2009 Stimulus Bill created the National Coordinator of Health Information Technology. This new bureaucracy is intended to monitor patient treatments and guide doctors in best practices. In the speech to the AMA, President Obama justified the need for such an organization by saying, "we do a better job tracking a FedEx package in this country than we do tracking a patient's health records."

The creation of a National Coordinator of Health Information appears to be a reasonable and prudent measure for delivering quality healthcare. Indeed, the collection, distribution, and dissemination of information are necessary for free markets to flourish. However, the Founders saw the government's collection and dissemination of information as inherently dangerous. In fact, it is exactly this sentiment that led them to adopt the First Amendment, guaranteeing Americans freedom of speech and freedom of the press. Essentially, the Founders believed and history has shown that if government can use its coercive powers to control the flow of knowledge and information that liberty and freedom are quickly eroded. Application of our constitutional principles to science supports the view of chemist and philosopher Michael Polanyi, that "scientists do and must follow personal passions in appraising facts and in determining which scientific questions to investigate." Freedom and the pursuit of happiness are essential for the progress and evolution of medical science.

Therefore, we should be extremely concerned with the creation of the Federal Coordinating Council for Comparative Effectiveness Research (CER). The CER is also a product of the 2009 economic stimulus legislation. The CER provides funding to compare different medical interventions and strategies with their effectiveness in terms of medical outcome and cost. Effectively, the CER will be the controlling authority determining which medical practices are economically prudent and medically effective – it defines the best practices. Enforcement of CER findings is vague and yet to be determined, however, it is clearly stated in the stimulus bill (pages: 511, 518, 540, 541) that there will be penalties for those doctors and providers who are not "meaningful users" of CER findings. This clearly discredits President Obama's claim that the government will not be "dictating the kind of care" patients will receive, and the legislation amounts to a coercive use of government power that infringes on the rights of doctors and patients alike. Even without penalties, the CER is an unjust use of the power of government because it stifles scientific freedom to develop alternative best practices.

Preventative care is the third leg of the "elegant solution" offered by proponents of government-planned healthcare. Claims that cost effectiveness and health quality will be improved by embracing preventative medicine seem believable. Who has not heard or repeated the axiom, "an apple a day keeps the doctor away?" Along with President Obama, 2008 presidential candidates Hillary Clinton and Mike Huckabee have also touted prevention as an elixir to cure the healthcare crisis, saving lives and dollars.

However, the experts are not so optimistic. During the 2008 elections, the New England Journal of Medicine (NEJM) found "that the broad generalizations made by many presidential candidates can be misleading. These statements convey the message that substantial resources can be saved through prevention. Although some preventative measures do save money, the vast majority reviewed in the health economics literature do not." Quitting tobacco use, improving one's diet, becoming physically active, and preventing alcohol abuse are all cost effective preventative actions that improve health. Certain medical procedures, such as screening for colorectal cancer and vaccinating against influenza, fall into this category as well. Nevertheless, evidence reveals the ignorance of political leaders who argue that preventative measures are more cost effective then treatment. In fact, the NEJM's exhaustive review of the literature showed the cost-effectiveness of treatment to be similar to that of preventative measures.[6] A 2009 letter to members of Congress from the Director of the Congressional Budget Office (CBO), Douglass W. Elmendorf, cited the NEJM study and others in reaching a similar conclusion, that the widespread adoption of preventative measures may actually increase healthcare costs.[7]

In retrospect, once a person falls ill, prevention is often viewed as a more appealing proposition than treatment. Given the choice, very few people would rather undergo bypass surgery than take a pill each day for the rest of their lives. But such prevention is much easier said than done. Prevention impacts a person today, tomorrow, and for the rest of his life, while treatment – if ever even necessary – takes place down the road. Such logic explains why, despite the known risks, people continue to use tobacco. Therefore, even if preventative measures are freely and universally available, many will choose not to implement them. Even for those who do consent to the prescribed preventative measures, many will never know if the burden was worthwhile.

Ironically, successful prevention leads to individuals' living much longer, consuming a greater amount of healthcare than their fellow citizens, and thereby actually increasing costs. Therefore, not only is it difficult *but gov't can't do this*

REINVENTING THE RIGHT

to motivate people to adopt preventative measures, it may even result in higher expenditures over the long run.

For preventative measures to be adopted by all individuals, guidelines would have to be developed and individual actions mandated by the government. Prohibition was justified as a preventative health measure on a similar basis. Not only was outlawing alcohol an abject intrusion on the rights of Americans, but such government action also ran contrary to the natural force of competition. As a result, competitive economic forces led to the development of a black market and the rise of criminal gangs of bootleggers. Prohibition was repealed as an outright failure. Many argue the War on Drugs is failing for the same reasons, and ever-increasing "sin taxes" on tobacco have also begun to create black markets for counterfeit Marlboros. We see time and time again that not only is the mandating of individual actions beyond the legitimate powers of government, but it also is woefully ineffective and ends up costing the government more money than it saves.

The trinity of eliminating waste and inefficiency, promoting information technology, and preventative care are billed as an "elegant solution" to the health crisis. But the claims of cost savings do not even stand up to light scrutiny, and the parsimony of the plan is lost in its details and requirements. Moreover, to be successful, all three elements would require frightening abridgments of individuals' liberties. We once again see politicians making promises and political judgments based on what sounds good rather than that which is right or that can be demonstrated to work.

Healthcare is dynamic, and the subjective, governmental reorientation of the delivery of care is fraught with both foreseeable pitfalls and unintended consequences. The most immediate and obvious impact would be the addition of 46 million to the ranks of the insured. The stated intention of the various plans being floated is to have every American covered by some form of health insurance. However, according to the CBO's study of the reform plans being crafted in Washington, only a net 16 million additional people would receive coverage. Moreover, the CBO concluded that some who currently enjoy the freedom to select the best fitting private insurance would be forced to switch to the government plan and some will lose coverage all together.[8] The healthcare plans being debated are far from a panacea and will not have the advertised effect of eliminating the problem of the uninsured.

Regardless of the exact number, expanding the pool of the insured will place more demands on the healthcare system. There are no plans to expand the supply of medical care, so upward pressure will be put on prices. Ironically, this conflicts with one of the plan's primary justifications: that it will reduce healthcare spending not only in the aggregate, but also on a per case basis. This natural force – higher demand leading to higher prices – can only be short-circuited by artificially limiting access and putting up barriers. Regardless of what the politicians say, government-planned healthcare will require that treatment and care be rationed and the CER guidelines will determine how.

Despite assertions to the contrary, rationing is the only way to accomplish the goals of government-planned health care. An honest assessment reveals that forced adherence to government mandated best practices will inevitably limit options available to doctors and patients, resulting in a de facto system of rationing. Rationing means fewer tests, imaging, procedures, and treatments for those who truly need them. Without exception, government-planned healthcare rations. In the United Kingdom, the National Institute for Health and Clinical Excellence (NICE) defines "best practices." The Guardian, a British periodical, describes how NICE works: "Health ministers are set up, designed to ensure that every treatment, operation, or medicine used is the proven best. It will root out under-performing doctors and useless treatments, spreading best practices everywhere." The treatments that have been "rooted out" include medicines that prolong the lives of people with certain breast and stomach cancers as well as certain proven treatments for Alzheimer's, back pain, and arthritis. Medicines that prevent blindness are even withheld from anybody with two eyes! The most horrific contribution of NICE is the codification of the "quality adjusted life year," a mathematical formula that states that $22,000 is the limit that can be spent to extend life six months.[9] Precisely this type of logic, mixed with the coercive power of government, created the Nazi and Soviet eugenics programs in the twentieth century. We deplored the ideas then. Now we call them a solution.

In an eerily similar vein, Tom Daschle, President Obama's first choice for Secretary of Health and Human Services, argues that senior citizens should accept the health problems that come with age instead of treating them.[10] Moreover, President Obama stated that the healthcare crisis lies in the, "crushing...cost of Medicare and Medicaid..."[11] Correspondingly, cost savings from these programs can come only at the expense of the chronically ill and elderly, who account for the majority of healthcare expenditures, mostly in the last few years of life. This is not the sort of reform that Medicare and Medicaid require. It is reprehensible to tell our seniors to pass quietly because it is their duty.

Proponents of government-planned healthcare argue that rationing is present in the current system. They cite as an example health insurers that refuse to cover certain procedures and medicines. But there is an important distinction to be recognized here. Is a treatment unavailable because the government denies access to it or because an individual made the choice to buy an insurance plan under which the treatment was not covered? No system is perfect, but one in which decisions are made by patients, doctors, and the people who pay the bills is inherently more just and efficient than one where choices are made by bureaucratically designed formula. This method is preferable because the individual is free to purchase the type of insurance they desire, whether it includes a high or low level of coverage. Many employers offer a range of policy choices as well. Scarcity means that not everyone can have everything – whether we are talking about healthcare or any other good. But throughout history, prices determined by the forces of competition have always directed goods and services in a way that is both morally superior to and far more efficient than government dictates.

The combination of less money available to perform more services and the CER guidelines that harshly limit doctors' autonomy will result in fewer of our brightest young Americans choosing to become medical professionals. Of course, the government has developed other plans to incentivize people to become doctors, primarily by subsidizing their educations. The coercive hand of government never rests. Even so, it is not likely that these incentives will counter the aforementioned negative influences and increase the supply of quality medical professionals. Only the free market can facilitate the competition that ensures that the most capable providers of any service will fill that role. Finally, such incentives only encourage people to enter the medical profession and have no bearing on whether they choose to stay, a decision upon which the lower income and decreased autonomy will have the greatest influence.

With lower spending, higher taxes, and more demand, profits will fall for all companies involved in the medical field. Financial resources and entrepreneurs will migrate to industries that have greater potential for solid returns on their investments. Entrepreneurial endeavors and profit seeking – not government rules and regulations – have led to humanity's great advancements, particularly in the field of medicine. The United States has the world's most competitive marketplace for healthcare, which is testified to by the fact that between 1996 and 2000, the US accounted for nearly 50% of the world's medical patents, more than six times the number of the next closest nation.[12] This is free market capitalism at its best, creating solutions that make our lives better. The unintended consequences of limiting potential profits are unimaginable, but it is certain that medical advancements will slow. The inventions and innovations that entrepreneurs and capital make possible have permitted the treatment of previously untreatable conditions, saving countless lives and improving welfare. We must ensure that these forces can continue to operate and give us breakthrough advances in the future.

Politicians repeatedly assert that healthcare spending is too high, is increasing too fast, accounts for too much of GDP, and will eventually bankrupt the nation. They insinuate the preposterous proposition that some diabolical conspiracy exists which drives up healthcare costs. Spending on healthcare has increased because there are more treatments, medicines, and technologies available today than ever before – adding years to life and life to years. Spending would certainly be lower if medical advancements had ended with the founding of the nation. Leeches, bloodletting, and wooden teeth sound barbaric, but they were the best treatments of the day. As absurd as this might sound, it is effectively what the proponents of government-planned healthcare are proposing – limit and suppress advancements in medicine to control costs.

Video games also cost a lot more today than they did in the 1980s, when Atari's "Pong" was seemingly the only title available. But what contemporary gamer would support a government intervention to end "out of control" spending? Would gamers accept the "Coordinating Council for Comparative Effectiveness Research" limits on access to new titles and would game companies like Nintendo, Microsoft, Sony, and EA Sports invest in new products if such a regime were in place? When the cost of doing business increases, less is produced and advancements and productivity gains are forfeited. Advancements in healthcare are dramatic and provide great benefits for consumers, resulting in longer lives, less suffering, more accurate diagnoses, and better cures. Instead of slowing progress by killing the profit motive, government should encourage risk taking and entrepreneurial activities that address humankind's health needs by curtailing unnecessary regulation and making it easier to comply with the remaining governmental requirements.

The driver of these advancements is profit seeking. Politicians lament the fact that, in comparison to other "rich nations," the US spends a higher proportion of its income on healthcare. But such complaints ignore the fact that US citizens have more discretionary income to spend on healthcare to begin with, which fuels entrepreneurial activity and the development of medical advancements. The US economy bares the economic burden of developing medical advancements not just for our country but also for the entire world. For example, it costs approximately one billion dollars to develop a new drug. The benefits of this new drug's development are spread much more evenly throughout the world than its costs. If companies are unable to recoup their investment and make a substantial profit on their endeavor, they will never develop the solutions in the first place. Proponents of government-planned healthcare disregard the evidence that an economy's ability to innovate and develop solutions to society's problems is directly related to the freedom of its markets. Like ostriches with their heads in the sand, they simply believe that government will provide benefits without cost, something that has never occurred in the world's history.

The miasma emanating from this argument is suffocating. Government intervention will stifle competition and kill incentives for risk taking and risk capital in medical ventures. The discovery of new treatments and new medicines will slow at best and stop at worst. People will remain chronically ill or die when they could have been saved. At its core, this is the truth of the world our opposition seeks to create.

Politicians can be counted on to make the most expedient choice, not necessarily the best one for all concerned. This certainly seems to be the case considering the lack of priority placed on tort reform within the healthcare debate. The ability to sue and recover damages from doctors and institutions that are truly guilty of medical malpractice is necessary for the proper functioning of the marketplace. However, the barriers and burdens of bringing a lawsuit are too low and encourage frivolous and malicious suits that dramatically increase the cost of medical care by increasing medical malpractice insurance premiums and encouraging the practice of defensive medicine.

Additionally, multi-million dollar punitive damage awards have created a situation where a good-faith medical mistake (or even just an unfortunate outcome) has become a lottery ticket. Attorneys and litigants court the juries for these multi-million dollar judgments. After all, it is argued, the doctor's insurance company can afford to pay. This dynamic drives insurance premiums through the roof and forces doctors to perform a multitude of expensive, unnecessary tests in order to protect themselves in the event of a lawsuit. Medical malpractice insurance can cost over $250,000 per year for an OB-GYN.[13] This impacts everyone – we all pay for it in the form of increased insurance premiums and taxes that pay for the unnecessary tests that doctors must conduct. A great first step to decreasing healthcare costs in America would be to reform our tort system by capping the non-economic damage awards that juries can give. This would decrease healthcare costs for all Americans while redirecting diagnostic resources to more efficient uses than simply ensuring that doctors do not get sued.

Tort reform is badly needed in the present situation and the need will only grow as government-planned healthcare takes shape in this country. One of the stated goals of any proposed reform system is to reduce medical spending, which can only occur if fewer tests and procedures are ordered. However, that means an increased risk that the doctor will not make the right decision. This will open doctors and providers to increased risk of medical malpractice charges and increase their insurance premiums at the same time that their incomes are diminishing. We cannot predict all of the possible consequences, but we can expect that doctors will be forced to avoid and refuse difficult cases, harming those who need care the most.

There is no shortage of examples of the private sector's ability to provide superior alternatives to publicly provided services. Among these is education. President Obama, his predecessors, and many families across the country send their children to private schools for a variety of reasons, including safety, tradition, and quality. At the root of the decision is a personal recognition that public education is inadequate. A number of communities throughout the nation have initiated voucher programs in order to increase access to private education and force competition within the public school system.* Ironically, government-planned healthcare is a move in the opposite direction. Just as the privileged are accused of being afforded more opportunities because of private education, the same will be said of healthcare if a government-planned program is implemented. When an individual has maxed out their allotted amount of care under the government's health plan, the privileged will utilize the private healthcare market just as Canadians do when they are denied care by their government health insurance program. The will to live is strong and most will do what it takes to survive. In the future such a system would create, only the people with means will be able to move past the barriers and limitations of government-planned health insurance and receive the care they need. Again, we find the proposed solution breeding less, not more, equality.

Healthcare choices are highly personal and are often a matter of life and death. It makes sense that decision-making should lie with the patient through consumer-driven programs. Moreover, where government involvement is necessary, emphasis should be placed on promoting free markets and the forces of competition, which provide the best quality of care, efficiently and equitably. Efforts to provide everything to everybody achieve the opposite: lowering the quality of care for everyone. Furthermore, social leveling contradicts human nature at its most basic level and can only be achieved through coercive measures that are antithetical to our founding values. The problem with American healthcare is not too little

* Of course, many of the same ideologues that argue for government-planned healthcare also argue against voucher programs – despite their demonstrated success in increasing the cost-effectiveness of education and raising academic achievement.

government involvement, but rather our refusal to respect the individual responsibility for safeguarding our own health.

Proponents of government-planned healthcare speciously argue quite the opposite. They claim that government is uniquely qualified to ensure a strong and competitive marketplace through the provision of a public insurance option, which will keep the insurance companies honest. Superficially, it is reasonable to assume more competitors are good for the market place. However, the government is not a typical market participant. Government does not have the same pressures or constraints that a business has and therefore need not be run efficiently. The power of taxation and the lack of any balanced budget requirement mean that the federal government need not worry about costs, expenses, or making positive financial returns. Politicians do not make business decisions; they make political decisions. The government has a variety of ways to game the system, hide costs, and limit competition, giving it an unearned advantage over private insurance (and one that has no economic justification).

Government has the ability to disrupt the marketplace by pressuring vendors, subsidizing inefficient activities, and effectively legislating winners and losers. Despite the promises of politicians, the government has no intent to compete on equal terms with private insurers. The vanity of politicians and the powerful desire to make good on campaign promises impair this possibility, especially when the coercive power of the government can ensure the politically desired outcome. In fact, the government touts its so-called bargaining power as a way to decrease costs. If a private entity heralded such bargaining power it would be branded a monopoly and promptly prosecuted. Such is the nature of government's "competition." Ironically, in the spirit of nurturing a competitive healthcare insurance marketplace, government may mandate certain expensive spurious treatments, set premiums, and regulate sales and marketing, thereby making the cost of providing private insurance prohibitively high. In so doing, the politicians will destroy the competition they claimed to be fostering and herald in a new era of healthcare inefficiency under the fist of the government.

A study completed in the 1980s by the National Health Service of Wales United Kingdom (NHSW) showed that a large majority of women of childbearing age were unaware of the risks posed to a child by a mother's consumption of alcohol and tobacco during pregnancy. This lack of knowledge persisted despite widespread scientific evidence and public educational programs. In contrast, prior to the creation of NHSW, women of childbearing age had a relatively greater understanding of critical preventative health measures important for delivering a healthy baby. Women were more knowledgeable because individual responsibility required it. By the 1980s, taking responsibility for one's health was greatly diminished because of the existence of the NHSW. Armed with this knowledge, the UK began to introduce market-based solutions into the healthcare system, which in a limited manner improved patient health and satisfaction. Without any incentive to take responsibility for one's own health, communication suffers and results in a deficit of knowledge and poorer health for society as a whole.

Government-planned healthcare is the wrong direction for reform and is a prescription for universal dissatisfaction. Consumer-driven free market solutions hold the keys to lower spending and expanded healthcare coverage. Although the current system is preferable to any government-planned healthcare reform, it is similarly flawed as consumers have limited control and bear limited responsibility for key decisions. This is a result of consumers' paying only a fraction of their total health bill, leading to a system in which the one who pays the bill gets to call the shots. Moreover, when the price is nominally nothing, as is the case in many insurance plans today, consumers have no incentive to restrain their consumption of healthcare. This phenomenon is similar to the lack of respect with which drivers use rental cars, and is directly observable in healthcare with the aforementioned NHSW example. The end result is much higher insurance premiums for everyone.

The other half of the economic picture is that the marketplace demands expensive and inefficient services, partly as a result of defensive medicine and the desire to "leave no stone unturned" when investigating a health concern. The former should be addressed with tort reform, while the latter's solution is directly compatible with taking responsibility for one's health. The instinctive will to survive is integral to human nature and instead of opposing it, healthcare reform should leverage it by creating a system that rests on individual responsibility. Prior to the creation of a national health service, the women in Wales were not dependent on government for support; instead they had to take responsibility for their lives. In effect, they had the freedom to take responsibility. Similarly, Americans need to take responsibility for their health. This means putting the consumer in charge and firing the nanny – our immense, tutelary government.

There are many ways to achieve this objective. For example, we can increase choice in healthcare insurance and allow people to customize insurance plans to fit their needs. Health Savings Accounts allow people to combine high deductable insurance, which insures against catastrophic health expenditures, with tax-exempt savings accounts that can build up over time and be used to pay for smaller health bills and procedures not directly covered by health insurance. These are some of the ways that the private market is making health insurance affordable, even without tort reform or reform of the massive government liabilities we face in Medicare, Medicaid, and SCHIP. A perfect example of the private market tackling the toughest healthcare challenges is unexpectedly found in the aisles of Safeway, a large grocery store chain.

In 2005, Safeway, a self-insured company, believed that it could achieve more control over its health costs utilizing market-based solutions. As a result of the 1996 Health Insurance Portability and Accountability Act (HIPAA), which allows employers to base premiums on relevant behaviors, Safeway followed the policy of the automobile insurance industry and charged high premiums on the activities that resulted in higher health costs. The program is voluntary and covers 74% of Safeway's non-union employees. The variables Safeway measured were tobacco use, weight, blood pressure, and cholesterol levels. If an employee passed these screens, they were given a discount on the base premium. If they did not, the premium stayed unchanged and they could be tested again in 12 months. If they showed improvement after the 12 months, they would receive a refund from their base premium. The program has been highly successful, as Safeway's health costs have remained flat while other corporations in America have seen their healthcare costs rise 38% from 2005-09. Moreover, smoking rates of Safeway's employees are only 70% of the national average. Employees are requesting additional incentives and the company wants to implement them but federal law prohibits it. In the Wall Street Journal, Steven A. Burd states that, "at Safeway, we are building a culture of health and fitness...[and] we believe that personal responsibility and financial incentives are the path to a healthier America."[14]

Personal responsibility should be the cornerstone of healthcare reform. Our healthcare system should nurture the forces of competition and the ingenuity of entrepreneurs to develop affordable and expanded healthcare delivery systems. The Founding Fathers understood that the rights to life, liberty and the pursuit of happiness are the bedrock of a great society. History, human nature, and nature itself affirm these principles, and attempting to find success while abandoning them will only lead to disappointment and ultimate failure. This nation was born out of the rejection of tyrannical control. We revolted over the taxation of tea. We refused to acquiesce to unjust government control of our money. But healthcare reform is about the control of our very bodies – there is nothing more sacred or unique. If government can control how you treat your own body, is there any power at all that it will not take?

Adam Oszustowicz earned a BA in History and a BA in Political Economies of Industrial Societies from the University of California, Berkeley; he subsequently earned an MBA and an MA in International Affairs from the George Washington University. He served as a financial consultant to the Department of Veterans Affairs, where he developed a template that serves as both a teaching tool and an analytical resource for financial managers of the Veterans Health Administration, which supports the agency's long-term goal of utilizing financial market strategies in allocating funds. Adam is an officer of a medical service company.

XII. FREEDOM TO CHOOSE:
Reestablishing Excellence in American Education

by Paloma Zepeda

Nearly 2500 years ago, Plato said, "There are really only two fundamental questions: who gets to teach the children and what do we teach them?"

Today, these two questions should still drive anyone interested in having a profound impact on America's economic future and the future of freedom in our country. Conservative proposals for education can seem scattershot: private school vouchers, charter schools, the movement for high-stakes testing, No Child Left Behind and high mandatory standards, moral education and proposals for educating religious children in secular public schools – quite a varied litany. But if we take a step back, we see a thread of capitalism running through all these proposals. Each of them is based in the free market of both resources and ideas.

Capitalism protects individual liberty at a fundamental level. In a free market system, each man chooses the purpose and rewards of his labor, and determines for himself his own best vocation. In state-controlled economies, the government administers tests to young children and selects a future for them – doctor, bilge pumper, gymnast. The state views education merely as a tool, enslaving each child from an early age and depriving him of access to information that would allow him to control his destiny. A biased and narrow education deprives individuals of the ability to determine their goals independent of the aims of the state. This is why an independent and responsive education system is a fundamental protector of capitalism while rigid, governmentally controlled systems fundamentally threaten it.

A successful educational system's protection of capitalism in turn protects liberty: a high-quality education allows us to choose our own employment and, therefore, our own destiny. Education similarly under-pins our republican system of government. Without a thriving debate to inform a participating citizenry, the republic devolves into oligarchy. It need hardly be said that like the free enterprise system, our system of representative government is a protector of individual liberty. But while the ideals of republicanism – of participation, of representative decision making – are often found within the educational system, the ideals of our other guardian of liberty, capitalism, are not.

A strong education system, like a strong market economy, is comprised of both private and public actors. Yet too often, our system draws arbitrary lines that favor the public provision of substandard education over private provision of superior quality education. The fundamental problem with our public education system is a lack of choice for parents, which leads to a lack of accountability for schools and teachers, and ultimately, a dearth of learning for students.

Programs like private school vouchers are an important step toward increasing choice for parents, which leads to beneficial competition in the education sector. Vouchers provide low and middle-income families with a subsidy to cover the partial or total cost of private or parochial school tuition for their children. Opponents of vouchers argue that they drain necessary resources from public education. Public schools are funded on a capitated basis, meaning they receive funding based on average attendance. So if one student decides to go to another school then it is true that the school she leaves may lose money. Proponents of performance-based funding recognize this reallocation of resources from a poorly performing school to a thriving one as a good thing. Moreover, at the state and federal level too, money assigned to one cause could have plausibly been used for another. But this is the nature of all government spending, which is necessarily constrained by the limit of tax revenues and the debt ceiling. Since all funding is limited, is it really so unfair to assign a budget priority to educational access?

Voucher programs across the country are consistently oversubscribed and parents are eager to gain this choice for their children. Clearly, at least some parents are "voting with their feet." One almost wonders why it is acceptable for students from wealthy families to go to private school, but it "deprives public schools of funding" when programs such as vouchers and other school choice mechanisms offer the same opportunity to students from less well-off backgrounds. It is perfectly acceptable, not to mention critically important to maintaining a quality and cost-effective education system, that public schools compete for their capitation-based funding.

Schools should not only compete on educational quality, but also on content. Parents who wish to send their children to religious schools or to ensure that their children are taught certain moral values, should also have choices in the educational system. Parochial schools should be on an equal footing with secular schools in terms of access to resources – and secular schools themselves should not be forced to adopt the moral values of far-flung bureaucrats just because someone in Washington thinks that a belief that God created the world is quaint. The price for being poor should not be a mandatory abandonment of one's family values once a child sets foot outside her home.

In much the same way that underfunded voucher programs fail to provide significant competition for the entrenched public school bureaucracy, charter schools also don't provide an accountable and competitive alternative for parents and students. Charter schools are schools run outside of the traditional school system, with funding from that same system. Additionally, these schools may accept private donations. Charter schools generally do not charge tuition and are run by an independent board subject to governmental certification. School quality and financial health certification requirements vary by state. Like vouchers, charter schools propose to let students and parents "vote with their feet" by providing an alternative to the local public school – a laudable goal. However, the governance of charter schools needs to be more rigorously enforced. Too many districts don't act to close charter schools that fail to meet mandatory educational quality requirements. Although educational disruption should be avoided, creating these semi-public entities and then exempting them from accountability is as anti-capitalist and anti-child as one could imagine.

Rejection of accountability has led to many of the injustices inherent in our current educational system. The stories are all well-known and well-understood. Too many recent immigrant children are caught in failing schools and too many children of color are likewise underserved. A recent

McKinsey study showed that a persistent racial achievement gap has created the economic impact of a permanent, severe recession. But this is not the only achievement gap that hampers our prosperity – the achievement gap between the highest-performing and lowest-performing states likewise has the same effect on GDP as a recession.[1] The inequalities in our current system impact all children. We can propose program after program, but without accountability these staggering and costly gaps will remain.

Accountability in education begins and ends with standards. Standards for student and teacher performance are a necessary component of assuring that a rigorous curriculum is taught by qualified educators in America's schools. Standards ensure that students learn to read, to write, to do math, and to understand our national history. Standards are necessary and should be developed by the states in order to prepare students to compete in a research-driven economy. Although when No Child Left Behind was ushered in, standards were a contested and partisan issue, the value of high educational standards seems a consensus position now. But while No Child Left Behind forced a recognition of the importance of high standards, it did not adequately address the core issue – where should standards come from, and how should they be enforced?

Our Founders envisioned the states as laboratories of democracy and enshrined into our Constitution the principle of federalism. Under federalist principles, the American people endowed the national government with a defined set of limited, enumerated powers in the Constitution. Any powers beyond those specifically given to the federal government fall entirely within the province of the states. Federalism protects liberty by protecting against the overreaching of any one branch of our federal government – it is part of the uniquely American system of checks and balances.

In the same way that federalism animates our constitutional structure, it should also inform our education policy. Any national education structure should seek only to encourage each state to develop better and more effective standards. Just as the states can be laboratories of democracy, they can also be laboratories of innovation in education. This "federalist" approach also best responds to differing local needs: as the previously mentioned McKinsey study found, children across the states are at dramatically different levels of performance and readiness to enter college.

A national standard for "educational adequacy" ignores these disparities and may well underestimate what "adequate" means in a high-performing state like Texas while dramatically overestimating the systemic capabilities of a struggling state like Alabama.

Only by allowing states to identify standards that reflect the reality of their present circumstances and to determine for themselves the pace of progress toward higher standards can we ensure that all states maximize progress and bring forth the potential of each American child. This approach will be all the more effective because it leverages the clear economic incentive for each state to have the best-educated, most-employable high school graduates and a strong public university system driving economic innovation. What state wouldn't envy Massachusetts' biotechnology hub or the economic engine that is North Carolina's Research Triangle?

Just as states should develop standards, they should also enforce them. Each state should judge for itself the success or failure of its standards. Although national research will be valuable to each state's understanding its relative competitive position, national enforcement of local standards is an ineffective and inefficient tactic. The appropriate role, then, for the federal Department of Education is as a national aggregator of best practices. This is a function the Department already performs and should represent its principal mandate. A national system of free, high-quality education need not be run by a regulatory behemoth. One need only look as far as any current national report of educational outcomes to see that a massive federal bureaucracy is not in itself capable of making our educational system succeed – and that it may even hamstring our school system's innovative potential. Centralization of educational policy in the hands of the federal government robs our children of the unique talents and devotion to student success of educators and administrators at every other level. With the Department of Education thus repurposed, it will be up to the states whether to validate their standards by using practices like high-stakes testing.

High-stakes testing does not need to be immediately implemented in the transition to standards-based education. Proponents of the testing argue that it is a necessary component of any system purporting to have standards. Otherwise, how does one understand and communicate the value of a credential such as a high school diploma? But an internally administered high-stakes test is not the only way to evaluate such a credential. The educational system already has two externally administered high-stakes tests that attempt to evaluate the quality of a high school graduate's education for the purpose of college admission, the ACT and the SAT. An alternative test, the GED, also attempts to validate the standard of a high school education.

However, because SAT, ACT, and GED scores are not reported by classroom, teacher, or subject matter, they don't give a window onto teacher performance. High-stakes tests would be administered by teachers to their particular classes of students instead of to undifferentiated groups of individuals like the SAT, ACT, or GED. Therefore, the advantage of this system is that it will allow evaluation of teacher performance in addition to student achievement. Unlike SAT, ACT, or GED scores, high-stakes tests administered by the school would give schools a view on both student *and* teacher performance.

Because ACT, SAT, or GED testing does provide a window into individual student performance, educational policymakers already have some data on student progress even in the absence of high-stakes testing. If high-stakes testing is slowly phased in after high educational standards are in place, the SAT, ACT, and GED are sufficient to serve as metrics of student performance during the transition. Because these tests don't give data on the performance of a particular classroom, however, an independent mechanism for evaluating teachers will also need to be developed. Teacher evaluation is a useful aim in itself. Thus, independent teacher evaluation need not cease once high-stakes testing is phased in. High-stakes testing will be an important part of standards-based education, but market-based testing alternatives can help ease the transition to such a testing model without forcing children to get caught in a test for which they are unprepared.

With a strong standards-based "floor," schools will be able to independently evaluate their staff and administrators and will be free to take action based on their findings. Education at its worst seems to be a line of complacently grazing sacred cows standing shoulder to shoulder barring students from playing in a field of innovation. In the prevailing model, the teachers who have hung around the longest are the most highly compensated and earn the most favorable benefits, regardless of performance or qualifications. There are better, more innovative, performance-based ways to compensate teachers that reward the best teachers, not merely the oldest.

Dramatic increases in teacher pay, tied to performance standards and increased responsibility, might be the first step toward a solution. In fact, one such model is being currently implemented at a charter school in New York City where teachers will be paid $125,000 per year – the effect has been predictable, the best and brightest teachers (and some who have never taught before) are applying for a shot to educate New York's children.[2] But the best schools will get even more creative to motivate teachers and reward the best. For example, as twitter user @JoshAronovitch suggested to Newark, New Jersey Mayor Cory Booker, why not give teachers a significant signing bonus that vests over time based on performance? Any innovative solution, however, will likely find a significant obstacle in the teacher's union.

The teacher's union should take the responsibility for developing substantively rigorous qualifications for membership and lead the campaign for subject matter expertise. To subordinate this goal to any other purpose represents a serious misapplication of priority and does a grave disservice to our children. The teacher's union should be the first to object when a music teacher is teaching algebra. And, if a union member does not meet the high standards for membership, the union should no longer consider that teacher a member.

Teachers are professionals, and any organization of educators should make continuing professional education a mandatory condition for membership – just like it is made mandatory for doctors by the American Medical Association and for lawyers by the American Bar Association. Ensuring teacher quality is a process, and the union should be at the forefront. Too often, programs aimed at educational improvement look at a "failing school" and make the decision to close that school. But this decision is only necessary in a world where you cannot fire teachers for unacceptable performance or reward superior teaching with merit-based pay. Closing schools is one of the most harmful things that can happen to a child's educational progress. But if schools were able to fire underperforming teachers, the entire school need not close – linking a teacher's job to performance serves students by more than just ensuring educational quality, it protects educational continuity. If entrenched teachers do not like the prospect of having their jobs depend on their performance then so be it. Education is not about them.

Educational continuity must be protected for students – but more of the same for teachers and administrators is just whistling past the graveyard. Within the ranks of teachers and administrators, we would do well to apply business professor Clay Christensen's principle of disruptive innovation. In a recent article for CNN.com, Christensen cites alternative certification in particular as a method that applies this principle of disruptive change.[3] Alternative certification organizations offer different standards than traditional teacher certifications to validate teacher competence, generally more quickly and at a lower cost to applicants. Although alternative certification is not accepted by all states or all school districts, those districts who open themselves up to alternatively-certified teachers are giving themselves that much more of an advantage in the fight to raise teacher quality. Teacher quality is about the educational qualifications and pedagogical skill of the candidates who get through the certification process and into the classroom in the first place, not just a battle to raise teacher pay. Any certification that accurately predicts a teacher's ability to succeed in the classroom should be embraced by parents, administrators, and teachers alike in pursuit of a top-notch education for children.

Despite the cries to raise teacher pay and increase system wide expenditures, we've ignored a central truth: garbage in, garbage out. Equal funding won't make equitable results, so let's stop pretending that pumping more money into failed systems through a redistributive federal policy will improve anything at all. Studies have shown that beyond teacher quality or parental involvement, the best indicator of student success is small class size. Decreasing the student-teacher ratio will take a funding commitment, to be sure. But class size is the driver here, not cash investment.

The most infamous statistic in this regard is perhaps that the Washington, DC school system has highest expenditure per pupil in the nation while producing the lowest educational outcomes.[4] This statistic is not an anomaly. State-by-state analysis shows that expenditure per pupil does not predict educational success.[5] Indeed, Texas schools are quite successful while maintaining lower costs than many of their neighbors. Eventually, an increased financial investment in education may be necessary. But a dramatic, immediate increase in funding will only make our current failed system a more expensive failed system. This is a trend borne out by recent history. An investment in better practices, rather than more money for money's sake, can increase the effectiveness of the system we have without writing blank checks that perpetuate systemic problems.

Capitalist principles can help us overhaul our education system at the systemic level, but capitalist incentives applied at the level of the individual student have also met with initial success. Our educational system provides long-term benefits, to be sure – if a student completes high school, he or she becomes qualified to attend college and is better able to obtain gainful employment. But too often schools and teachers fail to communicate incentives to students at all. Any business school student can tell you that aligning incentives with objectives increases employee performance. Why not apply this principle to students to help them make the educational progress critical to their future success?

In Roland Fryer's studies, he pays low-achieving students to reach certain academic benchmarks. Though this is an oversimplification of his methodology, he generally found that low-achieving students, when offered financial incentives, can improve their performance.[6] Critics have said that paying students for learning corrupts the educational process and robs students of achieving the true joy of learning for learning's sake. One cannot help but note that some of the people making these particular objections are professors who are – wait for it – paid to learn. Anything that helps students achieve more should be tried – and once it's tried, if it works, it should be implemented. Even the so-called "heretical" idea of paying students. Some might argue that turning the students into a pay-for-performance "workforce" of sorts will only open the educational system to more regulatory chaos. Would students be able to unionize? Can a unionized student challenge the teacher who sent him to detention, and sue for back pay? Extending arguments to the limits of reason can make any proposal sound like a fool's errand. Schools must remain able to discipline children, and giving incidental financial incentives will not impair that pedagogical imperative.

What will impair our ability to teach our children is refusing even incremental, scientifically proven change by clinging to sacred cows. Even if monetary incentives were not implemented, America's public education system in the recent past has undertaken efforts which actually have the exact opposite effect by deemphasizing quantitative, competitive grading scales in the classroom. It is imperative that we reverse any such trends that hinder the system's pursuit of its primary goal: allowing students to achieve their maximum potential and preparing them to thrive in an increasingly competitive world. Today's students are tomorrow's leaders of industry, government, and the education system itself. As such, it is in America's interest to embrace the commonsense need to show students meaningful incentives to commit themselves to their education.

So what happens when we get rid of the ineffective orthodoxies in education and embrace capitalist principles? Perhaps we'll finally have schools that once again serve as social integrators of the American fabric, bringing students from all backgrounds together in a venue that allows them to realize their potential while forming pro-social relationships with both peers and authority figures. No longer will parents be stuck without choices, with too many disadvantaged children trapped in dangerous, decrepit institutions. Our education system will allow parents to choose how to educate and transmit values to their children, without unnecessary interference from multiple layers of expensive bureaucracy. Schools will compete with one another to provide the best education, retain the best teachers, and maintain fiscal stability. Locally run and funded schools will be responsive, lean organizations that consistently evaluate their employees' performance. Teaching will be a profession like law or medicine, with rigorous entry requirements, remunerative pay, and professional ethics that require a commitment to consistently updating and improving curricula and teaching methods. A high school diploma will mean something economically valuable to every graduate, and companies across the globe will recognize that America once again has the best-educated workforce in the world. Perhaps some of these goals are decades away, but we cannot afford to let this daunting span of time diminish the will to seek improvement, beginning today.

Additionally, the capitalist principles of competition and pay-for-performance have a proven ability to unleash the powerful forces of entrepreneurship and innovation to solve problems better than any bureaucratic structure ever could. By increasing parental choice and accountability for schools and teachers, we align the incentives of administrators and educators with those of children and parents. When this is done, the truth is that we do not know the exact shape that our educational system will take – but we do know that it will employ the most efficient and effective methods of educating children for the future that they face. This is the beauty of American-style capitalism: the profit motive gives birth to innovations and advancements that no one can predict and that fundamentally improve processes and organizations. Our children should be so lucky as to learn in an educational system that embraces these principles and harnesses the power of the free market.

The capitalist principles espoused in this essay prepare our society to offer the best answers to the two questions that Plato posed at the beginning of this essay. Parents are allowed to choose for their children the education they think is best. Thus, parents will choose who educates the children. And because parents have the freedom to choose their children's educators, there will be no subjectively defined curriculum set by bureaucrats. Children will be, in the broadest sense, taught what they need to know. And as the world changes, and as what children need to know changes, the education system will change as well. In this way, the education system becomes what we know it can be: a stalwart defender of individual liberty, capitalism, and America's representative democracy in the twenty-first century.

Paloma Zepeda is a member of the Harvard Law School Class of 2010. She currently serves as Editor-in-Chief of the Latino Law Review. After graduating from Harvard College, Paloma worked as a management consultant with Monitor Group, where she advised pharmaceutical, grocery, and telecommunications companies on business strategy. She is the author of a blog, bikinipolitics.com, a former staff writer for the Harvard Political Review, and has worked as a researcher for both Applebee's America, an examination of American politics during the 2004 election, and Randall Kennedy's forthcoming work on the 2008 election.

XIII. SERVE AND PROTECT:
A Federalist Approach to Police and Crime Policy
by Bryan Jiral

A young man stands silently on the street corner. He watches the nearly empty street before him, excited by the prospect of making a couple hundred dollars. A car pulls up in front of him and the passenger window rolls down.

The driver appears nervous. The young man is cautious, but when the driver flashes a wad of cash, he reaches in to his pocket and pulls out a small plastic bag. Within seconds, flashing lights flood the street and the sound of sirens echo off of buildings as three local police vehicles fly around the corner to join the unmarked car, whose driver is now on the sidewalk, weapon drawn. The man on the street is handcuffed, read his rights, and ferried to the police station. A federal prosecutor is already there to meet him.

Within weeks, the young dealer is given a sentence of 10 years. In court, he begs for a lighter sentence, promising to provide information on his supplier, who he claims distributes to half the dealers in the city. He even promises to testify against him. But federal guidelines give the prosecutor little leeway, and he can do nothing.

Six months later, just blocks from the site of the dealer's arrest, a 14 year-old girl sits in her kitchen as her mother helps her with her homework. A bullet bursts through the wall of her home, striking the teenager in the head and killing her instantly. A turf war over drug territory has recently exploded. During the alleged shooter's trial, he brazenly brags to supply drugs to half the dealers in the city.

He could have been taken off the street.

———

Police and crime policy does not drive voters to the polls en masse in the same way that many of the issues covered in this book do. It does not engender the same intensity of spirit as most of them. But perhaps it is a mistake that it does not. After all, our individual safety is a paramount personal concern. Shouldn't it also be critical to each of us in our capacity as voters? Could it be that we've reached a point where many of us take our ongoing security for granted? If so, a reordering of our collective list of priority political issues is warranted. The episode above illustrates that more so than with virtually any other responsibility, the government's failure to implement effective police and crime policy has the potential to dramatically impact any one of our lives at any time. Perhaps it is time we acknowledge the crucial nature of this policy area, educate ourselves on the various policy prescriptions in play, and demand that our government responsibly make the decisions necessary to keep Americans safe from those who seek to do us harm.

In order to properly frame a discussion on police and crime policy, establishing a historical perspective is necessary. We must recognize that the principles upon which America was founded have been essential to attaining the level of achievement our nation has enjoyed. This essay seeks to employ these principles to develop a foundation upon which our government can craft policies most likely to guarantee the safety of all Americans.

The American nation is one of the most unique in the entire world. A country of farmers and merchants, we won independence by defeating the world's preeminent superpower. Having shed the yoke of tyranny, our Founders created a new nation based on the simple yet revolutionary premise that all men are equal, endowed by the Creator with unalienable rights. This principle infused America's founding documents. In the Declaration of Independence, the Founders articulate the guiding and defining purpose of governments: "To secure these rights, Governments are instituted among Men, deriving their just powers from the Consent of the Governed." In order to effectively fulfill such a mandate, the government would thus be charged with clearly defined, essential responsibilities. One of the most important and most visible of these responsibilities is the protection of citizens' rights from criminals. The words of the Declaration reveal a firm understanding that for liberty to prosper there must also be order. The government thus has the responsibility of ensuring order to guarantee liberty. The government's police function exists to maintain this ordered liberty so that all Americans can enjoy the freedoms we were guaranteed at our nation's founding.

The nation our Founders created was deeply influenced by the memory of British rule. Claiming the divine right of kings, the English monarchy's will was considered final and complete submission to that will was expected. The Founders took concrete steps to ensure that such tyranny could never again dominate the lives of free Americans. They divvied up the national government's responsibilities between three branches so that no single branch was omnipotent. They divided power even further between the federal government and the states, with the Constitution's Tenth Amendment guaranteeing that each state retained all governmental authorities not expressly enumerated to the federal government. But before any of these actions, our Founding Fathers enshrined in the Declaration of Independence the notion that ultimate sovereignty originates within the citizenry, guaranteeing a government of, by, and for the people. Out of the practical implementation of these ideas emerged the system of checks and balances and a federalist division of authority between the national and state governments, which have been central to American governance ever since.

What does this mean for the creation and enforcement of crime policy? Under a federalist system, any powers not constitutionally assigned to the national government are retained by the states, to include those necessary to protect us from criminals. This allows each state to enact laws that reflect both the unique problems that it faces and the collective will of the state's residents.

But in order to guarantee that all Americans would enjoy equal protection of their rights, the Constitution mandated that whatever state laws may be, they would be executed faithfully, in accordance with the principles which underpinned the establishment of the new nation. The Fourth, Fifth, and Fourteenth Amendments protect citizens' rights to due process and legal representation, and prohibit unreasonable searches and seizures. These amendments guarantee uniformity in the execution of law, but allow each state to determine the substance of its laws. For example, police may find marijuana in two different homes, one in Texas and one in California. Texas statutes make such possession a crime, while California law allows for a legitimate prescription that makes possession legal. Despite these differences in legal substance, the Fourth Amendment requires that a search warrant be obtained based on probable cause to justify police entry into either home.

These amendments are not meant to bind the states to the whim of the federal government, but rather to set the parameters within which the states administer their own laws. This ensures that the police carry out investigations in a manner consistent with constitutional principles. A federalist approach to police and crime policy ensures laws are enforced by authorities best suited to do so, without allowing the police carte blanche to infringe upon the rights of free Americans. Such a system ensures that the police are strong enough to protect our rights, but never strong enough to take them away.

In order for the government to effectively enact and execute laws that keep Americans safe from criminals who would violate the rights of the innocent, it is imperative that we employ these federalist principles. There must be as much local control as possible. Laws should reflect the unique characteristics and problems of the communities they are designed to protect. A law may be wildly successful in one place and a total failure in another. As we will see, federalization of crime policy too often discounts this fact, to the detriment of innocent Americans who rightfully expect protection from the actions of criminals. Locally focused crime policy – a hallmark of effectively employed federalist principles – provides three distinct benefits over a national "one size fits all" policy. Namely: it allows a community to efficiently allocate both fiscal resources and law enforcement assets; it places more accountability on those in office by subjecting policies and officials to review at the lowest level; and it lets local police and prosecutors utilize their knowledge of each community and its unique characteristics.

The lower the level at which laws are enacted and enforced, the more efficient such laws will necessarily be. While this discussion is by no means exhaustive, it should help to illustrate the inefficiency that results from over-federalized crime policy. First, the massive size of the federal budget makes it difficult to identify budgetary constraints, much less develop policies that fall within such constraints. Sadly, this encourages the federal government to enact policies essentially by trial and error. In contrast, states and municipalities must operate within clearly defined fiscal limits. Indeed, almost all states have some sort of statutory balanced budget provision, and the small size of local government budgets requires that efficiency is made a priority.

Secondly, by virtue of their smaller populations and nearer proximity to the low-level crime that accounts for the majority of criminal behavior in the US, states are best suited to quickly assess the effectiveness of a new policy. As such, local and state governments can scrap a law quickly if it does not work. Compare this with the bureaucracy entailed in federal processes, which makes shifting course quickly next to impossible. Federal programs and policies often take years to implement and even longer to assess, resulting in massive expenditures while yielding few results.

Finally, the complex nature of the federal bureaucracy virtually ensures that policies which emerge from it are equally complex. This is particularly true when the federal government seeks to dictate appropriate action to the states. For instance, a crime bill passed by Congress may contain so many unrelated subsidies and monetary incentives that a state's governor has little choice but to institute the policies, even if doing so requires replacing existing laws that have already proven themselves effective. Ultimately, federal crime policy has few objective benchmarks for success, is developed with very little input from the communities it ostensibly aims to help, and is very hard to reverse, even when such reversal is necessary to the point of being pure common sense.

By diffusing authority to enact and enforce crime policies to state and local governments, we also benefit from dramatically increased accountability. The level of access citizens enjoy to a county sheriff or a state legislator increases the likelihood that criminal statutes appropriately reflect unique, local characteristics. When a local or state policy proves ineffective, the communities can band together for a change. Whereas a community can hold its local government accountable for failed policies, members of Congress largely escape blame for policies that originate in Washington but whose failures are felt locally. Massive financial war chests and self-serving relationships with special interest groups are enormously powerful guarantors of reelection for incumbents. This safety evaporates at the local level, as does the ease with which improper sweetheart deals are worked into legislation. Thus, a law enacted in a state legislature and enforced by local police departments is inherently more likely to achieve its intended objective than one that emerges from the more highly politicized federal bureaucracy.

That this may lead to the existence of different laws in different states should be perceived as a positive effect. As an example, consider the variety of concealed carry gun laws between states. In Texas, by completing a ten hour safety course and successfully passing a background check, a resident may carry a concealed pistol on their person at all times. The law is based on the belief that guaranteeing this right to a broad swathe of Texans will deter criminals, and its existence has led to a reduction in violent crime in many areas of the state.[1] In Illinois, the legislators annually vote down a concealed carry program. The operating assumption and public belief here is that fewer handguns in public will necessarily be safer.[2] Both policies reflect the characteristics and the will of the population. This is a critical element of American representative democracy that illustrates the foundational principle that ultimate sovereignty lies with the citizenry.

A locally focused court system is also inherently more accountable than one in which federal criminal jurisdiction is too heavily weighted. An effective law, written by a state legislature to address targeted problems, and implemented by state and local law enforcement officials, may still be undermined by an ineffective prosecution. Though not chosen in the sexiest elections, a local district attorney exercises the discretion that often determines the sentences recommended to judges, and even whether a specific case is prosecuted. A misuse of such discretion will generally guarantee that a local district attorney is replaced at the next election. Greater accountability is also a byproduct of judges who are either elected or locally appointed, as opposed to being granted the lifetime tenure enjoyed by federal judges. A judge issues warrants, presides over trials, establishes admissibility of evidence, and ultimately determines sentences for those found guilty. While judicial elections may cause some inconsistencies and at times allow for political pandering, they also ensure that judges who pass judgments not in line with the spirit of the locally crafted laws do not remain on the bench for long.

Empowering local prosecutors and judges thus joins the legislative and enforcement mechanisms of federalism to foster a spirit of accountability that is most likely to keep a free citizenry safe from criminals. Such accountability allows a law to reflect local characteristics in all phases of development and implementation: from writing to enforcement through prosecution and sentencing. If it does not, the legislator that wrote it, the sheriff or police chief that enforced it, the district attorney who prosecuted its violation, and the judge that interpreted it can all be made to feel the sting of public outcry.

Lastly, state-centric, locally focused crime policy allows law enforcement to leverage relationships with area residents and capitalize on their familiarity with both the geography and the people. Most federal agents are headquartered in major cities and operate throughout large geographic areas. Compared with this, the beat-walking police officer is undoubtedly better situated to establish a rapport with both the people he is sworn to serve and those most likely to be associated with criminal activity. This rapport is invaluable and will increase the speed of collection and the reliability of information necessary for police to protect innocent citizens from those criminals who would do them harm, from mugger to murderer. In addition to the working relationships that the presence of local law enforcement fosters, familiarity with a community's nuances further aids in the speed of investigations and effectiveness of criminal deterrence efforts. An approach to crime policy that relies too heavily on federal agencies that are unfamiliar with the people or the territory for which they are responsible sacrifices the ability of local authorities to take advantage of their unique knowledge in order to provide the best possible protection of the rights of innocent residents.

The discussion thus far has centered on the notion that empowering state and local governments to execute police and crime policy is fundamentally in accordance with the Founders' vision of effective representative government. But we must not discount the federal government's legitimate role in protecting the nation as whole. As movement of people and items across state lines has become increasingly easy, various federal law enforcement agencies have begun to play a progressively larger role in combating crime that transcends state borders. In these instances, federal involvement is not only helpful but essential. Federal assistance may also be necessary in situations where state and local authorities simply do not have the resources necessary to deal with a particular problem. The existence of terrorist cells operating covertly within the US provides an example of such a challenge. Transnational terror groups are unlikely to restrict their dangerous activities to a single city, county, or state. Further, the spectacular attacks that a terrorist group seeks to achieve make the counterterrorism mission too broad, too expensive, and too manpower intensive for local authorities to accept in its entirety. As such, anti-terrorism efforts provide an excellent example of the type of law enforcement responsibility for which the federal government is best equipped.

But while exercising such responsibilities, the most appropriate role is for federal agencies to serve as facilitators, fostering cooperation and ensuring full use of the myriad capabilities of local and state agencies. The expansionist bureaucratic tendencies that too many federal agencies embody must be resisted. In exercising legitimate authority, no agency should be allowed to forcibly expand its jurisdiction. Acknowledging the supreme objective of guaranteeing the safety and security of innocent Americans leads to the recognition that law enforcement agencies at all levels of government must rely on each other, with each contributing its own strengths and leaning on the others to shore up its weaknesses.

Having established a constitutionally appropriate role in crime policy for the federal government, a brief discussion of inappropriate intrusions on the sphere of local law enforcement authority is warranted. Recent trends reveal a dangerous level of federalization of crime policy. These new developments are not only inconsistent with constitutional principles, but they also have very clear negative impacts on the effectiveness of crime fighting. To illustrate this, we can look at three recent actions of the federal government. First, federal sentencing guidelines have hamstrung US Attorneys and seriously hampered the overall goal of crime reduction. Secondly, federal anti-gang legislation has led to wasteful spending and jurisdictional confusion. Thirdly, federal carjacking statutes have blatantly overrun constitutional limits on federal power and usurped authority from the local law enforcement officials best suited to combat such crimes.

Federalization of crime policy necessarily reduces the caseload of local district attorneys and makes the various United States Attorneys' offices the primary prosecutorial authority in a wide array of cases. These attorneys are much more likely to be heavily influenced by federal sentencing guidelines created in Washington. These sentencing guidelines were originally styled as mandatory, until the Supreme Court wisely judged that they violate the Sixth Amendment. Nonetheless, they remain in place and must still be calculated when a sentence is determined.

While minimum sentences may seem good on the surface, such a policy severely weakens the discretionary authority needed to flexibly and effectively prosecute criminals. For instance, when a low level drug dealer is arrested by the local police, a district attorney must first decide whether or not to prosecute, and then must determine how to do so in order to achieve the greatest possible reduction of drug-related crime in the area. The prosecutor may offer a reduced sentence in exchange for the defendant's cooperation and testimony against his supplier. Removing a so called "dime-bagger" from the streets is a positive development, but taking down a major player in the local drug ring is much more beneficial. Such achievements are possible if the prosecutor has the flexibility to provide the defendant with incentives to testify against others. But when the prosecutor is hamstrung by regulations, he does not have the freedom to broker the deals that lead to the arrest of such "big fish."

It is much more likely that a local district attorney will have the flexibility necessary to achieve such success. The local prosecutor has greater awareness of regional criminal trends and is not beholden to the arbitrary decisions of Department of Justice bureaucrats. Because his actions are not as strongly dictated by federal sentencing guidelines, the district attorney is more likely than a federal prosecutor to degrade the local illicit drug market. Viewed in this light, federalization of crime policy becomes tantamount to attempting to kill a snake by wrestling with its tail, while empowering local prosecutors facilitates efforts to cut off its head, thereby removing the danger. The hierarchical structure of local gangs also makes local empowerment critical. A gang member who faces twenty years in prison but is offered a reduced sentence in return for testimony against his bosses is infinitely more valuable than one who spends two decades locked up, only to be replaced in the gang's organization. But in anti-gang efforts too, the federal government has impeded progress toward the overall objective of protecting innocent Americans from violent crime.

In 2005, the US House of Representatives approved a bill that, in addition to making sentencing guidelines mandatory, would have authorized vast sums of money to designate "high-intensity interstate gang activity areas" and allocated federal law enforcement resources to police these areas. Like minimum sentencing guidelines, this bill is superficially appealing.

However, the bill did not define what constitutes a "high-intensity interstate gang activity area." The ambiguous nature of the bill left the door wide open to further emasculation of local authorities, the negative impacts of which would have been felt throughout the country. The language of the proposed legislation would have taken away most of the limited discretion that even federal prosecutors have when trying a gang case. Furthermore, the proposed money for federal agencies to combat gangs would raise jurisdictional conflicts, inevitably reducing the ability of local law enforcement to eliminate the large number of gangs which operate locally.

Certainly, when gang activity crosses state lines, the federal government should play a central role. But its focus should be on the facilitation of local law enforcement's investigatory efforts and supporting prosecution by local attorneys. Finally, as was discussed earlier in this essay, ultimate success in combating crime depends largely on the relationships that the local police and detectives have within their communities. A strong trust between citizens and law enforcement is particularly essential in eliminating gang activity, which terrorizes and intimidates entire communities. Federal anti-gang legislation is fundamentally flawed, and the ongoing safety and security of all Americans requires that we ensure such proposals are not allowed to degrade the heroic efforts of our local police officers and prosecutors.

Finally, federal carjacking statutes represent another example of congressional good intentions gone wrong. Article 1, Section 8, Clause 3 of the Constitution authorizes the federal government to regulate interstate commerce. However, the language of the 1992 federal carjacking statute twists the clear language of this constitutional clause to wrest investigative and prosecutorial jurisdiction from local authorities with respect to a particular crime. The bill extends federal authority to any carjacking in which the "...motor vehicle has been transported, shipped, or received in interstate or foreign commerce."

But carjacking does not represent an overwhelming danger that requires federal government involvement and there is no reason to believe that state and local authorities are incapable of enforcing carjacking laws. Deliberately manipulating constitutional language to manufacture new federal authority is not only wrong, but it also adversely impacts the fundamental citizen protection capability of local and state law enforcement personnel.

A pragmatic approach to crime policy that allows states to request federal assistance is necessary. But allowing unwarranted federal infringement upon local jurisdiction is fundamentally opposed to the federalist principles upon which our nation was founded. Carjacking is indeed a serious offense, but the punishment demanded by the statutes leaves little room for prosecutorial discretion, and requires a subordination of local investigatory authority that undermines pre-existing rapport within local communities.

So how would an American society in which police and crime policy were guided by federalist principles look? Responsibility and authority of the states would be maximized and federal agencies would play a valuable but clearly defined role in facilitating and enhancing local law enforcement efforts. Criminal activity that transcends state borders or poses a national challenge would fall within federal jurisdiction. State legislatures would be free to determine the scope and focus of their own laws and those laws would be implemented according to their original intent. Constitutional protections would ensure that all laws respect the fundamental rights of individuals. State and local law enforcement officers and prosecutors would be empowered to fulfill their critical mandate of guaranteeing security for free citizens. Beat-walking police officers would build relationships within our communities, and district attorneys would be free to exercise human discretion to resolve human problems. Crime policy crafted at the lowest reasonable level would mirror the values and characteristics of each community. The unique advantages of local and state authorities would be leveraged in concert with supportive federal efforts, and the security of our rights as free Americans will serve as the supreme objective of the government's comprehensive police and crime policy.

Practically applied, federalist principles set the stage for dramatic successes in reducing crime in America. Operation Falcon II provides an excellent example of these principles in action. A joint operation between the US Marshals Service and state and local authorities, Operation Falcon II employed nationwide coordination and capitalized on the dedicated resources of the federal agency while simultaneously exploiting the relationships and community awareness of local authorities. The operation primarily targeted violent sex offenders and resulted in the arrest of more than 9,000 fugitives from justice.[3] This remarkable success was facilitated by the coordination efforts and assistance lent by the US Marshals, but was ultimately determined by the ability of local authorities to leverage local knowledge. Agencies at various levels of government possess strengths and weaknesses, and cooperation such as that embodied in Operation Falcon II provides the best means of jointly leveraging strengths while mitigating weaknesses.

In light of such an extraordinary law enforcement success, it would be a disservice to Americans' security not to apply similar federalist principles to the prosecution of those arrested. By allowing local prosecutors discretionary authority and ensuring federal support for the ambitious prosecution efforts required as a result of successful law enforcement operations, we can rest assured that the efforts of our courts system are aligned toward the supreme objective of securing the fundamental rights of all Americans. The complicated nature of making and enforcing laws does not negate the task's importance. Rather, complications are indicative of the importance of getting it right; often the most crucial problems a society faces are also the most challenging. But in order to succeed, two changes must take place. First, each member of our society must recognize the threat criminals pose not only to our nation as a whole, but to our own communities, our families, and ourselves. The scenario which began this essay paints this picture vividly. Secondly, it is imperative that government is guided by the principles laid out in our nation's earliest days. State and local officials must retain the authority to act in the best interest of the states, counties, and municipalities that they were selected to serve. The federal government must play its traditional role of assistance and coordination, bringing to bear the resources of the entire nation when necessary in the struggle against those who would do innocent people harm. Only then might the American people begin to enjoy the safety and security that free men and women deserve – the safety and security that makes the rights to life, liberty, and the pursuit of happiness truly unalienable.

Bryan Jiral is currently pursuing a JD at the Baylor School of Law where he is also President of the Law School's Federalist Society. After law school, Bryan intends to serve as a JAG officer in the Marine Corps or a prosecutor in a District Attorney's office. Bryan completed his undergraduate studies at Texas A&M University where he graduated in 2007 with a degree in agricultural leadership.

XIV. YES, UNLESS:
A Just Approach to Immigration
by John E. Katsos

Our constitution serves as a roadmap to the powers of government. Immigration is one area in which the Framers of our founding documents believed the federal government must have absolute control. They enshrined this belief into Article I, Section 8 of the US Constitution. Immigration is a natural responsibility of the federal government, as citizenship itself is inherently a national concept and a standardized immigration policy contributes to the security of our nation as a whole. Moreover, individual states do not have the resources to handle citizenship matters on their own. Our constitution represents the pinnacle of smart and correct governance: powers are enumerated and then they are separated, allocated to the various branches and levels of government. Our system provides enough flexibility for rapidly developing circumstances while giving deference to individual freedom when it does not infringe upon the greater good. This essay suggests a similar approach to structuring immigration policy: one of balancing and enumerating multiple layers of policy for the purpose of promoting the greater good and strengthening individual freedom.

The Immigration "Problem"

As with many aspects of daily life, travel has morphed dramatically since the founding of our country. Planes, trains, cars, and boats have all made travel faster and cheaper than even our parents could have ever imagined. Yet our immigration policies have not changed with the times. As a result, our immigration laws have been flouted repeatedly and openly, not just by illegal immigrants, but also by American citizens who employ them and pay for their illegal transport.

In the interest of full disclosure, I am decidedly pro-immigration. Thomas Jefferson was wrong when he said that the tree of liberty needs to be replenished by the blood of tyrants. Instead, in America, the tree has been sustained by the sweat of immigrants. These immigrants have come both voluntarily and involuntarily from places as far away as Africa, Asia, and Europe, and as near as a stone's throw across our own borders. The immigrant's story is one of triumph by the force of will. We are all familiar with the immigrant's story because it is our own. Each one of us holds pride in our ancestors' struggles. It is a common question in America: where are you from? Often, this question is not intended to ask where in the US you call home, but rather, from what part of the world our great country has inherited you and your family. At some point, someone not very different from ourselves and carrying the same blood, hopped out of a car, stepped off a boat, or exited a plane, with little but hopes and dreams to guide them.

Today, there are people like our ancestors doing exactly the same thing. They are probably doing it as you read this. The fundamental difference is that the majority of those coming to America today are doing so illegally.

The Department of Homeland Security (DHS) estimates illegal immigration in a series of yearly reports. These estimates started in 1980 and have continued annually, with the most recent data coming from January 2008. This most recent DHS estimate tells us that approximately 11.6 million people are currently in the US illegally. Of those, only 37% (4.3 million) have entered since 2000. 70% of the total illegal immigrant population is of "working age," between the ages of 25 and 55. More than 75% of the total illegal immigrant population journeyed here from North America, Central America, or the Caribbean.[1] Meanwhile, the US legally allows fewer than 2 million temporary workers under a variety of visa programs. The largest of these – the H1B visa program – is subject to a maximum cap. When we talk of illegal immigrants as criminals, their crime consists of coming to our country without one of these visas.

From these statistics we glean that 63% of our illegal immigrant population has resided in the US for almost a decade. This fact indicates two important considerations as we frame the immigration discussion. First, 63% of these immigrants have demonstrated a desire to stay in America for the long haul, despite their illegal status. Secondly, the rate of illegal immigration has actually increased during each of the last three decades. More immigrants are coming illegally each year, despite beefed-up border security and increased deportation proceedings.

Illegal immigrants represent about 3% of the current US population. For a group that gets so much attention, it is not a very large part of the whole. The status of illegal immigrants, however, remains a stain on our country's immigration laws and a burden on our society. If many of these same immigrants were in the US legally, they would pay taxes, report crime in their neighborhoods, participate in their communities, have strong incentives to adopt American culture and language, and enjoy the opportunity to advance their lots in life as legitimate members of American society. Some measure of illegal immigration will always be with us. These immigrants will continue to come and stay illegally no matter what changes are made in our laws because they are used by illicit enterprises that cannot survive without their presence. But by addressing the core deficiencies of our system that actually incentivize immigrating illegally; we can dramatically stem the tide.

No single solution will solve this problem, but a comprehensive plan that effectively enforces fair laws can do so. America needs a method of sorting the illegal immigrants who benefit our society from those who are a burden to us. America needs a means of encouraging those who wish to come for productive purposes to enter and stay legally. Finally, America needs a way to eliminate the enterprises which illicitly bring immigrants to the US and employ them – flouting the rule of law.

This summary implies something very simple about our existing immigration policies: the system is broken. We need a new way to think about immigration that provides both short and long-term solutions. The policies we embrace must be specific, flexible, and strike a balance between fairness and freedom. They must, in essence, be carved in the mold of our Constitution. This brings us back to the very purpose of this essay and, indeed, this entire book: conservative solutions to America's problems.

Our Conservatism's Approach

Society should engage in a balancing test when assessing future policy goals: on the one hand should be individual freedom and on the other should be the greater good. If the balance produces a close result, we should opt for the policy that enhances individual freedom. We define the "greater good" in terms of equality of opportunity, justice, and fairness. We recognize individual freedom as those collective items enumerated and referenced in our founding documents, namely: life, liberty and property. As Americans, all of these principles should be familiar. For conservatives, equality, justice and fairness are very important, but the balance tilts in favor of life, liberty, and property (and our rights to do with them as we see fit). Indeed, the former can only exist when the latter are protected.

We seek to maximize both the greater good and individual freedoms utilizing the rule of law as our mechanism. The rule of law simultaneously ensures that justice is done, while restraining our fellow citizens and our government from unnecessarily interfering with human creativity and ambition, the fruits of freedom. The rule of law alone can strike the delicate, but necessary, balance between individual liberty and the greater good that allows our country to remain both ordered and free – a shift in either direction is detrimental. When the rule of law does not reign supreme, the concept of individual freedom can be co-opted by those who apply it selectively, as happened when our country experienced the horrors of slavery and then of segregation. Without the rule of law, the concept of the greater good can be twisted to strip individuals of their most basic rights, as seen in our nation's troubling memories of forced migrations and mass internments. No political party was to blame for these tragedies – it was extremism, the lack of balance in policy decisions, which led to them. In framing our discussion of immigration, balance is the key.

At the heart of the illegal immigration challenge is the fact that our current system is not equipped to handle the demands for visas and citizenship of those wishing to enter and stay in America. Our population of 11.6 million illegal immigrants poses two dramatic policy questions for our generation: how do we stop people from continuing to come illegally; and what do we do with those who are already in America illegally? By seeking balance in immigration policy, we can identify the answers to these questions. Employing an understanding of these answers in a calculated and efficient manner reveals the series of policy suggestions presented in this essay.

How do we stop people from continuing to come into America illegally?

As noted before, conservatism dictates a balancing of outcomes between the greater good and individual freedom. When these two interests balance closely enough, we err on the side of the policy that offers the strongest protection for individuals' freedoms. In the context of immigration, it is in the national interest to allow immigrants to constantly refresh our society while also denying entrance to criminals, terrorists, and any others who would do our nation harm or burden our social system. In our embrace of individual freedom, we acknowledge that individuals should be able to move freely into and out of America for purposes of work, vacation, family visits, study, and other legitimate ventures. Our goal, then, should be to incorporate this freedom of movement to keep the tree of liberty constantly refreshed with a system that can effectively keep out those who might do damage to our society.

At this juncture it is important to clarify that immigrants generally are not and should not be viewed as "those who might do damage to our society." Neither are members of a particular race, religion, nationality or ethnicity particularly prone to damaging our nation, thereby warranting wholesale exclusion. Instead, we should require an objective reason particular to the individual seeking entrance that justifies his exclusion. Furthermore, the proposition that all illegal immigrants are only interested in illegal activity is baseless. A basic assumption of this proposition is that even if these people had a viable way to enter the US legally, they still would choose against it. The sad fact is that many people who immigrate illegally have no viable *legal* path to America, other than through temporary migrant programs subject to arbitrary numerical restrictions (such as the cap on H1B temporary working visas). If we reform this process in the mold of the "Yes, Unless" approach described below, many of those who might otherwise enter America illegally would instead choose to do so in accordance with our laws.

A major danger of illegal immigration is that even a well-intentioned immigrant who enters illegally can easily be sucked into a criminal world of gangs, government fraud, human trafficking, and the like. The purpose of the policies outlined in this section is to dissuade immigrants from ever coming into America *illegally* by offering them an alternative that is beneficial for both the immigrant and American society. This goal should form the basis of our entire approach to immigration reform: bringing well-intentioned immigrants out of the shadowy underworld created by our arbitrary immigration laws to benefit both the immigrant and America. Once this is accomplished, we can formulate an effective way to deal with those illegal immigrants already present in the United States and those who continue to come here in contravention of our new, fair laws.

"Yes, Unless"

Our current immigration policy allows an immigrant only to enter the US if they satisfy certain criteria. In essence, the process begins by denying admission, but then allows certain classes of people to enter. Thus, today's immigration procedures could be described as a "No, Except" policy. We say no to all, except for a lucky few, who often receive their select status arbitrarily. To preserve individual liberty while also ensuring a positive outcome for the rest of the population, the policy must change to one that begins by allowing entrance unless a clear reason exists to deny a person entry. This would send the message to potential immigrants that "Yes, you may enter our country unless there is a reason to exclude you" – a so-called "Yes, Unless" policy. This method will make our society more open for Americans and immigrants alike, while also allowing us to document those who might pose a danger to our nation.

The "Yes, Unless" policy requires a number of components. First, upon entry to the US, all immigrants will provide information concerning their anticipated place of stay, their anticipated duration of stay, and their anticipated employment. This expands slightly upon the information for which we currently ask. A potential immigrant will then have to present a form of government-issued identification from his home country, such as a passport. This identification will be "tagged," marking it in a way that indicates it was checked and approved by a Customs and Border Protection (CBP) agent before entry. Finally, the immigrant will be photographed and fingerprinted.

This process should sound familiar – it is borrowed from the current process for immigrants entering on I-94s, also known as temporary stay visas. At embassies around the world, consular officers perform local and

US background checks, fingerprinting, and photographing. The difference with our proposal is that, while an immigrant will have to state his purpose for visiting the US in much greater detail, he does not have to apply as a certain class of immigrant – all immigrants of this type would simply be treated as temporary residents. This system provides two main advantages over the current one. First, it significantly reduces the burden for the potential immigrant and dramatically increases the efficiency of the consular officer. This ease of entry will increase the likelihood that immigrants, especially skilled laborers and students, decide come to the US. In so doing, they will strengthen America's labor pool and make our universities even more competitive internationally. Secondly, by removing arbitrary numerical restrictions on the absolute number of immigrants we allow to enter, unskilled laborers who might otherwise take the risk of entering illegally will have a viable legal alternative.

As a part of the administration of this program, an immigrant's initial stay will be restricted to two years, with the opportunity to renew twice for a total of six years. Upon expiration of his temporary resident status, an immigrant will be required to leave for at least 180 days before being able to re-enter America. For example, an immigrant will not be allowed to stay in the US for six years, fly back to his home country for a week, and then return to the US. These time restrictions allow the flexibility to accommodate different types of temporary immigrants and provide incentives for those who plan on staying for the long-term to seek citizenship. An example might help illustrate this point.

James, a student from Australia, plans to attend college in the US. After being admitted to an American college, he goes to the US Embassy in Sydney to obtain a two-year temporary visa. Though he is pursuing a four-year degree, he must apply for renewal of his visa after the second year. James' eligibility for residency is reevaluated in light of his behavior since immigrating. For instance, if he has been arrested during the initial two-year period, he very well may be forced to go home. If he has respected our laws, however, his renewal application will be accepted. After four years of college, James decides that he would like to look for work in the US in his chosen field, organic chemistry. He applies to a doctorate program and is admitted. After his 6 productive years in the US, he is given the opportunity to obtain a green card as a worker in a specialized field. America benefits from his scientific work and he benefits by taking advantage of the opportunity for personal fulfillment that our country offers to all people and that has attracted immigrants for centuries.

Some may worry that too many immigrants may flood the country under this system. Currently, an immigrant attempting to enter the US must show means of support while here. This requirement is fair and logical for anyone wishing to stay in the US for an extended period of time. If an immigrant loses his level of support, a cap on the amount of time that he is allowed to be on social assistance will force him to either find other means of support or return to his home country. By way of example, Congress might determine that three months is a reasonable amount of time to provide a person to find other means of support if he has lost his employment. He may turn to other family members, get a new job, or enter into training for a better job. If he is unable to find new means of support, he will be asked to leave. If he does so, no prejudice will be exercised against him if he seeks to return in the future. Refusal to leave, however, will result in deportation and his being barred from reentry.

This changed approach to our immigration laws will encourage all well-intentioned immigrants to come to America legally. If the process is open and objectively fair, honest immigrants will strongly prefer the legal route to the illegal one. Many of those entering America illegally do so for reasons with which we can all sympathize: attempting to comply with our laws is not likely to produce results and is significantly more expensive than coming illegally. This new immigration process will also allow us to more easily identify, locate, and deport illegal immigrants who previously attempted to enter legally and were denied for cause. During the process, they will have been fingerprinted and will have had a photo taken for identification. It is important to realize, though, that this system will only be effective if it is coupled with the judicious use of enforcement mechanisms such as deportations and enhanced border security.

"More Entrances"

Our current immigration system also suffers from a striking lack of border security. In 2008, Congress passed laws requiring that fences, both real and electronic, be built along our northern and southern borders. These fences are not bad things in and of themselves. They are, however, of limited effectiveness without also establishing more points of legal entry. As the DHS statistics cited earlier indicate, more than two-thirds of illegal immigrants are from other North American countries, primarily Mexico, Honduras, and Guatemala. Many of these enter America through uninhabited regions of New Mexico and Arizona. Virtual and physical fences serve as a hindrance at best in the face of this traffic. Actual CBP officers are needed to capture and deport those attempting to enter illegally.

Establishing more points of entry along these uninhabited stretches of border will have three beneficial effects that are unattainable under the current system. First, CBP officers will be placed in the locations where illegal entries occur and they will operate with an infrastructure to facilitate the capture and deportation of those attempting to enter illegally. Secondly, in much the same way that visible city policing efforts effectively deter criminals within our country, simply placing officers in strategic locations will reduce the tide of illegal immigration by lowering an illegal entry's chances of success and preventing many would be lawbreakers from even trying. Finally, more points of entry will allow those transiting the border legally to do so more easily, thus facilitating the "Yes, Unless" policies outlined previously.

This "More Entrances" approach does not necessarily mean more guns and walls at the border, but it does mean more border guards manning more points of entry. Anyone who has driven by car to Mexico and tried to reenter can attest to the arduous process of returning to America, even for American citizens! A giant fence with cameras will not solve this problem. What will, and what will encourage more people to choose the legal route to our country, is an investment in technology that can quickly and easily process individuals and vehicles upon their entry into America. When coupled with efforts to recruit and train more enforcement personnel, this will bring our border into the twenty-first century. Adding new points of entry along the border, staffed by CBP officers with state of the art equipment to scan individuals as they enter and exit is a significantly more efficient and effective border security plan than simply placing a camera on a tall post or erecting barbed-wire fence.

Our current system in which the legal route to the United States is inaccessible prevents hard-working, law-abiding people from entering America. People with specialized training who are highly educated choose the legal path because the types of jobs they seek require it. Unfortunately, our immigration system makes it difficult for even these people to enter America. But these are exactly the type of people that our nation should be striving to attract! Academics, engineers, doctors, accountants, and others want to enter America in order to work and raise their families. Our "Yes, Unless" approach will allow significantly more of these people into the country, a major advantage as America continues to compete with countries such as China who impose severe restrictions on the entrance of professionals. In order to promote the adoption of more enlightened immigration policies toward our citizens abroad, one of the "unless" restrictions curtailing a potential immigrant's right to enter America will concern the policy of that person's home country regarding American nationals. If that policy is highly restrictive or implements an unreasonable quota on immigrants from the US, we will impose a quota in turn. Looking at the other side of the coin, because Americans can travel to many European countries for pleasure without visas, we should consider loosening restrictions on European nationals traveling to the US on vacation.

Another example here might be helpful. The vast majority of immigrants to the US currently hail from Latin America. Let us assume Manuel wants to come from Honduras with his wife, Maria, and their two children. He is an unskilled laborer but has some knowledge of farming and would succeed here by tending to an American farm. Maria is also unskilled but is prepared to work whatever job is required of her to support her family. Neither Manuel nor Maria has a criminal background in Honduras and both want to start a better life in the US. They believe that they can earn better pay in America and that their children will have opportunities unavailable to them in Honduras. America also benefits as employers gain diligent workers and a neighborhood gains a new family that will pay taxes and contribute to the community.

Under the current system, it would actually be more cost-effective for Manuel and Maria to cross the border illegally than for them to comply with our laws and enter legally. And that is only if they are lucky enough to get a visa. The risk inherent in crossing and the risk of deportation would be moderate, but even failure would leave Manuel and Maria no worse off than they were before.

Under the combined approach of "Yes, Unless" and "More Entrances," the cost of illegal transport would rise in the face of the added barriers to entering the country illegally. The cost of entering legally would diminish substantially as volume would allow the government to charge less for each application. Our new system would also make the risks and complexity of illegal entry prohibitive for many would-be illegal immigrants. Coupled with a commitment to domestic enforcement mechanisms making it riskier to live illegally in the US, the benefits of coming legally would far outweigh the risks of coming illegally. Manuel and Maria's calculus would be changed. Under the old system, a shot at illegal entry was their best option. Under the new system, it makes more sense for them to come to America legally. The paramount achievement of our new system is this fundamental reframing of the decision that thousands of would-be immigrants face daily: "Should I enter America legally or illegally?" By changing their answer to that question we address the immigration problem where it starts. This is the only way to effectively address the challenge of illegal immigration – by pulling it out at its roots.

These proposals are forward-looking in the sense that they address the problem of stemming the tide of future illegal immigration. They do nothing to deal with those who are already here illegally. The next section considers this question in depth. It may seem strange that an approach to a future problem would be presented before the solution to an existing problem. The reasons for this will soon become clear.

What do we do about those who are already in the US illegally?

The "Yes, Unless" and "More Entrances" proposals explained above must be espoused by our government in order to effectively deal with illegal immigrants who are already in America. The reason for this is simple. If we implement these policy changes first, illegal immigrants who are currently in this country will be more trusting of government action toward them in the future. Some may argue that if these changes are enacted before a crackdown on illegal immigration, the illegal immigrants will simply leave and return legally, without any punishment. This is a very persuasive argument and one that can be addressed by doing something that is fairly unprecedented – screening those who are leaving the country as well as those who enter.

"Illegal Entry, Legal Stay"

When these policy changes are announced, illegal immigrants currently in the US will not leave immediately. The reason is in the numbers: 63% of illegal immigrants have been here for more than a decade. These people have families, friends, jobs, and property here. In short, they stand to lose a lot with a hasty exit. Our current system exhibits a laissez-faire attitude toward departing illegal immigrants. We allow them to leave unchecked because we assume it will be harder for them to return than it was for them to enter. This is naive and it wastes a valuable opportunity.

We should be screening those who entered illegally to determine how they entered, for whom they worked, where they lived, and which of their family members remain in the US illegally. This will allow us to make progress in dismantling the system of illegal transport, illicit employment, and safe haven locations that promotes illegal entry into our country. If they entered illegally, they will be photographed, fingerprinted, and questioned regarding these matters. If, during their time in the US, they kept out of trouble and worked an honest job, they will not be asked to leave. This seems anathema to many conservatives who value the rule of law. They illegally entered the country and did not pay taxes during their stay in the US, and now they will get off without consequence? Not quite.

Many immigrants entered illegally because the system was broken; our analysis up to this point has demonstrated that fact. If they committed crimes while they were here, they were punished, with one exception: tax evasion. If illegal immigrants choose to identify themselves to the authorities within a year of this program's announcement, they will be on the hook to the IRS for their back taxes, but will not be held accountable for their illegal entry. This system will essentially be a temporary "illegal entry, legal stay" system and it will provide a balance. These individuals will not be punished for illegally entering the country, but they will be punished for violating our laws once they were here. After this year-long period, all offers of amnesty will be off the table permanently.

The punishment for tax evasion will be placed on the immigrant's criminal record, but no jail time or parole will be served. Instead, a percentage of his pay will be garnished for the remainder of his working life, allowing the formerly illegal immigrant to pay off his debt to the government over time. Of course, the worker will also have the option of paying his debt in a single lump sum. Each monthly payment will amount to very little for the individual, but multiplied over decades of working and by the millions of formerly illegal immigrants, we will recoup billions of dollars over the next few decades. This will help America pay for the new security measures and system overhaul that will characterize our twenty-first century immigration policy.

Why, though, would an immigrant who came illegally and has been living illegally for years turn himself in? He would do it for better pay, better rights, and to claim protection under the law. Most illegal immigrants are currently paid significantly less than the minimum wage and work in conditions that fall far short of American standards for legitimate businesses. In the new system, these workers will be able to lobby their employers for higher wages and better working conditions in a system that recognizes their right to do so. Additionally, economic forces will put pressure on Congress to reconsider increases to the minimum wage that can be potentially crippling to American business, as we will no longer allow the convenience of an artificially high minimum wage to be purchased by the sweat of illegal immigrants toiling outside the system.

How would the government prevent an illegal immigrant from exiting the country outside of the established framework and returning legally without anyone knowing? The incentive for an illegal immigrant to turn himself in would be personal convenience – he would never have to leave the country. Those who are in the country illegally will take advantage of the aforementioned one-year period to turn themselves in, immune from prosecution. During this period, CBP, Immigration and Customs Enforcement (ICE), and DHS will be implementing their technology improvements and increasing their staffs to catch and deport illegal immigrants who do not take the government up on its offer. They will also begin individual deportation processes during the one-year period, offering those caught the option of leaving legally and returning legally. This carrot and stick approach will encourage illegal immigrants to turn themselves in and come out of the shadows.

Any illegal immigrants who do not turn themselves in during the period of amnesty will not just be deported, but will also have any American property they possess confiscated by the government. Additionally, they will be barred from ever returning to America. These extreme measures will be effective in dealing with illegal immigrants after the amnesty period. However, enforcing harsh measures before any period of amnesty would not just be cruel, it would be anathema to the protection of individual freedom. Such draconian measures without offering those affected a period of adjustment to the new immigration policy would drive illegal immigrants deeper underground and would be antithetical to our purpose of creating laws which balance individual freedom and the greater good.

Federalism in Action

A final major failing of our current immigration policy is that the federal government does not have a good relationship with many local law enforcement jurisdictions. From a conservative perspective, heavy reliance on just the federal government is usually not a good thing. In many situations, policies are simply better conceived, implemented, and their effectiveness evaluated at the state or local level. In the immigration context, however, our Founders gave the federal government responsibilities over naturalization and immigration because they realized the tremendous havoc that could be wrought if each locality controlled who could and could not enter into and stay within their jurisdictional boundaries. So, the final piece to solving the policy puzzle is to require local law enforcement to report the names and addresses of illegal immigrants who come through their offices.

Many cities currently have "asylum" laws that do not allow law enforcement to ask anyone about their immigration status. The motivation behind these statutes is well-reasoned despite their flaws in principle. These laws assume that for the maintenance of order, it is important for all citizens to feel safe reporting crime in their neighborhoods. If illegal immigrants fear that they will be arrested when they report a crime or when they come forward after witnessing wrongdoing, the safety of their entire community suffers. For the "illegal entry, legal stay" system to work, however, local law enforcement will have to identify and report, though not actively deport or arrest, illegal immigrants. This will require significant liaison between federal and state authorities, which will be facilitated by the federal government's show of good faith through implementation of the "Yes, Unless" and "Illegal Entry, Legal Stay" systems.

The federal government has employed effective methods to achieve local cooperation in the past. Federal funding will be tied to compliance in order to ensure that local law enforcement officials report the names and addresses of illegal immigrants. This will also benefit the implementation of the "Illegal Entry, Legal Stay" policy by identifying households where amnesty could be actively offered while enabling the eventual deportation of those who refused to comply with the new laws.

Conclusion

These four policies, implemented in concert, achieve the balance that we have sought for many years. Individual freedoms will be promoted by recognizing the dignity and rights of both illegal immigrants currently in America and those abroad who wish to enter America legally to start a better life. Simultaneously, the rule of law will be strengthened by ensuring that in the future we actually enforce the laws we maintain on our books. These policies promote the greater good by allowing for order and stability within society through consistent application of our laws, while also dealing fairly with the immigrant population.

To end, I will share a personal story. My family is from Greece. My father and his siblings were brought to America by their parents in 1955. Within a generation, we had lawyers, doctors, accountants, and, of course, restaurant owners, in our family tree. My family's story is marked by varying levels of economic success, resulting in poor, middle class, and wealthy members of the Katsos family. But most importantly, we all were able to choose our own destinies thanks to the opportunities America offers. And all of this was possible for my immigrant grandparents – neither of whom ever completed the fifth grade.

If my family's story were unique, I would have little reason to share it. However, my story is not unique. It is fundamentally American. The common fabric of America is woven from the many stories of leaving one's home to create a new and better life in this country. Moreover, we provide a beacon and refuge for the many people who truly need to leave their birth countries because of the tragic realities of famine, war, and repression. This is not to say that we should simply allow everyone into America. Such a suggestion is foolish. But immigrants who are willing to make the commitment to becoming a part of the American dream should have the opportunity to do so. We all have an immigrant story in our past, regardless of the language in which it is told and however distant in the past it may be. Within each of us is the identity of an immigrant. It is time we remind ourselves of who we are, and from where we come.

John Katsos is currently pursuing his JD and MBA degrees at the George Washington University in Washington, DC, where he will be awarded both in 2011. He has previously worked for the US State Department, a multinational oil and gas company, and a white collar frauds prosecution unit. Originally from Brooklyn, NY, John completed his undergraduate studies at Haverford College in Haverford, PA, where he earned a Bachelor's degree in Religion.

XV. NAVIGATING THE SHOALS:
Building a Conservative Foreign Policy Worldview
by Austin J. Knuppe

Reflection on the state of contemporary conservatism often elicits images of the Titanic. It's not hard to picture conservatives scurrying around the decks of a gigantic steamship after a collision with an iceberg causes it to tilt ominously toward the depths. The elections in 2006 and 2008 served as two such icebergs for conservatives. In the ensuing panic, many conservative leaders have done everything they can to establish their credentials with the base; some have gone so far as to discredit fellow conservatives who they believe are not being "true to the cause." Eyeing the pandemonium from afar, liberal commentators such as the New York Times' Sam Tanenhaus have been eager to conduct an autopsy of the conservative movement. Tanenhaus was brazen enough to pen an article in the New Republic heralding, "Conservatism is Dead."[1]

Is Tanenhaus right? Is conservatism dead? Should conservatives retreat to their think tanks, talk radio, and blogs, or is this crisis a chance to rearm, reorganize, and energetically prepare to take on the perceived liberal majority? The answer must be the latter, for we conservatives have trod this territory before. As early as 1954, William F. Buckley was aware of "enormous fissure[s]" in the broad conservative movement that he sought to build. He knew that his grand coalition of religious traditionalists, libertarians, and neoconservatives would have to face trial by fire before its political coming of age.[2] But contrary to what Tanenhaus argues, and what many conservatives fear, now is not the time to retreat. Rather, it is time for thoughtful conservatives of all persuasions to rearticulate our vision for a new generation of voters. With the Cold War twenty years behind us and almost a decade removed from 9/11, nowhere is this new vision more overdue than in the realm of foreign affairs. It is time to present a cogent worldview for considering problems and developing solutions to issues transpiring overseas.

This essay offers such a worldview. It is undergirded by a fundamental belief that the ideas and institutions at the core of our nation's founding provide a sure path for future generations to navigate the shoals of international relations. To accomplish this, we must address three fundamental questions. First, what is conservatism's relevance to contemporary foreign affairs? Secondly, what should be the key objectives of American foreign policy? And finally, how should America bring her power to bear to carry out her foreign policy agenda?

To answer the first question in short, conservatism is relevant because it seeks to preserve the values and institutions that have allowed Western civilization to flourish. Since our nation's founding, the American people have been the engine of creativity, prosperity, and progress in our nation, and indeed throughout the world. Our values – free markets, individual liberty, and equality before the law – provide a framework that allows individuals and associations to flourish. Our institutions – both in the government and private sector – ensure that citizens are able to present and exercise their values in the public square. These are just some of the values and institutions that have allowed the United States to prosper for over 200 years. Even Tanenhaus (conservatism's self-appointed eulogist) recognizes that, "at its best, conservatism has served the vital function of clarifying our shared connection to the past and of giving articulate voice to the normative beliefs Americans have striven to maintain even in the worst of times."[3]

This preservation of the past is in constant tension with the inclination toward change. Buckley famously argued that the conservative "stands athwart history, yelling Stop, at a time when no one is inclined to do so, or to have much patience with those who so urge it." Indeed, experience reveals that not all change is constructive to society. Russell Kirk, a prominent conservative thinker, puts it this way: "The conservative declares that he acts only after sufficient reflection, having weighed the consequences. Sudden and slashing reforms are as perilous as sudden and slashing surgery."[4] Conservatives are much more than anti-progressive luddites. Rather, we recognize that a certain set of values and institutions have allowed our civilization to thrive. Moreover, we understand that these values and institutions were developed based on a particular conception of human nature and a profound respect for the lessons of history. It is to the analysis of these two forces that we now turn.

Diverse as the world's population may be, there exist specific modes of thinking, acting, and feeling that are universal. The Enlightenment-age philosopher Thomas Hobbes noted that prior to the creation of societies, humans existed in a state of nature where life was "solitary, nasty, brutish, and short." In the political arena, this mode of behavior leads to anarchy, where individuals seek to compete and survive, unrestrained by laws and social mores. The British conservative, Edmund Burke, agreed with Hobbes' shadowy assessment. Hobbes' framework gave Burke the necessary tools to dissect the French Revolution, leaving Burke with distaste for radical change and revolution. Burke concluded that the French revolutionaries' actions would not restore liberty, but that the Americans' revolution was the proper model of societal reorganization because of its newly formed government's distrust of even its own power.

Many of the Founding Fathers subscribed to a Hobbesian view of human nature and felt strongly that such a belief should provide the foundation for constructing a new form of government. In Federalist 51, James Madison made this clear as he reflected, "If men were angels, no government would be necessary...In framing a government which is to be administered by men over men, the great difficulty lies in this: you must first enable the government to control the governed; and in the next place oblige it to control itself." While Madison believed that civic virtue could evolve out of good governance, he was always skeptical of political power without firm tethers to restrain it.

History has repeatedly borne out Hobbes' assessment of human nature, namely that people have a propensity toward evil when a legal, moral, or societal framework does not properly restrain their passions. Among the most powerful, and certainly the most dangerous, of universal human conditions is an overwhelming desire to obtain and maintain power. A cursory glance at the Cold War establishes this point. Communists – from the Soviet tyrant Joseph Stalin to the Chinese dictator Mao Zedong – claimed over 100 million victims in the twentieth century.[5] These individuals destroyed the legal tethers that restricted their power and recreated a state of nature by instilling despotism and fear. Visiting the concentration camps of Europe, the gulags of the Soviet Union, or the killing fields of Cambodia reveals that Hobbes' state of nature is no piece of fiction.

Other times, people become so accustomed to the wealth and prosperity provided by their government that they abrogate their responsibility for civic virtue – the attitudes and habits of an individual that are conducive to social harmony. In these situations, the citizenry's lackadaisical attitude towards individual liberty removes the most crucial obstruction to lustful pursuit of power on the part of the government. The citizens of Rome were so thoroughly satisfied with the government's provision of entertainment and religious holidays – referred to by historians as "bread and circus" – that they allowed the slow erosion of their individual liberty. Cicero, Rome's greatest orator, tells us that this erosion not only led to the rise and abrupt assassination of Julius Caesar, but also the transition from a republican to a totalitarian form of government. The historian Edward Gibbons has written that Rome finally fell under the weight of its own imperial ambition because of a series of foreign policy blunders in the Middle East. Sound familiar?

American foreign policy will likewise run aground if her citizens do not zealously guard their individual liberty from their government. Two centuries ago, Alexis de Tocqueville observed that fostering liberty – or what he called "the habits of the heart" – is the only way to cultivate civic virtue. Conservatives are keenly aware that these habits must be taught and protected, because they run contrary to human nature.

In addition to reflecting on human nature, we must also cull the annals of history to develop our foreign policy worldview. Studying the lessons learned by previous generations allows the past to inform our decisions in the present and direct our path in the future. Here again, Edmond Burke proves to be a faithful guide. In his *Reflections on the Revolution in France*, Burke "argued that each individual's private stock of reason is small and that political decisions should be guided by the accumulated wisdom of the ages."[6] An application of the wisdom of the ages must be at the core of a conservative worldview.

Students of history realize that the past plays the role of soothsayer. Conservatives must listen to this sage's advice: building an empire abroad often leads to civil decay at home. The colonial British provide the most demonstrative example of this lesson in recent memory. At one time, it was said that the sun never set over the lands of the British Empire. After World War II, however, the Brits went bankrupt and were forced to surrender much of their colonial territory. Here in the United States, conservatives must reckon with the fact that many of our heroes, including Ronald Reagan, drove up the national debt through deficit-financed defense spending. Sadly, a limited and targeted use of deficit spending against America's enemies has ballooned into full-fledged fiscal irresponsibility on both sides of the aisle. With the current condition of our economy, the chicken is coming home to roost. Considering America's financial condition and her exploits in the Middle East, she would be wise to reflect on the experience of other world powers that landed in the dustbin of history. Do we really think that we can somehow pursue similar nation-building policies while avoiding the same forces that brought earlier empires to their knees?

History also reveals that the American experiment is utterly unique in the scope of the human experience. It is the exception in world history, not the rule. The past also shows us that our experiment with American republicanism is not easily exportable. It did not work when President Johnson tried to bomb the Vietnamese into being good democrats and odds are that creating constitutional republics of the American brand in the Middle East will ultimately fail as well. American democracy has been uniquely successful because it has as its bedrock the rule of law. The interplay between the Constitution, our court system, and our law enforcement and military provide a stable framework that eliminates anarchy while protecting individual liberties. This interplay is unique in our world's history, where sectarian violence, religious wars, and corruption have been the norm. In fact, it has been over two hundred years and our Republic is still a work in progress.

To review, conservatives understand that humans act in their own self-interest and will do so to the neglect of their neighbors if a legal, social, or moral framework does not restrain their passions. History demonstrates that governments act in a similar fashion toward individuals. They are prone to overstretch and seek empire if their citizens do not guard their individual liberty. America as a country has prospered because of the delicate balance between individual liberty and the power of government. History also warns us that trying to export our political experiment to other nations is a fool's errand. The discussion thus far has given us the tools to approach a complex situation, analyze actors' motives, and predict their actions based on a comprehensive understanding of human nature and the fundamental lessons of history. It is now time to turn these insights toward the analysis of foreign affairs.

Foreign policy consists of the goals a nation's government seeks to attain abroad, the values that give rise to those goals, and the means used to pursue them. History has seen these goals take the shape of territorial expansion, financial gain, or political strength. Values can range from ab stract aspirations like democratization, to more concrete objectives, such as combating human trafficking. The means used to pursue a nation's goals are diverse as well, comprised of military strength, political pressure, and economic coercion. Often multiple goals, values, and instruments are used simultaneously, making the study of international affairs complex and inter-disciplinary. With such a dizzying array of considerations, what principles define a genuinely conservative approach to foreign policy?

First, we must acknowledge that since the conception of the modern conservative movement, there has been a cadre of intellectuals, policymakers, and politicians who have all accepted the conservative label. The truth is that conservatives espouse a plurality of ideas regarding the most effective way to conduct diplomacy. Candidates in the 2008 presidential campaign reflect this diversity. From former Governor Mike Huckabee to Congressman Ron Paul, conservative policymakers have embraced dramatically different approaches to foreign affairs. Our goal is to reconcile this observation with our pursuit of an inclusive foreign policy worldview. The good news is that this diversity of opinion is an asset as we interact with other nations because it ensures that a single approach or paradigm does not gain a monopoly in policy making. It has been said, "Where all think alike, no one thinks very much." In big bureaucracies like the US State Department, groupthink can cripple our efforts at conducting successful diplomacy.

By grouping together conservative diplomats of different persuasions, America can form a foreign policy that is nuanced, addressing different issues with different tools. The process of considering these differing opinions and approaches is an exercise in discernment. Russell Kirk describes this process under the auspices of prudence – the virtue of being able to judge between actions to choose the appropriate ones at a given time. Kirk would certainly consider our pursuit of a conservative worldview as a worthwhile enterprise.

While conservatives differ in the mechanics of how foreign policy should be conducted, we generally agree on the fundamental purpose of American foreign policy. This recognition forms the basis of our shared conservative worldview. For conservatives, the purpose of American foreign policy is to preserve and advance America's national interest, generally defined as securing for all Americans the three unalienable rights listed in the Declaration of Independence: life, liberty, and the pursuit of happiness. Take a minute to reflect on these three rights before dismissing them as quaint or arcane: life – one's ability to live securely and to make a living; liberty – one's ability to associate, worship, and speak as one pleases without threat or coercion from the government; the pursuit of happiness – the ability to seek out personal and professional fulfillment in life. The Declaration is a good starting point for defining the national interest because it was crafted by those who acknowledged the faults of human nature and had a profound respect for the lessons of history. This vision is innately conservative because it seeks to preserve the values and institutions that have allowed American society to prosper.

Thus, what makes our foreign policy truly conservative is not the means used to execute it but rather the ends sought. The rest of this essay deals with the approach that we should take to effectively achieve the goals of a conservative foreign policy. The approach should be qualified as "political realism" and I recognize that other conservatives may disagree with these methods. We should remain confident that a vigorous debate over the conduct of diplomacy will only strengthen our approach and enhance our ability to attain our goals in foreign affairs. Realism is only one of many paradigms, but an understanding of the complexity of the international system makes clear that it offers the best worldview for foreign policy decision-making in the twenty-first century.

We now consider our second fundamental question: "What is the purpose of American foreign policy?" In order to put our worldview in the proper perspective, we first must examine what the left indentifies as the main purpose of American foreign policy. After this discussion, we will delve a bit deeper into how conservatives propose that America approaches diplomacy in order to achieve her foreign policy objectives.

Many progressive liberals contend that the purpose of US foreign policy is to promote social justice through the mechanism of international organizations like the United Nations. One blogger for the Huffington Post, the flagship blog of the Left, explained the overall purpose of a liberal foreign policy as follows: "It declares that the United States will abandon its self-centered conduct in the world community and embrace cooperation. It argues there must be major changes in the way internal US politics are conducted: the military will no longer be treated as sacrosanct; efforts will be redoubled to diminish America's role as a weapons manufacturer; the political power of corporations will be reduced; and environmental and worker-protection laws will be strengthened."[7]

In international relations, political scientists qualify this worldview as liberal internationalism, or more simply, idealism. Idealists hold that states operate not only on their capacity to promote power, but also to promote philosophical norms. Idealists also view a state's actions in terms of progress, believing that the system of international relations can be fundamentally transformed as the states that comprise this system embrace certain "transformational values." In the recent past, neoconservatives embraced idealism as they attempted to achieve this transformation through the exportation of freedom and democracy to the Middle East. A liberal application of idealism is poignantly illustrated in the next paragraph. Regardless of where he falls on the political spectrum, the idealist's desired endgame is a peaceful and just world order through a transformation of the nations that comprise it.

Sandy Berger, former National Security Advisor to President Bill Clinton, wrote in Foreign Affairs: "[T]he United States should be seen as a peacemaker again, actively engaged in the resolution of conflicts from the

Middle East to Southeast Asia to Central and West Africa, helping to build the peacekeeping capabilities of other nations, and willing to contribute money and troops, alongside our allies, when our interests and values are at stake. Even when the chances of success are small, such efforts help reveal that American power can serve the common good."[8] Goals such as universal peace, values such as equality, and means such as multilateral cooperation reign supreme for those on the Left.

Our conservative vision of American foreign policy stands in stark contrast. The reality is that diplomacy operates under power politics, known as machtpolitik. Competition and insecurity are inevitable in the international system. Thus, every country seeks to protect its own interests over the interests of others. Think of a political version of Darwinism – only the fittest nations can compete and survive. Political scientists use this competition as a base assumption in their work, arguing that the natural state of relations between countries in the international system is anarchy. Sounds a bit like Thomas Hobbes, doesn't it?

In the Hobbesian arena of international relations, countries set their foreign policies based solely on their national interests, or the goals of a state that ensure its security and survival. These goals can be territorial, economic, or military and are often practical, rather than strictly ideological. Despite the panoply of opinions in the movement, conservatives of all stripes generally agree that protecting and promoting the national interest is the central purpose of American foreign policy.[9] As a further qualifier, we embrace a very limited definition of America's national interest: the securing and protecting of American life, liberty, and property. This definition clarifies our goals, ensuring that policymaking is modest and incremental.

The national interest is often contrasted to the common interest, or a set of goals that many nations or organizations share. Combating global climate change, for instance, is considered part of the common interest because carbon emissions cannot be contained within one country's borders. Staunch realists are leery of identifying or even defining the common interest, believing that just because nations face a common problem does not mean that they will seek a common solution. Other conservatives adopt this lingo of the "common interest," suggesting ways that the private sector can address negative externalities better than the government could.

Sandy Berger's sentiment expressed above reflects a worldview that values the common interest above the national interest. By elevating the common interest, many liberals hold that conflict and competition between nations will cease. In light of our discussion earlier about human nature and the lessons of history, this belief is as naïve as it is dangerous.

Conservatives believe that our elected leaders must promote the national interest before the common interest not because they are selfish or short-sighted, but because the presidential and congressional oaths of office – developed based on our knowledge of human nature and history's lessons – mandates this hierarchy. When an elected official takes office, he pledges to protect and defend the interests of the American people first. This simple reality reflects a proper understanding of the role of democratic government: those elected to higher office have the authority and responsibility to represent the interests of the people who put them there. To abrogate this role represents a statesmanship that is not merely incompetent, but also immoral.

Some conservatives are tempted to adopt an idealist worldview because of its concern for norms and values. In the debate between realism and idealism, many cringe at realism for its alleged crude pragmatism and power politics approach. Many believe that because certain values and institutions thrive here at home, that our government can export American freedom and democracy to better other nations. Some even view such use of America's international power as a moral imperative. Is our realist orientation, as many would say, simply political window dressing for abdicating our responsibilities to the world's less fortunate?

To respond, realists do not take issue with the goals of an idealist foreign policy. Democracy, freedom, and capitalism – these are the real world manifestations of the values espoused by many conservative idealists. As our nation's Founders anticipated, America is a unique political experiment in which our unprecedented vibrancy and prosperity as a society are rooted in our continued respect for these values. But our government's primary role is the protection of our national interest. Even if it were proper for our government to craft a foreign policy based on the worldwide expansion of these values, history has taught us that governments are simply not equipped to succeed in such an endeavor: remember the lessons learned by the British and Romans. But the vast community of private, charitable institutions is capable of spreading these values, often directing immense resources, for instance, to addressing humanitarian concerns. Time and time again, the private sector has been the powerhouse for providing international aid. Doctors Without Borders, Catholic Charities, and the International Red Cross have done more to transform world politics than USAID or the UN's World Food Program. At the end of the day, the private sector (primarily comprised of non-profits) has stronger incentives, better means, and a better track record than national governments in promoting social justice.

Finally, it should be noted that just because someone labels him or herself a realist does not mean he or she is necessarily conservative. Consider the late Harvard political scientist Samuel P. Huntington. Huntington was a staunch realist, but also a lifelong Democrat. He was a speechwriter for two-time Democratic presidential nominee Adlai Stevenson in the 1950s, a foreign policy adviser to Hubert Humphrey in the 1960s, and a humanitarian advisor to President Jimmy Carter in the 1970s. However, Huntington was also the author of the now infamous book, *The Clash of Civilizations*, in which he argued that certain cultures will suffer perennial conflict due to their demographics, politics, and geography. This book was derided by a prominent liberal academic as a "fictional gimmick," something worse than the "War of the Worlds."[10] Huntington's life demonstrates that the realist paradigm is nuanced and should be studied in so far as it helps us lay the groundwork for achieving our conservative foreign policy goals.

Now that we understand the purpose of a conservative foreign policy, let's spend some time analyzing how realists conduct diplomacy. Realists approach international affairs pragmatically. "Conservatism recognizes the primacy of power in international affairs; it accepts existing institutions; and its goals are limited. It eschews grand designs, because it has no universal value system that it seeks to impose on others," argues Robert Kaplan.[11]

The administration of Richard Nixon is an example of pragmatism in action. The capstone to the president's foreign policy agenda was the "Nixon Doctrine." The Nixon Doctrine emphasized that the United States would keep its international treaty obligations, with the expectation that a nation that was directly threatened would assume primary responsibility for providing the manpower necessary for its defense. In cases of emergency, the United States would offer military aid and protection under a nuclear umbrella. This provided diplomatic reassurance for our allies in the Pacific who worried about the American withdrawal from Vietnam. Nixon's now famous "trip to China" and renewed diplomatic efforts with the Soviets stand as two additional examples of his pragmatism. Despite the ethical misgivings the president had about both regimes, he pursued diplomacy because it served American interests better than the possibility of nuclear apocalypse. Based on the recognition that American power was immense, but also finite, Nixon realized the vital importance of diplomacy. Balance-of-power politics and regional stability were key pillars of the Nixon Doctrine, making his foreign policy quintessentially realist. Preservation of American life and resources were his primary goals, making his foreign policy distinctly conservative.

Ronald Reagan, typically known for his moralism, also had a pragmatic streak. The president's rollback of communism in the third world provides a great example of realpolitik. Reagan enjoyed his greatest success in Afghanistan, where covert support in arms and funds for the mujahideen resulted in the Soviets' evacuation of the region. At the height of support, the US was funneling $650 million annually to the insurgents through agents in Pakistan – a steep price tag indeed, but vastly cheaper in both blood and treasure than a direct conflict with the Soviet Union.[12] Support for Chilean dictator Augusto Pinochet and the Apartheid regime in South Africa provide further evidence of the pragmatism of Reagan's anti-communist strategy. Indeed, several of America's closest allies against the Soviets were ABC democrats (anybody-but-communists). This history may be unsavory for some, but these alliances played a major role in the full-scale collapse of the Soviet Union in 1989. Realism does not always dictate that America should form alliances with dictators and rebels, but it does prioritize problems based on who or what poses the greatest threat to our national security. Reagan correctly diagnosed that the Soviets were the greatest enemy to American freedom, and the president took the proper steps to eradicate the threat.

When military operations did go south, Reagan had the foresight to withdraw troops before the situation got out of hand. After a terrorist attack on a Marine barracks in Lebanon killed 241 soldiers in October 1983, Reagan followed the advice of his Secretary of Defense, Caspar Weinberger, and withdrew American forces from the Levant. The president would later recall, "Bloody Sunday" was "the saddest day of my presidency, perhaps the saddest day of my life."[13] Reagan's prudent actions and modest goals prevented further losses of American lives and resources, and sought to avoid entangling our nation in a protracted conflict in the Middle East.

If the realists' approach is pragmatism, their most likely pitfall is the cardinal sin of hubris – the overbearing pride to think that one can act without discrimination and avoid the consequences. Hubris is an ancient concept harkening back to the days of the Old Testament and to Greek and Roman antiquity. Herodotus' account of King Croesus is a perfect example. Croesus, king of Lydia (an ancient city in Asia Minor) was trying to decide if he should seek an alliance with the Greek city-states or go to war alone against Cyrus the Great of Persia. Seeking wisdom, the king went to the Oracle at Delphi, who told Croesus that "if he campaigned against the Persians he would destroy a great empire." Croesus took this as a blessing and went to war with the Persians without allies. He did destroy a great empire – his own.

How can conservative policymakers avoid hubris if their diplomatic strategy is based on realpolitik? Most importantly, realists can heed the lessons of history by limiting their definition of the national interest. By limiting America's commitments abroad, she can retain a modest foreign policy agenda that is based on prudence, not ideology. Critics bemoan this attitude as isolationist when, in fact, it leads to international engagement that is based on sound and clearly defined principles. Prudent foreign policy is a safer alternative for the United States because it eliminates confusion in our intentions as well as overextension of our resources.

As we have seen, the realists' approach is pragmatism, and their most likely cardinal sin is hubris, but what's their endgame? Our endgame is to create a world where concerns over insecurity are mitigated. Conservative realists favor stability and predictability of the international order because it is generally a more peaceful alternative to rapid or frequent transformation, whether such transformation takes the form of internally-driven totalitarianism (in the case of a Stalin, Hitler, or Mao) or externally-pressured democracy (in the case of Afghanistan and Iraq). At the end of the day, realists and idealists alike want the fruits of their labor in foreign affairs to result in peace. Conservative realists have the upper hand in this debate because we understand the ugly side of human nature and the lessons of history that allow us to better predict how states will interact on the world's stage.

Peace is best achieved through a balance-of-power paradigm, where nations ally to form a parity of power against a stronger country. In the interest of maintaining a balance of power, nations can either bandwagon with a strong country (think of Southeast Asia's relationship with China) or increase their own power to balance that of their adversary (think of Russia's adversarial relationship with the EU). Arch-realist Henry Kissinger argues that only after two world wars broke down the balance of power in Europe was the United States truly forced to play nation-builder in order to restore order in Europe and Asia.[14] Having two friendly neighbors to the north and south, and two oceans to the east and west, the US was not experienced in power brokering in such intimate circumstances. Instead of restoring the balance of power, America accepted unilateralism and chose to become the world's policeman. While this strategy worked for upwards of fifty years, 9/11 and the Global War on Terror demonstrate the limits of such a policy. Americans today would be wise to understand that trying to build an empire without end is better left to Greek and Roman mythology than contemporary global politics.

Kissinger concludes his definitive foreign policy tome, *Diplomacy*, by stating, "To be true to itself, America must try to forge the widest possible moral consensus around a global commitment to democracy. But it dare not neglect the analysis of the balance of power. For the quest for moral consensus becomes self-defeating when it destroys the equilibrium."[15] As history has demonstrated, balance-of-power politics is not perfect, nor does it claim to be. Instead of preventing or eliminating conflict, it is designed to limit its impact. But, when combined with a shared set of values, like in nineteenth century Europe, balance of power can lead to stability and order.

The discussion thus far has revolved around establishing the purpose and process of American diplomacy. In so doing, we have set the groundwork to discuss the third of our three fundamental questions: how should America bring her power to bear to achieve her foreign policy agenda today? We have developed our conservative worldview. Now let's analyze the current world through this prism.

First and foremost, conservative diplomacy needs to maintain a healthy respect and regard for the United States Constitution. The last fifty years of conservative statecraft support this argument. For example, the life of Republican Senator Robert A. Taft teaches conservatives that the separation of powers between Congress and the executive branch provides a framework for reaching wise and shrewd foreign policy decisions. In the post-World War II era, Taft was wary of the increasing scope of presidential power, having watched President Harry Truman lead the country into war in Korea based on what Taft saw as impulse. Taft's prescience is notable. Over fifty years later America still has troops on the Korean Peninsula and much of the tension is still unresolved. President Bush recognized this reality and first went to the Congress for a vote of approval before authorizing the use of force against Iraq. Unfortunately, our 43rd president did not learn the lesson of committing our nation to foreign wars without end.

Conservatives believe that subverting the Constitution to any other statutes or laws surrenders American sovereignty. It also surrenders the national interest to the dictates and whims of the common interest, which has no objective definition. Senator Robert A. Taft was suspicious of international organizations like the United Nations or even NATO because he worried that these obligations would undermine America's commitment to protecting, upholding, and defending her Constitution. President Nixon showed diplomatic prowess by reconciling the Constitution with America's treaty obligations abroad. The result was a peace settlement to end the Vietnam War.

George W. Bush preserved the primacy of the US Constitution during the Global War on Terror, refusing to surrender enemy combatants to the international community, or to place US troops under the jurisdiction of the International Criminal Court. Contrast this with prevailing sentiment within the Obama administration, where considerable support was mustered in favor of appointing Yale Law School dean Harold Koh as legal advisor to the State Department. Koh defines his worldview in terms of "transnational jurisprudence" – using tenets of international law and foreign legal precedent to inform jurisprudence on America's home turf. Based on the historical precedent of the last fifty years, conservatives were right to fear Koh's approach.

Regardless of how conservative administrations approach the separation of powers or prerogatives of the executive branch, all agree that liberty is only sustainable when buttressed by the rule of law. Though seemingly paradoxical, American freedom can only flourish when it rests on the foundation of order established in the Constitution. Conservatives believe that the Constitution, and the Declaration of Independence that preceded it, contain wisdom for the ages because they were influenced by our two pillars – a proper understanding of human nature and the lessons of history. Both of these documents have guided our country through the torrents of war and the brooks of peace.

Along with a robust support of the Constitution, today's conservatives must understand that diplomacy's center stage is the home front, not the outside world. "All foreign policy is local," argues the diplomatic historian H.W. Brands. In other words, decisions made in domestic politics are intimately tied to how America acts internationally. Domestic public opinion is often shaped by events that transpire on battlefields and in embassies throughout the world. Both Presidents Nixon and Ford keenly recognized the domestic dimension of foreign affairs and demanded energy reform because they knew that our addiction to petroleum would enslave us to foreign nations, handicapping our ability to defend the national interest. President Reagan removed troops from Lebanon after the Beirut bombing created a groundswell of negativity against the administration's Middle East policy. President George W. Bush used domestic sentiment in the aftermath of September 11, 2001 to build a platform for the allied invasion of Afghanistan and Iraq. All of these observations reflect that foreign policy is formulated in response to electoral pressures at home.

But domestic influence in foreign policy goes beyond public opinion polls. Conservatives recognize that domestic problems in energy production, immigration policy, and entitlement reform have profound international consequences. The problems in the energy sector are glaringly obvious. As of 2008, only one-third of America's oil consumption came from domestic production. The other two-thirds came in the form of imports from countries like Saudi Arabia, Russia, and Venezuela – nations that are openly hostile to US interests. Former CIA analyst Michael Scheuer warns that if energy security is not addressed soon, America may find herself fighting a nasty insurgency in the Niger Delta in order to protect petroleum assets in West Africa.[16]

Border control and immigration policy are additional concerns that have dire international implications. September 11, 2001 showed Americans that there is a price to pay for having porous borders. Currently, cities such as Laredo, Texas have more in common with the no man's land between Afghanistan and Pakistan than they do with the rest of the United States. Kidnappings, beheadings, and drug trafficking are commonplace in such border towns and our local and federal law enforcement assets are overwhelmed.[17] Foreign policy with NAFTA partners such as Mexico and other Latin American countries is wedded to how America implements immigration policy. A prudent foreign policy in Central and South America is contingent on wise polices at home.

The most disconcerting domestic trend that will prove ruinous for American foreign policy is the federal deficit caused by our massive set of entitlement programs. Since the New Deal and the expansion of state services under LBJ's Great Society, politicians have ignored the need to reform entitlement programs such as Social Security, Medicare, and Medicaid. American voters are equally culpable for not demanding that the government live within its means.

The facts speak for themselves. Entitlement programs eat up a whopping 8.5% of GDP, as opposed to the entire defense budget, which comprises less than 5% annually. If left unfettered, entitlement programs could consume 18% of GDP in the next decade, costing over one trillion dollars to adequately reform the system.[18] Without this reform, the entitlement system could cause economic meltdown as our nation's 78 million "baby boomers" reach retirement age in the coming years. Domestic economic constraints will undermine our influence throughout the world and guarantee that all future diplomacy will be hamstrung. It will be a sad day for Americans if the US Dollar is replaced by the Chinese Yuan as the world's currency of exchange.

Conservatives must learn the art of diplomacy and they must learn it better than their liberal counterparts if they hope to make a difference in domestic elections and international affairs. It is critical that we develop a worldview that can weather the ebbs and flows of American politics. Once our worldview is developed, we must clearly articulate why our conservative paradigm is the appropriate one through which to view a complex and ever-changing world. We understand that precious few have the intellectual foresight to accurately predict future trends in foreign affairs. At the end of the day, we are all looking through a glass darkly. Constructing a worldview not only helps one understand the first principles of conservative thought, but it also gives conservatives insight into how America should bring her power to bear in the years to come.

British realist Martin Wight once wrote: "Realism can be a very good thing: it all depends on whether it means the abandonment of high ideals, or of foolish expectations."[19] With this framework in place, conservatives can learn the lessons of Odysseus and the dreaded Sirens. Just as Odysseus clung to the mast of his ship to avoid Sirens' tempting melody, conservatives must cling to their high ideals without giving way to foolish expectations. Armed with this proper understanding of realism, our conservatism offers the best framework for conducting foreign policy in the twenty-first century.

From this point forward there is no excuse for the hysterical lifeboat mentality that pervades current critiques of the conservative movement. Likewise, we should not remain stubborn and pledge to go down with the ship. Rather, we should mend the holes in our vessel by arming ourselves with knowledge of human nature, the lessons of history, and the skills necessary for discernment. If we can do that, then the appropriate metaphor for our movement will no longer be a teetering steamship but a fortified warship, cutting through the sea unopposed.

Austin Knuppe is currently a research assistant at the Hauenstein Center for Presidential Studies at Grand Valley State University. Previously, Austin has worked at a number of think tanks in Washington, DC, as well as the Paul Henry Center for the study of Religion and Politics. He is an honors graduate of Calvin College, where he received his BA in International Relations and History. Originally from the San Francisco Bay area, Austin currently lives in western Michigan.

XVI. RECLAIMING OUR FOREIGN POLICY:
International Organizations and American Sovereignty
by Jesse Davis

Without a doubt, the United States is the world's preeminent economic and military power. For at least the time being, we are in fact the sole superpower. But we of the up and coming generations must understand how our nation gained this status, and how easily it could be lost. As will be shown, a conservative approach to American sovereignty is at the core of our international leadership and our ability to maintain it.

In many areas of public policy – particularly in the realm of foreign affairs – the right policy may not be liberal or conservative, Republican or Democrat. The unfortunate reality is that, no matter how proactive a nation's leaders are, the complexities of international relations often demand only reaction. Sometimes hard choices must be made between the lesser of two evils, with no room for strict adherence to party platforms.

Thankfully, the bulk of foreign policy decisions happen at a glacial pace. Peace talks, trade negotiations, and the formation of international alliances are notoriously time consuming endeavors. In most matters of diplomacy and foreign policy, we have the luxury of deep study, productive debate, and careful consideration. This opportunity for deliberation lets us track over time what works, what doesn't, and what matters most in foreign policy. From continued observation, two truths emerge. First, a nation's ability to preserve its sovereignty is the prime determinant of its overall success. Secondly, more often than not, the application of conservative principles offers American policymakers the best means of preserving our national sovereignty.

This is not a conservative playbook for foreign policy – volumes have been written on that topic from a wide range of perspectives. Rather, this essay presents comparisons, observations, and recommendations on issues that affect American sovereignty. Specifically, it examines American participation in a variety of international organizations including the United Nations, NATO, the World Trade Organization, and international judicial entities. Readers are invited to draw their own ultimate conclusions, but also strongly encouraged to recognize the opportunity and liability we face in a changing global atmosphere.

Sovereignty and Foreign Policy

Over the past three centuries, we Americans have learned a thing or two about sovereignty. From our revolutionary beginnings and our support of freedom abroad, we have learned that a nation's sovereignty is hard won, yet easily lost. Through the success of our ingenious republican system, we have learned that true sovereignty must rest with the governed and not with the government. From our sometimes bitter internal strife, we have learned that sovereign power must be exercised with the utmost care. But perhaps our greatest lesson is that which we learned first – American security and prosperity utterly depend upon American sovereignty.

As a faraway king taxed their goods and quartered soldiers in their homes, the Founding Fathers came to realize that America's destiny lay apart from the British Empire. Despite their animosity for the king himself, most did not rebel out of hatred for their former country or delusions of grandeur on the great frontier. They simply recognized that British and American interests could not be reconciled. Americans wanted ownership of the prosperity that hard work and the resources of the vast North American continent were certain to generate. But the British crown and parliament weren't concerned with American growth. Rather, they desired little more than lopsided trade, tax revenue, and further territorial expansion. Any other colonial success was ancillary to these goals. In the end, America could not mature while subjected to the British sovereign. For this reason, we Americans seized sovereignty for ourselves and made every citizen the equal of the monarch.

Thus, from the beginning, American success has stemmed from the understanding that our needs are not best met when we suborn them to the interests of other nations. One may notice, not coincidentally, that the lessons and foundational principles noted above are echoed throughout conservative political philosophy. However, the principles of republican governance, limited government, and the fundamental rights of man take on special import in the realm of foreign policy. To abandon any of these ideals is to erode the very sovereignty that has brought us to the pinnacle of world influence.

Despite the benefit of this knowledge, our nation's politicians have seemed more than willing to parcel out our national sovereignty piece by piece. We have already seen that an expanding government works against popular sovereignty in domestic affairs. Increasingly, we have begun to see what expanding international government means for our national sovereignty. That core tenet of modern liberalism, the notion that more government and more regulation can solve any problem, has been writ large on the international stage. Foreign dictation, not self-determination, threatens to control our future.

Today the conduct of the United States is constrained by our membership in several international political bodies, by our adherence to hundreds of treaties, conventions, and trade agreements, and by our maintenance of a huge number of formal military alliances. While many of these measures and organizations are of great benefit, others unreasonably restrict our ability to defend ourselves, prevent us from halting bloodshed abroad, and even dictate how we should administer our own laws. Each international agreement, for better or for worse, is a check on our nation's ability to act for itself. Thus, each is a check on our national sovereignty. Certainly there are good reasons for a nation to give up small portions of her sovereignty. Much sorrow and bloodshed have been avoided through international cooperation. Indeed, a world without regulation and fora for discourse would be as brutal and chaotic as Europe during the Dark Ages. But over time, as a nation cedes away her right to act in any number of small ways, those things she gives up reach critical mass. If she is not careful, she will have given away more of her sovereignty than she has retained.*

---

* There are some who find this concept impossible. They argue, as did Samuel Johnson, that "in sovereignty there are no gradations." Or, as his later American counterpart John Randolph would say more coarsely, "A state can no more give up part of her sovereignty than a lady can give up part of her virtue." Yet we know this to be false. The core genius of the American system itself is an intricate mechanism of dual state and federal sovereignty. Likewise, our international success could not exist in a world of absolute sovereignty, with no room for trade agreements or military alliances. As any red-blooded young man could remind Mr. Randolph, a lady has quite a lot to give up before her virtue is spoiled. However, if she is not vigilant, spoiled it soon will be.

So as citizens of the most powerful nation on Earth, we must approach foreign policy with exceeding caution. We must espouse responsible foreign policy which recognizes that international citizenship and national sovereignty are not mutually exclusive, yet protects the latter as its highest priority. A crucial balance must be struck between the two. We cannot give and give and give of ourselves, only to wake up one morning at the mercy of not one, but dozens of faraway sovereigns. Unfortunately, much of our current foreign policy treads dangerously close to this line. Many of the international programs in which the United States participates are relics of a bygone era and cannot adapt to meet modern challenges. In this way, the dead hands of the post-World War II era and the Cold War still maneuver the puppet strings of American diplomacy. Simultaneously, the United States avoids participation in some programs that could work to our benefit. It is time to reevaluate our international involvement and bring to bear the conservative principles that are so sorely needed in our foreign policy. Nothing less than our national sovereignty is at stake.

The United Nations

When the United Nations was founded in 1945, the world still reeled from the traumatic effects of World War II. Millions were dead, entire countries lay in ruins, and animosity between nations ran deep. At this time, there could be no nobler foreign policy goal than that of fostering cooperation and growth. The UN was envisioned and created as an ideal organization in which every country could parlay on equal terms. Each nation would have a voice and a vote on matters important to all. Comity and unity of purpose would flourish where intrigue and mendacity once held sway. Gone would be the days of imperialism and the Great Game between feuding powers. A new era would be born: an era of peace, security, and prosperity. Of course, to ensure that all this came to pass, a benevolent Security Council would preside over the organization. As the greatest among equals, the members of the Council with veto power would paternalistically shepherd the world into the *novus ordo seculorum*. War was to be outlawed, and no aggressive force allowed without the Council's blessing.

Of course, some measure of visionary idealism was necessary in those dark days. The world needed hope that the atrocities of war and famine could someday be forgotten. But UN proponents forgot all too easily that the use of force as a policy tool had been decried for centuries, and opposition to it had been codified in the Kellogg-Briand Pact of 1929. Neither fact had stopped Hitler and the Axis powers, all of which were among the 63 signatories to Kellogg-Briand. Within a decade, the body vaunted as the new hope of the world was drawn into the deadly interplay between rising superpowers. As the US and the USSR came to blows by proxy in the Korean War, the UN wisely chose to support the side of democracy and economic freedom. But in doing so, it revealed what jaded observers had known all along – whatever the forum, and whatever the overarching rhetoric, nations will ultimately seek to act in their own best interest.

There is nothing inherently incorrect in the structure of the UN. On paper and in concept, the organization does much to recognize the sovereignty of nations and acknowledge the prerogative of the powerful. Yet in practice, we see the failure of theory. For example, the "one nation, one vote" notion is egalitarian and inclusive in theory. But in practice it has too often reduced the UN General Assembly to a clearinghouse of small, poorer nation's grievances against the large and rich. Donee states wag their fingers at donor states, and pass recommendations to curtail more prosperous nations' success in the face of their own shortcomings. Nations poor in resources advance recommendations that the wealth of the few be shared among the many. Nations whose governments stifle innovation and growth use the UN as a platform to accuse democracies of sabotage.

UN humanitarian programs provide additional examples. For all the food, medicine, and clean water these programs provide, absurd amounts of money are wasted in overhead and bureaucracy. In theory, a worldwide cooperative should be the organization best suited to aid the starving, sick, and impoverished. Yet in practice, private agencies and direct infusions of aid from donor states have proven much more efficient. For example, World Vision International, one of the world's largest Christian charities, attributed only 13 percent of its 2008 expenditures to overhead and most of that figure to fundraising activities.[1] In contrast, at least one UN operation has posted an astonishing 85 percent in overhead costs.[2] Worse yet, bureaucracy is fatally susceptible to corruption, as the Oil-for-Food scandal proved in the 1990s and early 2000s.

Perhaps the most obvious example of diplomatic practice giving lie to theory is in the use of force. Some UN founders believed and some theoreticians maintain that strict regulation will ultimately extinguish the resort to force. In theory, if cooler heads prevail we will have no need for brutish wars. For this reason the UN Security Council was given exclusive jurisdiction over the use of force in international affairs. By the strictures of the UN Charter, Article 2, no nation may employ force without the Council's permission, except in self defense. This provision has led to the deployment of UN "peacekeepers," a multinational, ostensibly military group charged with preventing the unsanctioned use of force. Yet in practice, when an organization announces its intention to remain weak and impartial, its moral authority becomes irrelevant in the face of determined force. Without the use of force as a real possibility, UN action against aggressors will continue to fall into the familiar cycle of vague talks, meaningless monitoring, ineffectual sanctions, wasteful peacekeeper deployments, and ultimately, UN embarrassment. In the Balkans, peacekeepers watched impotently as Serbian troops stole UN weapons and matériel and used them to carry out genocide. In Darfur, rather than abandon the use of force, the Sudanese government launched a new genocidal offensive the day after a deployment of peacekeepers was announced.[3] In Iraq, the UN allowed decades of atrocities before one nation had the courage to end them.

The very first UN engagement, the Korean War, provides a fitting study of the organization's cycle of failure. Although an armistice was signed in1953, North and South Korea remain technically at war. The two countries have not been idle. In the almost sixty years since the war's outward end, South Korea has boomed and become one of East Asia's most vibrant democracies and prosperous economies. Meanwhile, communist North Korea has seen her allies dwindle away and has descended into poverty. Only the most powerful North Koreans enjoy a first-world standard of living, and the nation depends completely on food aid to stave off famine. As Department of Defense officials regularly point out in press briefings, the stark divide between the two half-nations is outwardly visible. At night, from high above, one can see the lights of South Korea shine brightly while only a few miles away the North Korean darkness is palpable.

This harsh dichotomy is partly due to what scholars call the chilling effect. Studies have shown that negotiating ceasefires without remedying the underlying animosities sometimes perpetuates conflict. It bottles up aggressions and saves them for another day. In the intervening time each side continues to one up the other, until eventually fighting breaks out again. More importantly, the Korean conflict remains at a technical stalemate today because North Korean leaders know that their bluster and aggressive moves will be met not with strength, but with concessions and appeasement.

North Korea has massed what some analysts call the world's largest conventional artillery on its southern border, and the UN Security Council has allowed it to do so. North Korea has sponsored terrorism, run massive money counterfeiting operations, and denied its citizens' human rights, and the UN Security Council has allowed it to do so. North Korea has tested long range ballistic missiles and developed the nuclear technology to arm them, and the UN Security Council has allowed it to do so. Granted, every few years the Council will pass new sanctions to goad North Korea into negotiation. Every so often the "Hermit Kingdom" will promise to halt its transgressions in return for aid or lighter sanctions. But the end game is always the same. North Korea makes threats, and the UN blithely dances along to its tune.

Today, American forces still guard the 38th parallel, the last battle line in the world's most enduring conflict. They stand ready at the Demilitarized Zone, with rifles and tanks pointed north, to protect a thriving democracy from a tyrant the world willingly enables. Stalemate and starvation are the legacy of the United Nations' mission to control the use of force. As of this writing, North Korea has restarted the production of weapons-grade uranium, has tested a nuclear device more powerful than the bomb dropped on Nagasaki, and has launched a missile capable of hitting Japan. In response, South Korea has joined in a US backed anti-smuggling program aimed at containing whatever weapons of mass destruction the North builds. Infuriated that the South would stand up to its threatening posture, North Korea has withdrawn from the 1953 armistice and technically re-declared war. Not surprisingly, analysts don't believe North Korea wants a real fight. Many recognize recent events as simply its most dramatic bid for international attention yet. Of course the Security Council has condemned the North Korean action, just as it has before. But if action is to be taken against the aggressor, the task will surely fall to the US.

Why has this been allowed to transpire? Why has the grand community of nations not halted North Korean lunacy and ended the decades old conflict? Because the basic failing of the UN as a peacekeeping body is that nations will always act in their own best interest. North Korea will do whatever it deems necessary to get what it wants. China, as the regional power broker and a veto-holder on the Security Council, will not allow further Western involvement within its sphere of influence. The remaining Security Council members do not have the resources, clout, or political will to bring North Korea to heel. And so the competing interests at the UN have left the US guarding the world's most fortified border.

As a result, the United States must look to her own best interest. It is in our best interest to work for a more peaceful, more cooperative world. But good intentions are meaningless unless one has the courage to act on them. Thus it is also in our best interest to work outside the UN framework when necessary, and reform it as we are able. Some have envisioned the UN as a world government, but it is clear today that the organization cannot and must not function in this role.

In fiscal year 2009, United States gave almost $600 million to the core budget of a body that dictates our international conduct, often to our detriment.[4] Regular, mandatory contributions by the US represent 22 percent of the overall UN budget, far more than any other nation.[5] In addition, in 2006 the US provided 27 percent of UN peacekeeper funding, to the tune of almost $1.5 billion.[6] And these astounding numbers don't include further billions in direct aid to other UN programs. Instead of bankrolling the mechanism that undermines our sovereignty, it is in our best interest to salvage what we can from the UN and leave the rest to history. Rather than strengthening the UN into a world government by expanding it, we should use our diplomatic currency to build up the areas in which it excels and demolish those in which it does not. The UN is an excellent forum for dialogue, but an exceedingly poor vehicle for action. It is rife with bureaucracy and blame-placing. Why not then let the UN be the venue for the multilateral discourse that will always be slow and clumsy, and leave matters of action to the organizations that are better suited for it? At the very least, procedural roadblocks should be removed to allow action by other bodies and individual nations. It is in the best interest of American sovereignty to reclaim the lost opportunity of the UN as an international forum and abandon its hope of world regulation. As with any form of political organization, the UN's mandate should be limited to its core competencies.

The North Atlantic Treaty Organization (NATO)

The North Atlantic Treaty Organization, NATO, is another child of the post-World War II era. Founded in 1949, it is a collective defense organization and essentially an alliance of the Western powers. As Lord Ismay, the first Secretary General of NATO, once said, the original goals of the organization were to "keep the Russians out, the Americans in, and the Germans down." This rather blunt statement aptly summarizes NATO's aims. At the time of its founding, the former Allied nations needed the strength of an ascendant America, feared the spread of communism from the USSR, and dreaded the eventual return of German military ambition. So, the victors of the Second World War declared their mutual defense and vowed that "an attack against one of them…shall be considered an attack against them all." In retaliation, the USSR and her allies signed the similar Warsaw Pact in 1955, and for the next 30 years these agreements formed the battle lines of the Cold War.

As time went on, American supremacy in the West became clear, and the German threat waned. When this occurred, the basic and enduring function of NATO became opposition to Soviet expansion. American land bases, air facilities, naval bases, and missile installations were constructed across Europe and around the world. Military spending on both sides escalated to epic proportions. Rapidly expanding nuclear arsenals mushroomed into mutually assured destruction, the ability of each side to destroy the other many times over. But when the Berlin Wall fell in 1989, the core mission of NATO fell along with it. Russia appeared ready to join the ranks of democracy, and the Soviet threat was no more. Russia agreed to allow East Germany to rejoin the democratic Federal Republic of Germany, on the condition that NATO would not expand its membership further east. Suddenly, after decades of readiness, NATO found itself without a war to fight.

In the following years, NATO adapted to the new power structure in a series of treaties on conventional forces in Europe. It scaled back active deployment, and recreated itself as a worldwide peacekeeper. It undertook its first ever military action to enforce UN resolutions in the Balkans, and later accepted offensive missions in the 2001 invasion of Afghanistan, and training missions in Iraq. The organization sought expansion by granting membership to several formerly neutral and Warsaw Pact nations. Currently, NATO membership stands at 28 nations, including the former Soviet states and allies Hungary, the Czech Republic, Poland, Estonia, Latvia, Lithuania, Slovenia, Slovakia, Bulgaria, Romania, Albania, and Croatia. The Ukraine and Georgia are also pending members.

It would seem to be acceptable, since the West won the Cold War, that it should set the tone for the future. With the Soviet threat gone, new missions must be formulated. As nations grow into mature democracies, they naturally want to join the grand alliance of free nations. Yet all is not as it seems. From its inception, NATO had the firm and immediate purpose of checking Soviet aggression. With that purpose gone, the idea of mutual defense becomes much more nebulous. The NATO missions in Iraq and Afghanistan seem to indicate a counter-terrorism mission, yet this goal has not been codified by the decision-making North Atlantic Council. The September 11th attacks were ruled sufficient to invoke mutual defense for the invasion of Afghanistan, but will future attacks in other countries mean the same? When a bus explodes in London, must we as good allies invade Yemen?

Expansion presents its own challenges as well. As more Eastern European nations join the club, the chances of NATO participation in a conflict increase dramatically. For example, Georgia has been notified that it will someday receive an invitation to join NATO. But in 2008, outright hostilities broke out between Georgia and Russia. Russia now occupies key territory in South Ossetia, and has no intention of returning it to Georgian control. If this conflict had taken place only a few years later, NATO nations may have been obligated to defend our Georgian ally. A new Cold War or even a new World War could have resulted. As columnist Pat Buchanan points out, precisely this type of no-questions-asked agreement has drawn major powers into needless and premature conflict before. Yet if NATO did not respond to such aggression, it would lose all credibility among its smaller members.

Additionally, the West has seemingly abandoned its promise to stay out of Russia's backyard after the reunification of Germany. In 2008, relations reached crisis levels as NATO and the United States moved forward with plans to place missile defense systems in Poland and the Czech Republic. Actions like this further increase the likelihood of diplomatic tension and perhaps military conflict between NATO and Russia. One can only fear the involvement of other world powers in such a conflict, including nuclear-armed nations like China, India, or Pakistan.

The maintenance of a massive military alliance made sense during the Cold War, when the fall of one ally could have portended the fall of Western democracy. But today, the continued growth of an organization which represents over 70 percent of worldwide military spending seems self-defeating.[7] A loose political or trade alliance is one thing; the commitment of the United States to defend far-flung allies like Estonia and Latvia is quite another. In such an expanding and binding alliance we have given away much of our military sovereignty and the opportunity for nuanced discretion, but we have gained little in return. The time has come for a reformation of the NATO agreement, including a clear statement of its modern mission, reexamination of mutual defense obligations, and the cessation of expansion before the former goals are accomplished.

International Trade

Despite the attention we give the political side of foreign affairs, perhaps the strongest ties between nations are economic. A century ago, President William Howard Taft coined the term "dollar diplomacy" to describe a phenomenon that has been known since ancient days. The use of force may cow an enemy into submission, but fostering bonds of trade and economic interdependence will make even a fierce enemy into a strong ally. This realistic, fundamentally conservative view has informed most major foreign policy decisions since the end of World War II. By engaging in economic cooperation, we give up little in the way of American sovereignty in exchange for great gains in influence abroad, international stability, and prosperity at home.

It is no accident that major nations have not engaged each other in all-out direct conflict since the widespread adoption of a trade-centric, globalist worldview. Thomas Friedman humorously labeled this peace bolstered by trade the "Golden Arches Theory of Conflict Prevention," and postulated that no two nations with McDonald's restaurants ever went to war. While his theory has a few holes, especially as Big Macs become available in the most far-flung and dangerous parts of the world, the central premise holds true. For all the grand ideals and fraternity of international organizations, economic interdependence builds the most lasting peace. Common sense tells us why this is so. If one nation produces wool, and its neighbor buys the wool to manufacture blankets, both nations benefit. Why doesn't one nation take over the other by force, and have all the wool and blankets it needs? Not because of any particular sentimentality or morality, but because both nations know that the cost of war is dramatically higher than the cost of peace. The first nation knows it will have to use its wool-producing resources to take over its neighbor, by conscripting sheep farmers into military service and weapons production. Even if it does take over the manufacturing nation, it must then rebuild the factories it may have destroyed and learn the process of making blankets, not to mention enforce its will on the citizens of its conquered neighbor. The manufacturing nation faces a similar set of costs, including a "guns or blankets" dilemma in its industrial sector. The benefits of peaceful trade are clearly superior to those of war.

As the global neighborhood becomes smaller and distance an ever diminishing obstacle to the exchange of goods and services, we see the hypothetical above played out repeatedly on a hugely complex scale. If one replaces wool with oil and blanket factories with refineries, the real-world application is immediately apparent. Yet we still see conflicts over oil and other valuable resources throughout the world. These conflicts occur because those who control the resources choose not to maximize their trade opportunities. In Iraq, Saddam Hussein controlled a vast supply of oil, which he traded greedily only with certain partners and allies. He kept his oil wealth bottled up among the Iraqi elite and squandered it on war with Iran rather than investing in the infrastructure of economic development. As a result, the Iraqi nation withered away until Saddam's greed led him to invade Kuwait in search of more oil.

Contrast the Iraqi experience with that of Saudi Arabia. The House of Saud has leveraged its oil wealth into regional and world influence. The Saudis do not resort to force to meet their ends, because they know that trade with other nations ultimately reaps much more success.

The best policy for world peace, then, is world trade. The international community's largest effort to facilitate world trade was the General Agreements on Tariffs and Trade of 1947, which has evolved into the current World Trade Organization (WTO). The WTO represents more than 95% of all world commerce, and seeks to establish a regime of free and fair trade.[8] Although the WTO has a forum-like structure, it functions more like a managed exchange or mediator between nations. If a country's tariffs are too high to allow reasonable trade, or if it subsidizes an industry too much to allow fair competition, the WTO will issue a ruling that such activities should be curtailed. Unlike the UN's all-inclusive attitude, membership in the WTO is limited to nations that demonstrate a willingness to engage in free trade and display a measure of economic stability. As a result, the WTO is an exemplar of an international institution molded specifically to its purpose and, more importantly, limited to it.

By obeying the rulings of the WTO and making concessions to our trade partners, we do give up a measure of American sovereignty. However, the ultimate benefits of global trade are immeasurable. Just as in other areas of foreign policy, a small part of our self-determination can be sacrificed to make great gains. The trick is to avoid the slippery slope of outright charity, as opposed to mutually beneficial trade.

As we recognized the common sense benefit of international trade, we must also recognize the common sense drawbacks. One persistent criticism of the WTO is that it helps the rich get richer and the poor get poorer. Yet as John F. Kennedy and Ronald Reagan agreed, "a rising tide lifts all the boats." Responsible management is necessary to see this promise through. Unregulated, international free trade can result in the same inequities that in the past have led to labor riots and trust-busting in our domestic economy. The most recent round of WTO talks is aimed at ensuring fair trade alongside free trade. Just as regulation in the United States seeks to prevent unrestrained capitalism from forcing labor prices far below a working wage, WTO regulation seeks to prevent less scrupulous nations from prostituting their poor to increase foreign trade. Macroeconomic benefit can be gained without selling out microeconomic interests. This is not to say that trade partners must accept inferior goods at inflated prices in an altruistic pursuit of subjective "fairness." Rather, the global marketplace can and must support trade that is free – based on the laws of supply and demand, unencumbered by excessive tariffs and duties – and fair – in which nations do not collude to push their rivals from the market place or take advantage of a rival's poverty. Furthermore, through limited regulation it is hoped that the forceful dominance that pervades military affairs will not overtake trade affairs. The rich nations will not simply get richer, and the poor poorer. Rather, each nation will benefit according to what it contributes, and the rising tide will lift us all.

An additional drawback is that when a nation is a valuable trade partner, our usual policy elevates that nation's political status above others. We often overlook political differences with such nations, to the point that we are willing to ignore human rights issues in favor of healthy trade. The US – China relationship is a current case in point, as are relations between Iran and western European nations like Germany and Italy. As important as free trade is to world stability and prosperity, both are undermined by policies divorced from reality. We cannot tolerate that China censors, imprisons, and kills her citizens for their political views. We cannot tolerate that Iran seeks a nuclear weapon or that Saudi women are brutally oppressed. Yet we can solidify lasting change in each nation with Western trade. A careful balance is necessary to open those nations and others like them to our beneficial influences, while not condoning their nefarious actions. Pragmatically speaking, trade talks and political talks cannot be carried on in a vacuum from one another. All the cards should be laid on the table and sorted through. Even though this approach may result in a piecemeal path forward, in the end it will result in a more lasting partnership than economic or political discussions could forge alone.

International Justice

International justice is perhaps one of the most controversial areas of foreign policy. Each nation that values its sovereignty jealously guards the right to prosecute its own citizens. The United States maintains Status of Forces Agreements with each county where our troops are stationed, in part to ensure that we have the final word on how our lawbreakers are punished overseas. Extradition treaties between most nations make the return of prisoners a matter of international law. Diplomatic crises can erupt when the judiciary of one nation seeks to enforce its laws on a visitor from abroad. Indeed, a monopoly on the confinement of and violence against her citizens is a hallmark of a sovereign nation, and a right worth defending on the international stage. Sometimes, however, no sovereign is willing or able to prosecute a mass murderer or a war criminal. Sometimes a sovereign nation is complicit in atrocities that cannot go unchecked and unpunished. The international community has offered solutions for dealing with such criminals when their home countries do not, but dogmatic arguments that misunderstand the nature of national sovereignty have rendered the most ambitious of these efforts impotent.

Day to day justice is an internecine affair. The average bank robber or murderer does not flee to another country, nor does he operate across international boundaries. In the United States, even the most complicated interstate crimes are dealt with in a fairly routine interaction between dual state and federal sovereigns. Criminals who flee to other countries are usually returned without incident. In Europe and other regions where cross-border crime is more prevalent, organizations such as Interpol facilitate the apprehension of criminals and their return to the prosecuting country. But in the most heinous of crimes, those so atrocious as to be labeled crimes against humanity, the government of the criminal's home country may be a co-conspirator. Worse yet, the criminal may be the head of state of a government that promotes genocide, mass rape, and scorched earth warfare. Who is to prosecute these crimes?

Until the just a few years ago, war criminals and individuals accused of crimes against humanity were dealt with on an *ad hoc* basis. In earlier times, a victor would simply execute the vanquished offender. More recently, a winning nation or alliance would set up military commissions for the task, as was the case in famous post-World War II Nuremberg and Tokyo trials. But even in these carefully implemented and fundamentally fair trials, the winning military power was still responsible for enforcing justice against the losing party. To put this state of affairs in perspective, if the American criminal justice system ran this way, a theft victim could only find justice if he captured the wrongdoer himself and physically forced remuneration.

Only at the close of the twentieth century did the international community take a collective step toward the adjudication of crimes against humanity. In 1993, a special UN tribunal was set up in The Hague to prosecute and adjudicate genocide and war crimes perpetrated during the Balkans conflicts. In 1994, a similar tribunal was created to deal with crimes committed in Rwanda. The need for the courts was clear – the home governments of those regions were either unwilling or unable to fairly decide how their war criminals should be punished. Even now, some criminals prosecuted in these special tribunals remain local heroes who would have otherwise never been brought to justice. Finally, in 1998, many UN member states met in Rome and agreed to the creation of an International Criminal Court (ICC), with competency and jurisdiction in exactly this area of law. The ICC operates alongside but independent of the UN organization, wisely separating the criminal judicial function from the diplomatic clamor of the UN and placing it in more specialized hands.

Unfortunately, the ICC has received much criticism from the world's largest and most important nations. The United States, China, India, Russia, and Israel all have either refused to sign the ICC treaty or have withdrawn their support. The main complaint is that the court is merely another organ of an international community run amok, and a cover from which small nations may throw stones at their larger rivals. According to the critics, such a court is an unacceptable intrusion on the sovereignty of nations and their courts. This is a valid concern, as the reader of this particular essay has probably gathered.

However, the structure of the court and its governance are specifically designed to assuage such fears. In fact, before the United States withdrew from the treaty, our government had an enormous influence on its drafting. Largely at our insistence, the court can only hear cases within a very limited jurisdiction: genocide, crimes against humanity, war crimes, or crimes of aggression. To be prosecuted in the ICC, an individual must be a citizen of a nation which has signed the treaty, the crime must have occurred in the territory of a party to the treaty, and the case must be referred to the court by the UN Security Council or the state in which the crimes occurred.

Not coincidentally, this system parallels the subject matter jurisdiction and grand jury indictment requirements found in the United States and many other criminal justice systems. Even more familiar to Americans, an individual before the ICC is presumed innocent until proven guilty beyond a reasonable doubt. The ICC even has a public defender's office of sorts. The ICC was envisioned and functions as a court of last resort, to be called upon only when a national court system is not able to handle a case. If an individual is prosecuted in a national court system, or if a nation decides not to prosecute, the ICC cannot hear the case.

The short reach of the court is evident in its current caseload. Since it formally began work in 2002, the court has heard no cases, and the prosecutor has opened investigations into only four: crimes against humanity in Uganda; war crimes and crimes against humanity in the Democratic Republic of the Congo; war crimes and crimes against humanity in the Central African Republic; and genocide, war crimes, and crimes against humanity in Darfur. This would seem to indicate an international organization operating according to the principles of limited government and a pragmatic evaluation of world affairs. Rather than the tool of the meek against the mighty some feared it would become, the ICC is a venue to find justice in some of the world's most desperate tragedies. With the aforementioned critical safeguards in place, no nation loses sovereignty by supporting the ICC, but rather lends its voice to the ultimate sovereignty of justice.

By any measure, the world around us is changing. The global economy has ebbed and as it rebounds will be reinvented in a myriad of unpredictable ways. New regional power structures are emerging as some states fade in influence and others grow. The population of the world is growing most in the areas which have the least resources, and the new voices are added to the throng every day. Here at home, the hard choices of the Bush era have alienated old allies and made for sometimes strange bedfellows in the fight against terrorism. The Obama administration has heralded a new era of internationalism, one to rival the post–World War II epoch of cooperation. This change in leadership could become either an immense opportunity or a colossal liability to our foreign affairs. No one can deny the good that may come from increased engagement and a more positive diplomatic tone. Each of the international organizations discussed above holds great potential to affect positive change in the world. But likewise our leaders must recognize the thin ice on which they tread. A few minor concessions to our international rivals today could become abject disadvantages tomorrow. A sea change like we are currently experiencing only occurs once in a lifetime. The Founding Fathers employed the revolutionary power of global change to enhance the United States' international standing, as did our leaders following both World Wars. For our part, we today must seize upon this chance to reform our foreign policy in favor of American sovereignty, or risk losing it forever.

Jesse Davis is a former communications aide to Senator Kay Bailey Hutchison, specializing in military and foreign affairs. He observed the Slobodan Milosevic trial at The Hague, and has written on foreign affairs, international justice, and human rights law. He earned his BA in History and Political Science from the University of North Texas, where he also served as Student Body President. He is currently a law student at Baylor University, with an emphasis on criminal and public law.

XVII. THIS WE WILL DEFEND:
A Principled Approach to National Security

by John Amble

Conservatism is often defined by its adherence to the concept of small government. But a more accurate description would highlight, instead, a philosophical belief in *limited* government. More than a semantic irrelevance, the change in this one word illustrates the central conservative conviction that the limits of government should be defined in terms of scope, rather than size. Arbitrary restrictions need not be placed on the number of government employees, an agency's budget, or some other purely subjective measure. Conservative thought holds that the government's actions should be guided by a set of principles, and further, that these principles should remain the same as those upon which our nation was built. This is the essence of conservatism: that in a functioning society guided by a commitment to and defense of liberty, the government will be charged with a specific, clearly defined set of responsibilities. In short, we believe in a government with a small mandate, not necessarily with a small size. We expect that it will fulfill the responsibilities within this mandate effectively and fully. Nowhere is this distinction more obvious or more important than in a discussion of the government's responsibility to provide for the defense of our nation. It is a responsibility that is rooted in an eternal respect for individual liberty. It represents the most basic obligation, explicitly defined by the constitutional social contract under which the government was created by the American people. Americans deserve a government that commits to fulfilling this obligation completely. Our rights, and our liberty, would mean nothing without an institution to protect them.

For more than two centuries, the federal government has accepted this responsibility by fielding a national defense apparatus capable of both defending our sovereign territory and, when needed, carrying out expeditionary actions to secure the nation against external threats. Comprised of the military and various defense, security, and intelligence agencies, the particular characteristics of this apparatus are continuously changing. Its size and strength increase at times and decrease at others. The financial outlays dedicated to its maintenance vary from one budget to the next. The array of enemies against which it is aligned shifts regularly and frequently. Even its stated purpose is adapted as the world evolves.

It is imperative that our nation's political leaders ensure that such changes are singularly directed toward the consistent objective of securing our nation against immediate and future threats. Too often, however, the debate on the appropriate size, strength, and role of our national security apparatus is hamstrung by lingering tempers over previous military actions. But yesterday's perceived strategic failures or military setbacks do not negate the government's responsibility to combat tomorrow's threats. Our political leadership must be able to vigorously debate our future security policy unencumbered by emotional arguments over events of the past. The difficulty of this task is clear; its importance is enormous.

In order to guard against current dangers and prepare for those that might emerge in the future, a critical question must be addressed: what, exactly, should our national security policy aim to secure? Given all that is at stake, the answer to this question must include anything critical to the continued ability of the US to function as a free and open democracy. With this in mind, an effective government, guided by our nation's historical and enduring principles and acting on its responsibility to its citizens, must secure three things: the nation's territory, its people, and its interests.

Regarding the first of these categories, it is without a doubt the federal government's constitutional role to defend against and respond to any hostile infringement upon our territorial sovereignty. This principle serves as the most basic responsibility of our government's national security organization, and it has since the US's earliest days. Though the makeup of this national security organization has changed over time, the principle and the responsibility have not. For most of our history, America's geographic location provided us with natural protective shields. However, the Pacific and Atlantic Oceans are becoming decreasingly effective as barriers to attacks against our homeland. Immense technological progress – and more importantly, the vast proliferation of new technologies – have made us increasingly vulnerable within our own borders. As such, it is incumbent upon the government to take steps toward securing us against an ever-expanding set of threats.

If protection of our homeland comprised the limit of the government's national security obligation, disagreement about when to go to war would dissolve. By pledging to defend everything within and nothing beyond our borders, we would have total clarity in terms of when we should commit our forces to defensive action. Attractive as that possibility might seem, a policy based upon such a premise is simply incapable of producing security for our nation in the contemporary global environment. There was a time when this proposal may have been at least moderately effective, but only because most of what mattered to our nation could be found within its geographic confines. Additionally, as was stated above, we were able to rely on the vast expanses of the oceans as natural safeguards. Unfortunately, both of these conditions have changed. The lives of the world's people and the interests of its nations are growing more interconnected every day. For all of globalization's economic, political, social, and cultural benefits, it brings with it a host of responsibilities that our national security policy must address. To ignore the threats globalization poses to our security would be dangerously naïve.

Understanding the nature of our rapidly changing world, then, is critical to identifying that which – beyond our sovereign territory – the government has an obligation to protect. It is virtually impossible for an attack against our homeland to not also be an attack on the American people. Thus, implied in our government's homeland security responsibility is the duty to also protect the American citizenry within our borders. But what of American citizens in foreign countries? Should Americans abroad have their safety guaranteed by our national security policy? This is a legitimate and important question to ask. In search of an answer, consider the ramifications of a blanket refusal to act to protect our people abroad. Removing the threat of the most serious repercussions would inevitably make them targets of our enemies. The resulting vulnerability would strongly discourage virtually any travel beyond our borders. Such de facto isolationism would only foster an "us vs. them" mentality, making further conflict even more likely.

But by seeking to protect Americans against threats anywhere in the world, we can make an attack against our citizens too costly for our enemies. Our adversaries would risk a military, political, or economic response by the most resource-laden nation in the world. This is not to say that *military* action is required in every situation, but rather that keeping the option on the table is sufficient to send a powerful message to those who would do innocent Americans harm. The United States has a history of acting in accordance with such a policy. During the Boxer Uprising in 1900, we sent troops to the rescue of diplomats and civilians from the US and other nations under siege in China. Nearly a century earlier, a principal justification for declaring war on Britain in 1812 was their practice of forcing American citizens into service in the Royal Navy. The government's obligation to secure our people, at home or abroad, is even more crucial today. Ours is a dangerous world in which many of our enemies do not distinguish soldier from child, considering any American a morally legitimate target. Again, a military response may not be required, but should in all cases be considered a viable and valid option.

Beyond guaranteeing the protection of American territory and people, our government has an additional responsibility with respect to national security: that of securing our national interests throughout the world. In 1778, George Washington wrote that "no nation is to be trusted farther than it is bound by its national interest; and no prudent statesman or politician will venture to depart from it." His reasoning implies that a free citizenry will expect its government to act in accordance with its national interests, and further, that leaders who ignore these interests can and will be rejected by the people. This standard holds true in all areas of the government domain, to include ensuring our security. Put simply, it is a legitimate and critical objective of the federal government to protect from harm those institutions throughout the world which together comprise our national interests.

Discussion on this topic is highly controversial, but it need not be. If we accept the premise upon which America was founded (as embodied in the words of our first president), that the government is obligated to protect our national interests, then any remaining controversy can be attributed to the failure to expressly define our national interests. Those who oppose the application of our national might toward defending American interests abroad choose to portray such an effort as one of a playground bully flexing his muscle to take what he wants, regardless of whether or not the object in question is rightfully his. But a distinction must be drawn between (A) the justifiable goal of *protecting* our nation's legitimate, established interests, and (B) infringing on the sovereignty of other nations or the rights of their people in attempting to *expand* our interests without regard to the valid claims of others. The only way to differentiate between just and unjust applications of military power is to define our national interests. The most basic and most appropriate definition is this: those legitimate institutions or activities, within our borders or beyond, which contribute to our nation's economic prosperity, the sustainment of our democracy, or the continued freedom of our people.

The United States' government has a history of heeding George Washington's advice and acting to secure our national interests. But while it also has a history of at least informally defining such national interests in the terms described above, we as a society have failed to demand that such a definition be expressly and openly articulated. By defining our interests, we can put into perspective the very complicated foreign policy issues which our nation faces, and identify those occasions in which committing our national security resources to action is justified. Doing so will also make clear the government's historical precedent of relying on this definition to determine when to act to secure our national interests. Consider as an example the Barbary Wars of our nation's infant years, the so-called "Banana Wars" prior to World War I, or military action in Panama in the late 1980s. Along with countless others, each of these actions conformed to the application of our military power to protect our nation's prosperity, our democracy, or Americans' continued freedom. It is worthy of note that despite charges of imperialism, none of these led to colonial establishment of any definitional form. Our lack of serious colonial ambition sets us apart from virtually every great power this world has ever seen. This should be considered both a mark of national pride and a testament to the wisdom of defining our national interests in these terms.

Now, to return to a point referenced briefly above: that of the value of making judicious use of all instruments of our national power, beyond pure military clout. When the government accepts the responsibility of protecting American territory, our people, and our national interests, it is not presupposed that military action will inevitably be the best course of action. Certainly, a threat to any of these categories should be viewed as both a necessary and sufficient condition for our government to employ our military might. However, in many instances, diplomacy, economic sanctions, or some other measure may provide the most appropriate means for such protection. Diplomatic efforts ultimately secured the release of Americans held hostage in Iran from 1979-1981. But President Carter was certainly justified in his April 1980 decision to use highly skilled military operatives in a daring but unsuccessful rescue effort. And had the hostages not been released on the day of his inauguration, President Reagan very well may have chosen to undertake a much wider offensive to gain the hostages' freedom. Our very capability to undertake military action has set the conditions for nonmilitary solutions to take shape in numerous crises. Furthermore, when our government takes seriously its national security obligations by expressing unequivocally that our forces will be committed when necessary, such a posture will often prevent such crises from ever developing. By possessing both the power and the will to act, we may avoid many of the dangers which would most assuredly manifest themselves in the absence of our military strength. It is the foremost paradox in international affairs that the greater our efforts in building a strong, capable defense apparatus, the less likely such an apparatus will be forced into use. By taking precautionary measures, we can, in effect, contribute to a more peaceful world. This is the essence of achieving peace through strength.

But what if we detect an imminent threat before it does us harm? The world contains an almost unfathomable number of potential dangers to our national security. As these dangers have expanded, however, so too has our capability to detect them. Our society's advancement has provided us with a set of tools developed for the sole purpose of identifying looming threats to our security. In the event that we receive credible information that America is in danger, it is incumbent on our government to act. Preemption is at times a controversial topic, but unswerving opposition to preemptive action is both irrational and dangerous. If in 1941 credible evidence had made our government aware of Japanese intentions to attack Pearl Harbor, it would have been obligated to do everything within its power to derail the attack. Such an obligation would necessarily include taking preemptive military action. Blind resistance to the idea of preemption would have forced our government to sit idly by and hope that the forewarned assault would not materialize. Opponents who claim it is impossible to know with certainty when a threat is credible do so from an equally irrational perspective. What is the purpose of the myriad agencies whose mission it is to detect such threats, if we refuse to consider the valuable information they provide to our leaders? Ensuring these agencies' ability to discern those truly credible threats requires that they be given adequate resources to develop cutting edge capabilities and retain highly qualified men and women in their service.

Acceptance of the premise that it is the obligation of our government to defend our territory, our people, and our interests leads us to two critical questions. First, what, exactly, is the nature of the current and future threats against which our government must defend? And secondly, what tools are required in order to successfully fulfill these obligations? By answering the first question, we can prepare ourselves to answer the second.

It is clear that we live in an era of uncertainty. The tragic events of September 11th, 2001, render obsolete many of the underlying assumptions upon which discussions of geopolitical relationships are based. Many traditional paradigms of international relations assume that states are the primary actors on the world's stage. But the actions undertaken by religious fundamentalists from a number of countries force us to accept that non-state actors also play a pivotal role. Anybody who has traveled by commercial airline since 9/11 can attest to the effects on Americans' daily lives of transnational terrorist organizations engaging in asymmetric, paramilitary activities. But that fateful Tuesday morning did not signal the beginning of a new era so much as it forced the US to recognize a tactic the use of which had been on a dangerously steep rise over the previous two decades. The number of suicide attacks throughout the world increased from fewer than five instances per year in the 1980s to more than 80 in 2001 alone. The trend has continued to increase at this astronomical rate since 9/11, with 460 suicide attacks in 2005.[1] There are no signs that this frequency will diminish in the near future. The actions of nineteen al Qaida hijackers forced Americans to see what was already occurring throughout much of the rest of the world. As witnesses to evil, we were forced to acknowledge that we were no longer immune to violence and destruction steeped in hatred. Technological advances, combined with increased means of global communication and transportation, have brought the threat into the forefront of American consciousness. Indeed, the spread of such tactics has made our homeland, our people, and our interests as vulnerable as those of the rest of the world's people. And we must acknowledge that we are the most attractive target for terrorists whose fundamentalist beliefs leave no room for compromise. This is an adversary who yearns for America's total annihilation.

Americans have developed a full understanding of the dangers posed by terrorists willing to die in order to do us harm. From the moment our nation felt the vulnerability of victimhood, it was an impossible threat to ignore. But it is incumbent on our leaders to also recognize the evolving nature of the threat. While we have been made keenly aware of the potential damage that can be caused by suicidal operatives, we must also identify the even greater harm that our enemies seek to inflict by adopting new tactics. It is no secret that al Qaida has sought the means to acquire weapons of mass destruction. Our government must continue to develop tools which will thwart their desires. And if they succeed in acquiring such weapons, our security depends on the government's ability to ensure that they can never be used against us.

While threats from terrorist organizations are currently most visible, we must be simultaneously prepared to defend against attacks from an organized military apparatus of an independent nation-state. Focusing only on the most visible danger will inevitably leave us vulnerable. In an increasingly treacherous world, we cannot rely on our ability to adapt to a new threat once it has manifested itself. Today, it is too easy for our society to disregard the possibility of armed conflict against a conventional military as belonging to a bygone era. But let us not forget the long list of previous conflicts which were each judged by contemporaries as the "war to end all wars." These are the players on today's global stage: a China whose internal political stability depends on unsustainable levels of economic growth; a Russia whose actions trend more and more toward those repressive policies of its Soviet past; an Iran with nuclear ambitions; a Pakistan constantly on the brink of defeat from within by radical Islamism; an increasingly bellicose Venezuela whose government foments hatred toward the US in order to hedge its power at home. We must be prepared for any possible events which could lead to a conflict which nobody now wants. The relative likelihood of such events transpiring cannot be known. But the very possibility is supremely indicative of the complex world in which we live, and in which we must be prepared for all contingencies.

While these examples form anything but an exhaustive list of the threats we may face, they do represent the notion that danger may emanate from virtually any source, at any time. We must also recognize that our foes could make use of emerging technologies to cripple our ability to defend ourselves. As a society, we have become critically dependent on information technology. Our government in general has not avoided this dependence, nor has our defense structure in particular. But just as technological developments have increased our capability to conduct military and security operations, they have also led to a massive expansion in the tools which may be used to attack us. It is imperative that our government stay at the forefront of technological development in order to prepare for and respond to any such attack.

The emergence of new technologies has also become a vital element in commerce. Keeping in mind the trends toward greater globalization discussed earlier in this essay, it must be understood that an attack on the information infrastructure upon which most of the world depends would have massive repercussions for populations in countries around the globe. This infrastructure epitomizes our national interest as previously defined. It is indeed a legitimate institution which, as a pillar of global commerce, clearly contributes to our economic prosperity (not to mention the prosperity of nations throughout the world). For centuries, the oceans were considered by the nations of the world as global commons, owned outright by no country, but the use of which could not be restricted to anybody engaging in legitimate activity. Policing actions were the responsibility of all free nations, but the burden fell most heavily on those with the greatest naval resources. The internet and other information networks have become the new global commons. And while all nations play a role in their protection, our vast resources and overwhelming share of responsibility for technological development leave us shouldering the greatest burden. It is in our national security interest to do so.

The discussion to this point illustrates that the world harbors an immeasurable variety of dangers for us. It also demonstrates that the increasing complexity that defines our civilization amplifies these dangers. By recognizing these facts, we can begin to appreciate the level of preparedness necessary to ensure America's security. But above all this, we must also acknowledge that we represent the optimal target for a range of potential foes. The United States sits alone as the most outstanding example of a nation guided by the principle of liberty. We face menacing threats from those who loathe our very adherence to the virtue of freedom, and from those who despise us for the prosperity that this adherence has allowed us to achieve. Our enemies are constantly on the lookout for the slightest vulnerability, and we must recognize that threats may appear seemingly out of nowhere. Armed conflict has throughout history exhibited an unnerving propensity to occur when least expected. Consider that World War I, a bloody conflict which would involve virtually all the world's great powers and would claim 16 million lives, was spawned by a single event: the assassination of Austria's Archduke Francis Ferdinand by a Serbian nationalist. And now consider that our exponentially more complex world is marked by considerably more uncertainty than was the world of 100 years ago. To ignore the possibility of *any* threat is simply not an option. But what resources are required to deter and defend against the uncountable threats we might face tomorrow, next year, or in a generation?

First, the need for a robust military capable of dynamically shifting between high-intensity and low-intensity conflict is paramount. We must continue to maintain ground forces capable of defeating either an insurgent group in an urban environment *or* a conventional army on an open battlefield. Planning to meet one threat at the expense of preparedness for the other is potentially suicidal for our nation, regardless of which appears most likely to emerge in the near future. A symmetric war with another nation-state would also place immense demands on our naval and air forces. As such, we cannot neglect the high-tech strategic capabilities that they provide. Nor can we expect the luxury of time to develop such capabilities on short notice. We must continue to develop cutting edge weapon systems and guarantee superiority in these areas in the event that conventional warfare is thrust upon us at a moment's notice. We must also maintain our nuclear deterrent capability. The existence of our nuclear arsenal prevented America's complete destruction during the Cold War, when we stood toe-to-toe with another nuclear power bent on political and military domination throughout the world. Our deterrent capability protected our own nation and countless others who would have certainly fallen prey to Soviet expansion. We must be able to rely on such a capability to deter similar, future threats.

Secondly, intelligence and espionage agencies must be given the resources they require in order to operate effectively. Our very existence depends on these agencies and their ability to provide forewarning of emerging threats. That they also house both our most sophisticated network warfare capabilities and the greatest concentration of our covert operational resources makes them all the more critical to our national security. The performance of these entities has received much scrutiny at various times in our history, and rightfully so. But it must be pointed out that while their failures are the object of intense publicity, their successes are inherently rarely known by the public. The greatest of attention must be paid to their continued development in order to guarantee the contribution to our security that these agencies are required to make. At the same time, vigorous debate, based on our principles rather than politics, must continue in order to balance our national security interests with the civil liberties of Americans. Our citizenry deserves it.

Finally, we must strive at all costs to maintain our identity. The US was founded as, and remains, a capitalist nation with a republican style of government. Economically, our adherence to free market ideals has spurred the development of a vast pool of resources. At anytime our industrial might may become instrumental in defeating our enemies, as it was in World War II. Politically, our mode of government allows us to demand that our leaders act in accordance with the objective of preserving our national security. Those who don't will be replaced. The world is full of screaming voices which would have us surrender these ideals. But capitulation would inevitably degrade our nation's ability to fight and win the wars necessary for us to continue as a free and prosperous society.

This essay includes an acknowledgement of the many threats we face, as any honest discussion of national security policy must. But it is a discussion borne of optimism for our country's future. Since our nation's founding, the United States' government has overseen our progression from a hopeful newcomer on the world's stage to the most economically prosperous, culturally vibrant beacon of hope civilization has ever seen. This development has been enabled by, and indeed dependent upon, our absolute commitment to our foundational principles. It is incumbent upon our government to act in accordance with these principles and provide for our nation's security. Doing so will allow our society to continue to flourish and achieve the potential that we have only begun to approach. Time and again, our nation has proved resilient in the face of constant and evolving dangers. A government which accepts its responsibility for the security of our nation and undertakes an honest assessment of the likely threats to our society can promise continued resilience, continued success, and continued prosperity. This is the government that America deserves.

John Amble is a graduate student in the War Studies Department at King's College London. In 2008, he served in Baghdad, Iraq as commander of a tactical psychological operations detachment, where he was awarded the Bronze Star Medal for exceptionally meritorious service. He subsequently served as an intelligence officer at the Defense Intelligence Agency. His extensive military training includes resident professional courses at the US Army Intelligence Center and the JFK Special Warfare Center. Prior to his military service, he worked as a financial consultant for a variety of political campaigns in the Midwest. John is a graduate of the University of Minnesota.

XVIII. FREE MEN, FREE TRADE:
Embracing the Virtues of Globalization
by Matt Obenhaus

Perhaps one of the most difficult policies for the average American to support and defend is that of free trade. The trend toward globalization is often seen as a harbinger of the inevitable diluting of our culture, degrading of our national sovereignty, and loss of American jobs. A 2008 Bloomberg poll revealed that fully 50% of Americans believe that free trade harms America while only 26% believe it is good for our country.[1] Opponents of free trade have an arsenal of readily available anecdotes to support their view that globalization is a destructive force, harmful to America. The loss of manufacturing jobs and the perceived outsourcing of jobs by American companies to countries with lower cost labor provide the themes for many of these bromides. Both are widely cited by populist politicians and broadcast on mainstream media channels, and the negative emotional appeals of an unemployed American worker are hard to counter.

In contrast, the benefits of free trade and globalization are more diffused. They subtly benefit the American consumer and result in less obvious ways in increased wealth, variety, and output efficiency.* In addition, Americans have a natural inclination to believe that we can produce most things more superbly than any other nation. Therefore, patriotic Americans naturally question the logic of free trade. In their minds, we can produce everything we need, make it of higher quality, protect American jobs, and keep all of our dollars within our own borders.

This essay recognizes that a commitment to free trade is really the application of the basic principles of individual freedom and liberty to the phenomenon of globalization. Free trade also provides the vehicle through

---

* Any reference to consumers also includes businesses and producers that consume goods as part of their production processes.

251

which individuals and families the world over (Americans included) can reap the benefits of these basic principles. Such an approach to globalization is in fact the most effective and efficient way to maximize wealth and employment while at the same time maintaining America's commitment to individual liberties. The benefits of free trade and globalization will be discussed, with some deference to economic theories. Subsequently, this essay will deal with the issues that concern individuals and commentators most regarding free trade, such as trade deficits and loss of jobs. Lastly, I will discuss the policy implications of a conservative interpretation of issues revolving around free trade and globalization.

What is Free Trade?

In order to facilitate an effective discussion, a definition of free trade is necessary. In essence, free trade means allowing individuals and institutions freedom to enter into contracts for the delivery of goods and provision of services, irrespective of national borders. The crux of this argument rests upon the notion that those who freely enter into contracts do so for their own benefit and utilize their own property to fulfill their contractual obligations. Necessarily, then, a contract between multiple willing entrants is expected to benefit all parties involved, while also affording them the freedom to dispose of their own property as they see fit. Most importantly, an argument for free trade is an argument for individual freedom of choice; simultaneously, it is an argument against centralized governmental control of commerce, a historically typical precursor to totalitarian rule.

Theory of Comparative Advantage

Understanding the theory of comparative advantage is critical to understanding precisely why free trade is beneficial to nations. The theory states that nations should specialize in producing those products that they are relatively good at making, and trade with countries that are good at producing other goods. Each nation is said to have a "comparative advantage" with regard to the goods and services that it is relatively good at producing. Comparative advantages arise due to many factors, including but not limited to: size and education level of a country's labor force, its legal structure, its climate, and its natural resource endowment. However, the true essence of comparative advantage lies in the absolute limits imposed by time. Time is the ultimate limited resource, as there is only so much in which to produce the things that the people of America desire to purchase. If America tried to produce everything, it would not be able to specialize in the things it is relatively good at, and thus it would devote many of its scarcer resources to producing things it could more appropriately allow other countries to produce. These are resources that would have to be shifted away from our comparative advantage industries.

Even if America is believed to be the best at producing everything, called an absolute advantage, it still would make sense for America to specialize in production of those goods in which it holds the largest advantage. Russell Roberts, author of *The Choice,* uses the following example to illustrate this notion: while the CEO might be the best typist in his large company, he still hires a secretary to do the typing, freeing him to focus on making those major decisions to guide the company for which his position and training equip him alone to handle.[2] The same logic applies to countries engaging in international trade. Even though America may have an absolute advantage in producing steel, it may not have a comparative advantage in doing so. Producing steel could take away resources (land, investment, labor) from an industry in which America has an even greater advantage, such as pharmaceutical development and production. Essentially, comparative advantages allow countries to specialize in producing certain goods or services and trade for those in which another country specializes. In this way, each country ends up with more, through trade, than it could ever produce within its own borders, raising production and consumption in all countries.

By eschewing tariffs and other protectionist measures and specializing in its comparative advantage sectors, a country's economy will become much more vibrant, which inevitably leads to greater wealth for the country's entire population. In addition, the vibrant, dynamic economy is one that can constantly reinvent itself as newer, more lucrative industries bring newer and higher paying jobs to the nation. Though this often means shifts in the types of jobs available, it ensures maximum wealth for the economy, and by extension, higher wages for the people. Our country's sustained economic prosperity and high standard of living have resulted from our economy's timely transition from agrarian to industrial, and from industrial to technology-centric and service-based. While the forces which led to these shifts – coined "creative destruction" by the economist Joseph Schumpeter – strike fear in some, they have been essential to our historic economic growth and per capita wealth creation. Protecting these forces by maintaining free markets domestically and embracing free trade internationally allows a nation to shift resources to their most profitable uses. Such a commitment is absolutely necessary for America to maintain its position at the top of the world's economy.

Perhaps an illustration will clarify this theoretical concept. Assume that there are two nations in the world, Texas and California. Initially, they conduct no trade with each other. Imagine a California that has to grow cotton to clothe itself and beef to feed itself. Imagine a Texas that has to grow its own grapes, produce its own movies, and develop its own software. In California's case, land that is excellent for producing grapes and wine would have to be shifted towards producing other food crops to which the climate and soil may not be naturally favorable. In addition, labor would be shifted to produce these goods, at the expense of industries that could have more cost-effectively and efficiently used people's unique talents. If California has to produce everything for itself, it would increasingly rely upon people who do not naturally have skills in certain areas in its production. Actors would bale cotton and software developers would herd cattle. With this in mind, it is not hard to see that all of these theoretical shifts in production would result in fewer resources devoted to California's true comparative advantage industries – technology, entertainment, and wine, to name a few. As a result, wealth and overall output would be drastically reduced from what California could achieve if it traded with Texas.

Now assume that Texas and California agree to trade with each other. Before trading, the resources available within Texas made it able to produce beef relatively less expensively than California. California, in contrast, was able to produce computers relatively less expensively. Once trade opens up between these nations, Texas will have a comparative advantage in producing beef and will begin to export to California. In a similar manner, California will begin to export computers to Texas. In the short run, unemployment will result in the California beef industry and the Texas computer industry. In the long run, however, employment and production go up in the beef industry in Texas and computer industry in California as those resources that were devoted to inefficient production are reallocated to the country's comparative advantage sectors, fueled by both internal demand and demand from the other trading partner. Consumption and output go up in both countries as resources are allocated to more efficient forms of production. All consumers benefit with cheaper, higher quality beef and better, less expensive computers. Equally importantly, employment will go up in comparative advantage industries. The ultimate gain in employment in comparative advantage industries is conveniently left out of free trade opponents' arguments.

This simplistic model serves to illustrate the powerful effects of comparative advantages. Although the United States is much larger and has abundantly more resources than most countries, individual Americans still benefit greatly by focusing on our comparative advantages. For instance, free trade in the clothing industry allows us to import clothing cheaply while the highly skilled American workforce focuses its energy on developing and innovating new technologies across industries – a much more lucrative pursuit for both employers and employees. Meanwhile, the shoemakers and seamstresses making the clothing that we import have jobs that they would not have if we did not allow free trade. And if their government follows free market policies, those domestic industries will grow and form the basis for their own country's economic growth.

Despite America's large size, it remains bound by constraints on land, climate, and human resources. Trade barriers between US states would be seen as unquestionably foolish by sane Americans, as every state cannot efficiently produce everything that its residents need or desire. And yet, many in our country support the building of trade barriers between the US and other nations. Why? The answer can be found in the populist rhetoric employed by political leaders to play on Americans' fears. Though advanced economic theory is unquestionably difficult to understand, a basic comprehension by everyday Americans of such principles as those described above is immensely powerful. Armed with such an understanding, we can demand a stop to the fear-mongering which actually contributes to, rather than mitigates, a deterioration of economic opportunity throughout our nation. Forces of protectionism destroy beneficial trade between countries, which also destroys wealth generating activity not only in our own economy, but in those of our trading partners as well. Who would argue against policies that contribute to a higher quality of life for all Americans, while simultaneously helping to fight poverty and raise standards of living throughout the world?

Although trade may seem like competition between nations, it is more accurately described as a form of international cooperation. It allows countries to specialize, increase output, and trade for those goods that they are not well suited to produce domestically. The belief that international trade is a zero-sum game in which one country's lot is improved at the expense of its trading partner's is simply false. In fact, each country becomes better off by relying upon the unique skills and resources of the other nation. This is one of the basic lessons of economics: when multiple parties freely choose to specialize in production and cooperate, all parties benefit. In international trade, rather than the slices of the pie getting reallocated, specialization and division of labor allow the whole pie to grow.

Many policymakers naively try to implement this logic by utilizing government programs (and our tax dollars) to support or build industries that they believe are (or should be) America's comparative advantage industries. However, the less that the government is involved, the more likely it is that individuals interacting without restriction, within a legal framework, and with access to capital markets will direct capital and resources into comparative advantage industries. This is the purpose of free and functioning capital markets: to take capital from those who freely choose to invest it in order to fund those who have potentially profitable ideas. This is how America's comparative advantage industries were built – from farming to pharmaceuticals, from the automobile to the airplane, and from the personal computer to the mobile computing device. Who knows better when capital should be allocated to an emerging technology: an investor who has studied the proposition in detail and has put his personal fortune on the line, or a bureaucrat whose primary research tool is a public opinion poll and who is committing not his own money, but that of the taxpayer?

Herein lies the powerful convergence between Adam Smith's "invisible hand" and the theory of comparative advantage, a convergence that illustrates the true reason for the ascent of the American economy. The "invisible hand" allows for the development of new technologies and new industries that are more lucrative – for workers and investors alike – than older industries. Then, under the free trade framework, these become America's comparative advantage industries, the economy allocates to them the requisite capital and labor, and our trading partners are able to focus on the industries which we used to dominate. It is this progression that leads to increased standards of living for both our citizenry and those of our trading partners.

Benefits of Free Trade: Consumer Choice

When countries specialize in their comparative advantage industries, the result for each of us is lower prices and more choice. These facts should be obvious to even the most determined free trade opponents. It should also be obvious that when consumers are able to purchase more for less, the result is a higher standard of living. Individuals can spend less of their income as a percentage on meeting their basic needs and therefore have more money left over to spend on luxury items. Indeed, the less money a consumer requires for food and shelter, the more he or she has available for iPods and vacations. When countries engage in free trade, consumers are also exposed to a richer variety of goods.

Perhaps the best example of a global industry that illustrates the benefit of free trade to consumers is the automobile industry. Can anyone plausibly claim that American consumers would be better off today had the US auto industry succeeded in blocking the entry of foreign cars into America? The presence of Japanese and German automobiles in America has added to the choices that American consumers have and has reduced prices for American car buyers. The result has been an ever-growing percentage of Americans that owns and drives a high-quality and safe vehicle, coupled with a dramatic increase in quality and decrease in price of domestically produced cars. By blocking the entry of foreign competition into the US market, the government could have maintained the dominance of America's bloated and non-competitive automakers within our borders. However, such a move would have sacrificed the interests of every domestic automobile consumer to the lethargic dinosaurs that were the American auto companies. It also would have precluded American automakers from making the innovative, technological progress that later led to massive market-share gains internationally.

As detrimental to consumers as a protectionist policy focused on one industry can be, protectionism that targets multiple industries will have the even larger effect of tying up resources in inefficient industries, inevitably reducing consumer choice for Americans and diminishing the appeal of our goods to consumers in international markets. Ultimately, this will lead to a massive increase in the US cost of living and an equally massive reduction in American quality of life. There is no surer way to destroy America's position as the most innovative and dynamic economy in the world than to revert to the tried-and-failed policies of protectionism.

Benefits of Free Trade: Competition

Although competition may not inherently seem to everyone like a benefit, it is directly linked to consumer choice and reduction of prices. Competition drives innovation in business and keeps companies in tune with their customers. After all, companies with few competitors and many buyers have little need to innovate and listen carefully to market trends. They can remain profitable by producing little and charging a price that is high relative to their production costs. Consider the enormous advancement our society has made in recent years in the information and technology fields. Would access to computers and the internet be as widespread in America today if only one company held the means to pursue IT research and development, and if the government refused entrance to the market by foreign firms? Opening up markets to global competition reduces the market power of domestic firms and forces them to innovate in order to compete and survive against many competitors. Innovation is the fundamental driver of economic growth and development. A company that can succeed in a competitive environment is one that succeeds in developing new and better products, services, and ways to run a business.

Returning to the automobile industry, it is no surprise that the American automobile industry fought so diligently against Japanese market entry in the late 1970s and early 1980s. The Japanese were able to offer automobiles of high quality, lower price, and lower weight at a time when fuel prices were a major concern. Where would the American consumer be today had the Japanese not entered the American market? What innovations in car technology would the American car companies have failed to realize if they had not been forced to compete? We might today be driving cars which get only a few miles per gallon, are not equipped with airbags or other safety mechanisms, and don't come standard with power windows and locks, sunroofs, or CD players – all features that we now take for granted in new cars.

Benefits of Free Trade: International Cooperation and Peace

Humanitarians, as well as economists, should be promoting a free trade agenda in America. History has shown that countries that trade heavily with each other are much less likely to engage in warfare, as the nations naturally discover both mutually beneficial similarities and differences. High volumes of traded goods kept the young American nation from going to war with England immediately after the Revolution and mitigated many of the potentially disastrous long-term effects of the War of 1812. More recently, America's trade relationship with China is largely responsible for keeping us out of armed conflict over such thorny issues as Taiwan's pursuit of independence. And the European Union's very existence is based on the premise that further economic integration of Europe's countries will result not only in greater wealth, but also the eradication of warfare on a continent that has a long history of internecine struggles. The most current evidence of this is an attempt to bring formerly communist eastern European nations into the EU fold. Nations that are economically isolated are much more likely to have a natural hostility to the world, as rogue states such as North Korea clearly reveal. In short, societies with interdependent economies pay a high material price if they go to war with each other, making conflict seem even less palatable than it would otherwise be. Moreover, societies that trade together are inherently societies that interact with each other, which allows for a recognition of common humanity between citizens of each country. This is an important step in avoiding war and a truly valuable goal, made attainable in part by the adoption of free trade policies.

Does Free Trade Destroy Jobs?

One of the most common lines of attack on free trade is that it destroys domestic jobs as companies flock to lower cost sources of labor and domestic consumers and producers switch to lower cost goods or labor sources. The counterargument is that reduced trade barriers with foreign countries lead to increased exports and thus to increased jobs in the export sectors of the economy. For America, these export industries present the opportunity for the greatest possible profit and highest possible wages. And as jobs are created within the economies of our trading partners and their standard of living is increased, their demand will increase for goods that they could previously not afford. Americans whose jobs were originally lost will now find opportunities for higher wages in those industries where we have the greatest comparative advantage. Yet, the question remains whether the gains in export related jobs outweigh the loss of import related jobs. Some believe the solution is for government to pursue policies that boost exports while reducing imports. However, the evidence reveals that countries that make unilateral reductions in trade barriers see concomitant growth in both imports *and* exports.[3] The evidence also reveals that there is no statistical correlation between long-term unemployment and free trade.[4] Finally, statistical analysis shows that the long-term US unemployment rate has remained stable or fallen despite a tremendous reduction in trade barriers.[5]

In fact, the historical record actually suggests that free trade *increases* the amount of both manufacturing and service jobs in the United States. According to the National Center for Policy Analysis, between 1989 and 2004, corporations moved jobs to the United States at a much faster rate than they outsourced jobs. There was 82% growth in "insourced jobs" while only 23% increase in outsourced jobs. And manufacturing jobs in America actually doubled during that period.[6]

Even so, opening up a country's economy to the forces of globalization may very well result in some job destruction in the short run, and the most educated proponents of free trade recognize that some reallocation of prices and labor force is a necessary condition to greater domestic economic prosperity. This reallocation entails job and wealth creation in the comparative advantage sectors and job and wealth loss in comparative disadvantage sectors. An opponent of free trade might argue that the downsides to this reallocation will outweigh the benefits. Despite the potential negative reallocation effects, the overwhelming majority of economists still support free trade, based purely on the understanding that ultimately, more American jobs will be created, and higher wages will be paid.

Moreover, the short-term job losses that are the byproduct of globalization are due to workers being displaced from formerly viable industries in which America no longer has a comparative advantage. These workers are often unable to immediately transfer their skill sets to the new, comparative advantage sectors of the economy, leading to short-term unemployment. While this is unfortunate, there are many fixes to the problem that do not require us to forego the benefits of free trade. Chief among these is encouraging the retraining of displaced workers to develop their skill sets within the comparative advantage sectors of the economy. As a result, more workers will find higher paying jobs in industries that are more lucrative for American investors and producers – a true win-win proposition. To claim that displacement of workers from obsolete industries is reason to forgo the wealth-creating benefits of free trade is akin to arguing that an individual's lack of familiarity with computers means that he should continue to conduct all of his correspondence, work, and research with pen and paper. Such an analogy clearly illustrates the absurdity of the idea that we must sacrifice the tremendous benefits of free trade rather than promoting the retraining of displaced workers.

Will free trade agreements with poor countries lead to large increases in unemployment in low wage sectors?

An often utilized argument against free trade agreements is the fact that America will hemorrhage low wage jobs to lower cost producers. This line of attack was deployed against the North American and Central American Free Trade Agreements (NAFTA and CAFTA), among others. Yes, it is true that the average wage in Mexico is well below the average wage in America. When one looks at an hourly wage rate comparison, the low wage paid to a Mexican employee doing similar work can be downright frightening to an American in fear of losing his job.

In the case of NAFTA, the massive job losses never materialized. To be sure, some manufacturers moved operations to Mexican border towns, but NAFTA is also credited with increasing other manufacturing and service jobs as a result of increased demand for US products in Mexico (remember the section on comparative advantages for why this occurred). Why didn't all US manufacturing firms flock to the low-cost towns of Mexico? The reason relates to the measure of productivity. Often, wage standards vary widely between countries precisely because of differences in productivity, or output per hour, between nations' labor forces. Rather than looking at the standard hourly wage rate, a company contemplating moving its production would look at what it gets for that hourly wage.

For example, consider an American firm whose employees get paid $20 per hour, while potential Mexican employees get paid the peso/dollar equivalent of $5 per hour. Now imagine that a typical American worker can produce in 1 hour what it takes the average Mexican 6 hours to produce. Does the company really have an incentive to move its production to Mexico? The answer is obviously no, because the company would have to pay $30 to get from the Mexican employee what it gets for $20 from the American employee. This is the reason that there was no mass exodus of American manufacturing as predicted. Those firms that did shift operations did so to take advantage of actual comparative advantages that Mexico possessed. Meanwhile, many Mexican firms such as CEMEX and Grupo Bimbo expanded their operations and moved some corporate functions into America to take advantage of the highly skilled and educated American workforce for critical and high paying areas such as marketing, finance, and engineering.

Are trade deficits bad for America?

Another common attack against free trade is the fact that it can lead to large trade account imbalances. In current times, this line of attack is most often directed at China, as many feel that their "undervalued" currency harms our domestic producers and allows China to store up large amounts of American cash. This line of reasoning comes from a belief that if free trade is actually fair, countries should trade roughly an equal value of goods and services with one another. However, one must consider the converse of trade deficits, which is the capital account surplus. Whereas the current account measures trade in goods and services, the capital account measures trade in assets, such as bonds, stocks, or real estate. By accounting definition, if a country holds a current account deficit vis-à-vis another country, it must hold an equal amount in a capital account surplus.

To illustrate this concept I will use another two-state example within the United States. In this interstate trade scenario, we know that not all states will trade equally with one another. For example, we can assume that New York imports much of its citrus fruit, and perhaps a great deal of other manufactured goods. Therefore, it may run a trade deficit vis-à-vis other states across the country. Obviously, as one of the financial capitals of the world, one can expect to see the state of New York run a capital account surplus, as many take the money they receive from selling goods and services to the state of New York and invest in financial assets.

The same analogy illustrates what happens globally, where one can expect trade to be unequal between countries based upon trading patterns. The deficits/surpluses arise from a myriad of factors, but can be summarized by viewing the country's comparative advantages and collective preferences. Individuals in many countries collectively prefer current consumption whereas those in other countries may place a higher value on future consumption. These preferences may result from demographic factors, such as the nation's average age. In countries with aging populations, people will generally prefer to save more and thus have more to invest, whereas countries that have relatively young populations will tend to consume more.

Institutional forces are also important, such as uncertainty in future employment, political instability, or the extent to which the government has welfare institutions in place. Individuals living in nations that have a dearth of good investment choices will naturally prefer to invest in countries, such as America, that have superior investment opportunities. Once again this relates to the theory of comparative advantages, in that some countries have a comparative advantage in "producing" future consumption goods such as investment assets, while others hold a comparative advantage in producing current consumption goods, such as manufactured goods. The 2008-2009 financial crisis notwithstanding, America over the last few decades has continued to be a place where foreigners prefer to invest their money as the US is seen as a successful producer of financial assets. With a relatively young population, America has been a country that has preferred to save less and consume more. As a result, America continues to run a trade deficit (it buys more than it sells) and a capital account surplus (it receives more investment money than it gives).

Now to the issue of whether these forces are good or bad. After all, the thought of the Chinese government and its people storing up American cash and assets might seem reason for concern. But it is important to understand the forces involved in this scenario. Essentially, two basic events occur which lead to America's growing trade deficit with other countries such as China. First, American consumers or firms import foreign goods. Rather than foreign firms or individuals purchasing American goods with the money they receive, they choose to save it. Secondly, foreign firms or individuals take the American cash with which we buy their goods and buy American assets.

In the first instance, Americans are getting a great bargain: we're able to purchase tangible goods with paper currency without reciprocating with an offering of goods or services. In the second instance, perhaps people are afraid of what foreigners will do when they own a large percentage of American assets, such as real estate. Will they act collectively to damage the assets and thus harm America? One has to think critically about the incentives of foreign investors and their decisions to purchase American assets. Foreign individuals and firms invest in America because they believe that they will earn a profit from their investment. In some cases, they have invested monumental sums in order to attain ownership of their assets. Why would any rational investor or group of investors deliberately throw away their investment simply to harm Americans? These irrational fears of foreign ownership of assets reveal a lack of understanding of the basic economic principles discussed above. Such fears also ignore the benefits that American firms derive from allowing foreign investors to purchase assets in America. Such an infusion of capital allows for greater innovation and product improvement than would otherwise be possible.

Issues of Free and Fair Trade

Another commonly held belief is that the American government may at times need to level the playing field due to foreign firms' desire to sell below cost in order to enter the American market or to run an American firm or industry out of the market. Let us first deal with the logic of a foreign firm's selling below cost simply to enter the market. Even with lower prices, would a firm be able to sell below cost forever? Surely some American

264

firms would still sell and either make a limited profit or accept temporary losses. Eventually, the foreign firm would have to raise its prices to sell at a profit, resulting in a dissatisfied customer base. If American firms were able to stay in the market or reenter with ease, it is not likely that the foreign firm would be able to recover its initial losses before they again faced competition from American producers. In fact, this policy seems disastrous, and many economists are skeptical that companies ever truly make these decisions, let alone that such decisions would prove successful.

Instead, the "selling below cost" argument is often a tired canard that domestic industries utilize against foreign firms that have developed a true cost advantage. If a foreign firm is selling below a domestic firm's cost of production, the only way it can sustain success is if that price is still above its own cost of production. The result is that the foreign firm can afford to sell profitably at a price below which the domestic firm can sell profitably – a situation that only arises when the foreign firm has a true cost advantage over the domestic firm. It is too bad that government institutions often slap dumping allegations on the foreign firms on the basis that they must be selling at a loss simply because they are selling below the *domestic* firm's production costs. The commonsense question must not often be raised as to why on earth a foreign firm would sell below its own cost. And if that question were raised, the answer would generally be that the foreign firm is in fact *not* selling below its own cost, but rather is profitable by selling at a cost that the domestic firm cannot match. In the final analysis, this is exactly the type of competition that Americans should embrace: competition that forces domestic firms to improve their operations and deliver better, cheaper products to the American consumer. If any other course of action is taken, the end consumers are the ones who lose, as they are forced to pay higher prices for a good they could otherwise get at a lower cost.

However, there are some cases where foreign firms are able to sell at lower prices due to government subsidies, sometimes referred to as export subsidies. These situations may harm firms or industries in the United States, but as a whole, what is the end result of the foreign government's "generosity?" The American people are able to purchase goods more cheaply! Perhaps it would be better to call it an American consumption subsidy rather than an export subsidy. We can see these forces in action within

America, as well. Our agricultural subsidies force American taxpayers to foot the bill for cheaper food products for consumers all over the world.

Conclusion: American Policy Implications

The policy implications of a conservative interpretation of globalization strongly encourage less government involvement in the economy and heightened individual freedom. In order to foster economic growth both within and outside of America, policymakers should focus on reducing US tariffs, quotas, and subsidies, refrain from specious dumping allegations, continue to promote bilateral trade agreements, and work within the framework provided by the World Trade Organization to promote free trade across the globe. The most prosperous nations in the world's history, including America, have achieved such prosperity precisely because they have opened their borders to trade and have benefited from comparative advantages. By promoting free trade, policymakers encourage freedom of choice, economic prosperity, and political stability – not only in America but across the world.

Matt Obenhaus will graduate in 2010 with an MBA from the Tuck School of Business at Dartmouth. Matt spent four years in the United States Army as an Air Defense Artillery officer, achieving the rank of Captain. He received a BS in Agribusiness from Texas A&M University where he was a member of the prestigious Corps of Cadets. Matt is married to the former Rachel Isaacs and has a two-year old daughter, Ellison.

XIX. DISSOLVING COLLECTIVISM:
Taxing, Spending, and the
Rights of Man
by Patrick Wetherille

Recently, the media and many everyday Americans have begun to accept the mistaken notion that conservatism is associated with reckless economic policy. Large increases in federal debt levels, driven by tax cuts and Iraq war spending under President George W. Bush, have tainted an approach to economics that traditionally calls for fiscal restraint, balance, and fairness. No matter what you think of the recent actions taken by the popular strain of the Republican Party, it is important to dissociate those actions from conservative principles, which lay in the philosophy of classical liberalism.

Classical liberalism, not to be confused with contemporary liberalism, is rooted in the writings of John Locke, John Stuart Mill, and others. These men laid the foundation of the future conservative movement by developing a philosophy that recognizes the supremacy of the individual. This philosophy acknowledges the need to protect individual liberties and freedoms from the threat of an excessively powerful government or an oppressive collective. Their beliefs were developed in response to a specific form of tyranny – absolute monarchy – but they are an indictment of any government that seeks to abridge the freedoms of its people. James Madison fought to include a Bill of Rights in the Constitution because he recognized that even in a constitutional republic such as ours, the tyranny of the majority could threaten the natural rights of the individual – those rights and freedoms that God endowed in man.

In creating a federal separation of powers, the Founding Fathers sought to limit government's coercive power. They did this because they understood that tyranny is the natural consequence of the concentration of control in the hands of too few people. While this tyranny could manifest itself in the degradation of rights to free speech or religion, the Founding Fathers were also supremely concerned with the perils of *economic* tyranny. Indeed, stamp and tea taxes imposed without representation served as winds that fanned the flames of our own revolution.

Taxation without representation exploits the fruit of another's labor without his or her consent. Such a system is inherently unjust. The notion that economic reward should be directly related to economic output at the individual level is at the philosophical core of both classical liberalism and our conservatism. We don't believe that people should pay fewer taxes simply because we don't want to part with our own income. Truth be told, we are very happy to contribute to expenditures that are necessary for our government to uphold its fundamental obligations to the American people, such as the preservation of our national security. However, we believe that the government should only engage in coercive taxation to fund those initiatives that contribute to the protection of Americans' rights and that the free market cannot produce on its own.

Defense spending provides an excellent example of an appropriate governmental role. Imagine relying on a private market to provide for national defense. Competing military forces would have incentives to attack each other to eliminate the competition, inevitably violating citizens' rights to life and liberty in the process. Such a system would also fall victim to the classic economic free-rider problem: why pay for defense if your neighbor pays for it and you can enjoy the same protection? A private market for a military authority would inherently devolve into dictatorship and negate the very freedoms that governments are established to protect. This is why we form governments and give them monopolies on the use of force in society – so that a single body, selected by the people, is charged with protecting our unalienable rights. It would be wrong for government to abdicate its responsibility to secure, promote, and defend the individual rights of its free citizens. But on the flipside, it is also morally wrong for the government to exploit the power it exercises on our behalf to seize income for purposes other than those that fall within its proper domain.

Consider, as an example of such flippant exploitation of government's well-defined obligations, the mob museum proposed in 2009 to be built in

Las Vegas. The museum was to be paid for by the 2009 economic stimulus bill that was intended to facilitate our economy's emergence from recession. Thus, the museum would be funded by taxpayers from all fifty states. The question that immediately springs to mind is: why should the federal government pay for something like this? What benefit does an Alaskan hunter, a Nebraskan farmer, or a Georgian lawyer get from his contribution to the museum? None! Moreover, it is clearly an entertainment source that the private market could provide on its own. Assuming sufficient interest existed, an entrepreneur could arrange financing and launch the museum, charging enough for admission to guarantee himself a profit. If the interest is not there, no one would undertake the venture. If an entrepreneur moves forward despite the lack of interest, the museum would fail.

In this way, the fact that the mob museum does not exist in the private market already establishes that it is an inefficient allocation of resources. Because the idea exists yet has been rejected by free market entrepreneurs, we can assume that the financial support of those who benefit from the museum is insufficient to keep it afloat. That government sought to impose it despite the lack of market demand is an abuse of elected officials' sacred charge as the keepers of the public purse.*

Conservatives see the mob museum as wrong because of the dissociation between those who fund it and those who benefit from it. All taxpayers are required to pay for the museum, but only a small subset of Americans will enjoy it. This differs radically from national defense, for instance, in which the entire nation pays and the nation as a whole benefits. This example not only highlights what conservatives believe to be immoral economics, but also shows how such behavior is grossly inefficient. It is human nature to spend someone else's money with more profligacy than your own – if you didn't earn it, but you get to spend it, there's no need to exercise restraint. To avoid this, conservatives support free market principles as a means of ensuring both fairness and efficiency. We subscribe to the capitalist thesis first advanced by Adam Smith, considered the father of modern economics. He argued that free, self-interested individuals, acting in concert through a

---

* The mob museum eventually caught the eye of some watchful Republicans who sponsored an amendment to the stimulus preventing the money to be spent on "wasteful" items like the mob museum. Bowing to public pressure, President Obama and the Democratic leadership approved the measure, but would have gladly passed on that bit of pork to Harry Reid's home state in the absence of conservative protest.

market, will produce the optimal outcome in terms of both resource allocation and societal benefit. Our mob museum example is just one of many throughout history that buttresses Mr. Smith's argument.

In the mob museum example, we see Congress's capacity to allocate resources in ways that strikingly limit their potential. The money tied up in the mob museum could be returned to taxpayers to spend at their discretion. It could pay for food or an electric bill or new clothes. What the money might purchase in private hands is less important than the recognition that whatever the taxpayers would use that money for would give them more satisfaction than they could ever get from being forced to pay for a museum they will never visit.

Have you ever stopped to think about how often you are actually taxed? We are taxed with such frequency that we forget how often the government is making decisions about how *our* income should be spent. When you wake up and brew yourself a pot of Columbian coffee, think about the import tax you paid on the beans. When you get in the car and drive to work, think of the sales tax you paid on your car and the gas tax* you paid the last time you were at the pump. Got a cell phone? You pay a monthly tax on your plan. Property tax is a big one for those who own their home; even after you have moved from an apartment to a house and have paid off your mortgage, you remain a renter for life – and the government is your landlord. Of course we barely even notice the income and payroll taxes we pay. As comedian Chris Rock has pointed out, you do not pay those taxes – they take them; you get your check and the money is gone!

Then there's the last tax you'll ever pay: the death tax. You pay the government for the privilege of dying. Why? Do you cause some inconvenience to society by dying? Do you consume additional public resources you hadn't been using while alive? No! In fact, you're done using such resources – if anything, the government should pay *you* for dying. After all, you're no longer making use of public programs like Medicare and Social Security. You're done using roads or taking advantage of America's

---

* The gas tax is actually an example of how taxes should efficiently link usage and revenue. Gas taxes go to pay for public roads – so the more you drive and add to the wear of highways, the more you pay for their upkeep. The problem is that when it comes to the allocation of highway funds, Congress does a bad job of spending that money. Back-scratching can lead to expenditures like Alaska's famous "bridge to nowhere." When the politician's only incentive is to bring home the pork, the result is wasteful spending that unjustly penalizes the ordinary taxpayer.

expensive national defense. The real reason the government gets away with taxing you in death is that when you're dead, your political voice is conveniently and permanently silenced. Politicians like taxing dead people because dead people can't vote. But they do have money, which is a great way to finance things like a mob museum in Vegas.

This brings us to a discussion of three practical problems with a collectivist approach to economic resource allocation. First, as our population grows, it becomes progressively more difficult for Congress to respond to the individual preferences of the electorate. Secondly, as markets become more and more complex, it is unlikely that politicians in Washington will be able to determine when expenditures are efficient or inefficient uses of funds. Finally, political favoritism and corruption are inevitable in this system. When economic decisions are made for the collective, the average taxpayer is exploited to the benefit of special interest groups.

Over the past two centuries, America has grown dramatically. Our population has exploded and our economy has become far more complex than the Founding Fathers could have imagined. Yet our voice in government has shrunk. Certainly, great strides were made during the late nineteenth and early-to-mid twentieth centuries to enfranchise women and African Americans. However, when Congress capped the number of members of the House of Representatives in 1929 at its current 435, it began a general process of dilution that continues to shrink our individual voices to this day. The Founding Fathers considered accountability and responsiveness to be essential to effective government. In 1790, the average size of a Congressional district was 33,000. Today, the average district is home to over 650,000 citizens.[1] As the size of congressional districts has grown, *our* government has become virtually unaccountable to individual citizens.

At the same time, our economy has become immensely more complex. In 2008, the White House undertook a very public intervention in the automobile manufacturing market. To do so required months of study just to develop a basic grasp of the industry. Consider that the White House's administrative resources are far greater than those available to the average Member of Congress, yet we expect our representatives to make knowledgeable decisions on a massive variety of topics. While shared resources and a division of labor allow individual members and committees in

Congress to specialize on issues, at the end of the day, each House Member has less than a dozen staff to help him or her make decisions that impact over 300 million Americans. Imagine being responsible for making decisions that impact everything from orange growing in Florida, to software development in California, to investment banking in New York.

It took the White House months to prepare a deal for the auto industry with over 1000 members of staff in-house, not to mention hundreds of thousands of support staff sprinkled throughout the various agencies of the President's administration. Now imagine a single Member of Congress with a handful of staffers, only one or two of whom might possess any level of expertise regarding the industry. Can that Member make an informed decision on something like the auto bailout bill? Perhaps he or she could speak to the issue at a broad level. But does that Member understand the intricacies of the plan being considered? Most likely not. Has that Member actually read the bill in its entirety? Most *certainly* not...after all, such bills can be thousands of pages long! Coupling the decrease in responsiveness with the proliferation of issues and economic complexity, there is a real risk that members of Congress will get it wrong. They won't come to the most fair, most efficient, or most desirable outcome. In fact, history has shown they often don't even come close.

The automobile manufacturing intervention is a great example of how the government can do more harm than good. Looking at its financial statements, its investment decisions, or even just its product line, one can easily see that there is something wrong with a company like GM. Is government ownership a solution? Let's take a page from history by looking at another industry to answer that question.

Over the course of the twentieth century, demand for railroad transportation stagnated as travelers gravitated toward aviation and cargo found a new home in semi-trucks. Despite waning demand, Congress sought to save the railroads at the behest of certain constituencies who demanded it. Amtrak, the public/private hybrid, was formed to subsidize the railroads. Unfortunately, railroads have become the most subsidized form of transportation available. It costs taxpayers over $100 per thousand miles traveled by train just to keep those trains running. Compare that to $10 for the same distance traveled by airplane and $4 for buses.[2]

One would think that with government support, Amtrak would at least have good service. Wrong. Without any need to compete, Amtrak has failed to innovate in ways that even come close to our international peers. China, Spain, and France all have trains that top 200 miles per hour. The Acela, our fastest train, is capable of hitting 150 mph, but that fact is irrelevant since it averages only 86.

Now, after considering how the government takeover of Amtrak has cost the American people billions of dollars and has provided us with one of the worst public train systems in the developed world, do you think government should really be in the business of making cars? I think not.

In general, our conservatism embraces fairness by favoring a smaller role for the federal government. That is, we believe that the people benefiting from public expenditures should be the same ones who fund them. Throwing large portions of individually earned income into a gigantic pot that is reallocated and spent by 535 imperfect individuals in Washington – and expecting fair, effective, and efficient outcomes – requires a very large leap of faith. Fundamentally, liberals tend to have this faith while conservatives do not.

There is a lack of trust between many conservatives and their lawmakers. With a continuously diminishing voice at the Congressional district level and the proliferation of special interest groups (a 2005 study found roughly 35,000 registered lobbyists in DC, about 65 lobbyists for every elected official), it is no wonder that ordinary citizens feel disenfranchised.[3] While the mob museum example discussed earlier demonstrates the inefficiencies inherent in collectivism, it also highlights the rampant political favoritism that has become part of DC culture. The idea for a mob museum did not occur in a vacuum. At some point, local Las Vegas politicians began lobbying for federal stimulus money to appease their local constituency. Using that money for the museum would bring jobs and tourist revenue, making local interests very happy.

But is it right? Conservatives would say no – if Las Vegas wants it, Las Vegas should pay for it. Is it efficient? Conservatives would say no – if the private market failed to produce it, the mob museum would be an unprofitable venture in chronic need of public funding as a means of life support. The fact that a small but well-connected minority can co-opt our government into taking from the population at large to fund their whims is categorically unfair. To call this dynamic anything but what it truly is, theft, is disingenuous. To allow it to continue is wrong.

The problem with expenditures like the development of the mob museum is that the constituents who demand it appeal to their representatives by employing a warped definition of the concept of the "common good." In reality, rarely does it exist for this type of project. While there may be some ancillary benefits to the local community or even the nation, the costs borne by the taxpayer far outweigh the publicized upside, which usually consists of a specious argument that it will create jobs and boost the economy. The result is a dynamic in which projects supported by the best "talkers" and lobbyists are funded, instead of those that are the most beneficial and most efficient. When our government accepts that the pursuit of a nebulous common good justifies any and all uses of taxpayer money, it creates an environment where inefficiency and unfairness rule.

In exploring some of the reasons that conservatives prefer smaller, limited government, we have touched on the fundamental ideological differences between collectivism and individualism. Liberals tend to support the former, believing the state and its inhabitants should be viewed in the context of a political community where individuals are innately dependent upon one another. Their logical conclusion is that this mutual dependence, which can be used to justify virtually any state action, extends to economic policy. They argue that the collective, not the individual, makes better decisions about economic policy and the allocation of resources – which are not private, but common. But this concept is fundamentally at odds with an American government that in its founding invoked its individual citizens' natural rights to liberty and the pursuit of happiness. For if people are not free to do what they will with their own property, these very rights are meaningless.

Conservatives reject this collectivist view. While we acknowledge that communities are important,* we believe the individual's rights, decisions,

---

* In fact, conservatives embrace collective action in communities that are free-associations: those groups that you can choose to join or leave, such as religious organizations, political groups, social clubs, etc. However, conservatives are wary of power exerted over others in organizations that are not free-associations; namely one's nation. In nation/state membership, individual rights must be preserved to deter a tyrannical collective majority.

and freedoms are fundamentally more important than the prerogatives of the collective. We extend this reasoning to economic policy through the recognition that the individual almost always can make the best decisions about the use of his or her own income. Acknowledging that certain exceptions are required for the government to effectively carry out its constitutionally enumerated powers, conservatives are very reluctant to extend the role of collectivism in economics beyond that which is absolutely necessary to the functioning of the free market.

Now, what might be an example of such an exception? We already covered national defense. Development and maintenance of roads and public infrastructure provide another illustration of government's appropriate role. However, whenever possible, the private market should be used as a supplier. There's no reason for government factories to build jets when Lockheed Martin does it so well. But, the provision is public – the government justifiably levies taxes to finance defense and infrastructure.

In general, the exceptions should be limited to government provision of those services that allow the private market to work. Not coincidentally, these exceptions generally take the form of governmental protections of the life, liberty, and property of its citizens. Our founders acknowledged these appropriate functions of government in the Declaration of Independence, which highlights them as the singular reason that governments are "instituted among men." An effective national defense apparatus is necessary to preserve life and property from hostile actors outside the state. Private markets need a robust, fair system of laws to enforce property rights within the state and enable contracting between parties, a necessary tool to make markets function efficiently across space and time. Together, these build the foundation of private exchange. They manifest themselves through the branches of the military and through courts, law enforcement, and record-keeping done at a number of levels of government.

There are other exceptions as well. For instance, markets require good information to allow for informed transactions. However, if one party has more information than the other, consumers are exposed to exploitation and possible harm. The Food and Drug Administration is an example of an agency that is, on principle, justified in regulating certain markets. However, it is also possible for the actions of such agencies to be inappropriately influenced by interest groups that push an exploitative or unjust agenda, generally in pursuit of unearned advantages. The FDA is justified in banning a drug because it is unsafe. But if it were to ban a drug in response to political pressure, this would clearly be unjustified. The conservative approach to this dilemma is to inculcate in our public officials a sense of political disinterest and an allegiance to the welfare of all Americans. Those charged with public trust should honor that trust by making decisions that are indifferent to the specific constituencies and that maximize the well-being of ordinary citizens – or be removed. It is as simple as that.

Thus far, the discussion has focused primarily on what is right, rather than what is economically beneficial. Often, differences between conservatism and liberalism are written off as purely ideological. But within the realm of economic policy, liberal collectivism actually results in harmful outcomes that not only violate principles of fairness, but also lead to less efficient resource use for society as a whole.

We saw this in our mob museum example. Another case in point for a conservative, individualist approach to economics lays in America's so-called "entitlement spending" programs. These long-term fiscal obligations have a drastic time lag between taxation and use by individual Americans: you pay now and get your benefits in a few decades. Unfortunately, this method of operating is responsible for America's accumulation of the largest amount of debt the world has ever known; and we, the youth of our nation, will get stuck footing the bill. Current low-ball estimates show that the United States will owe more than $53 trillion over the next 75 years.[4] That's about $550,000 per household, according to former US Comptroller General David Walker. To better understand how we got into this hole, we need to explore entitlements in greater detail.

When you are young, the government takes your money and spends it immediately on those who are old enough to qualify for the benefit. So while the accounting promises to pay you back later, your benefits are entirely dependent on those younger workers who will be paying *your* way.

Looking at a specific case, consider Social Security, America's government-run retirement system. Essentially a pyramid scheme, Social Security promises you income in retirement for taxes paid during your working years. Sounds good, right? Only if you're at the top of the pyramid.

This collectivist approach fails abysmally as soon as population growth declines. As with any pyramid, when the bottom falls out, those at the top get paid and those at the bottom incur losses. That's precisely what has happened with Social Security. When the US experienced exponential population growth in the years immediately following World War II, Social Security was a great deal. Americans paid in a fraction of their actual retirement costs because there were so many more workers paying into the system than retirees drawing from it.

However, as population growth slowed, the deal got worse and worse. Congress had to raise payroll taxes in 1950 to compensate. They did so again in 1954. And again in 1957. Since Social Security's inception, Congress has had to raise the payroll tax 21 times, from its original 2% to its current 12.6%. Social Security was a great deal for the first few recipients. Ida Fuller, the first ever recipient of Social Security, only paid in $22 but received over $22,000 throughout her retirement.[5] However, as the costs have grown and the pyramid's base has shrunk, the average return has fallen. In fact, if you're a young male today, your projected return is actually *negative*.[6] That's right. On average, you would be better off putting that cash in a coffee can and burying it in the backyard for forty years.

Now, if Congress were to actually raise taxes to cover the projected shortfall, you might get a positive return – but the next generation would get an even lower rate of return. Many liberals have called such a tax increase a solution, but it simply passes the buck onto our future children. Remember, Congress has enacted this "solution" 21 times before, yet the crisis remains. At the end of the day, *there is no free lunch!*

Conservatives have a different approach to the problem. They ask why government is in the business of retirement planning in the first place. After all, there is a private market for retirement planning. Some argue that Social Security is necessary because it is "certain," implying that private savings are not. In fact, your Social Security benefits are anything but certain. The Supreme Court ruled in *Fleming v. Nestor* that you have absolutely no ownership over your Social Security payouts, despite your regular payments into the system. Moreover, Congress could easily draft and pass legislation to deny you benefits, as it has done before.*

---

* The 1983 reforms to social security included an increase in the normal retirement age and benefit cuts to those who wanted to retire at the original benchmark.

Some would have us believe that private savings are not enough to cover our expenses if we are lucky enough to live a long life. They argue that Social Security is necessary because it is perpetual; you won't run out of it if you live a long time. Again, in light of the facts discussed in the above paragraph, this statement is incredibly dubious. However, the private market can and does provide such security. For instance, perpetuities are financial devices that allow you to give the bank a sum of money at retirement in return for fixed payments for the duration of your life. Many are surprised by the accuracy with which actuaries can make the predictions necessary to plan for such programs, particularly when compared with the gross miscalculations upon which Social Security seems to have been planned. Congress, it seems, has trouble with even simple math.

Finally, some say that Social Security is necessary because people *won't* save for retirement. Conservatives tend to think that individuals are not this dumb – especially if we don't provide an institutional crutch that allows them to do so at others' expense. However, even if you accept this premise, the government could easily mandate forced savings – but not through a pay-as-you-go Ponzi scheme. Instead, Social Security could be transformed into a system that lets you save at least part of your contributions. By putting some of your money into traditional Social Security and some into a system of accounts, individuals would get better returns and would fund their own retirement rather than relying on future generations to pay for it. Moreover, while pay-as-you-go schemes are simply a way of redistributing existing income, savings help provide the capital needed to fuel economic growth. This approach has been successful in other countries, such as Australia, where a mandated savings component has strengthened the nation's pensions system. It can be done in America as well and it can help stave off some of the 50+ trillion dollars in debt that we are scheduled to accumulate over the coming decades.

While Social Security is a vehicle for retirement planning, it is far from ideal. It forces the redistribution of resources and foregoes the incentives for good behavior that ownership of any sort requires. Moreover, it is incredibly inefficient. There are clearly better ways to funnel resources for retirement planning that utilize government resources appropriately and leverage the power of individuals and of markets. While the moral issue may or may not sway you, the efficiency issue should.

Overall, the conservative approach to economics is one of fairness and efficiency. We believe that certain activities by government are necessary, but when corrupt politicians spend our money to deliver pork projects in return for votes, we object. We object because it is wrong for government to steal from taxpayers to suit the whims of special interests. And we object because such behavior results in a misallocation of resources, making the country as a whole less prosperous.

As a practical framework for avoiding such abuses, we believe that it is critical for costs and benefits to be as tightly linked as possible in the realm of public economics. At the federal level, Congress should only tax and spend on those items that benefit the whole country: defense, interstate roads, etc. At the state level, each state should provide for itself. The county should provide for the county, and the city for the city. Why can't Las Vegas pay for its own mob museum? Shouldn't Alaska pay for its own bridges to nowhere? By linking revenue sources to expenditure beneficiaries, the government will better disaggregate those areas that truly warrant government intervention from those that are rife with cronyism, political corruption, and pork-barrel spending.

While this task is not easy, it is the right approach to government and it is a hallmark of conservative economic philosophy. A recent example of this, the rejection of stimulus funds by a handful of governors, deserves applause. Whatever your opinion of Keynesian economic theory, the stimulus was a hastily written bill, full of politically motivated spending, and a gigantic liability to every taxpaying American, current and future. By rejecting the money, those governors took a principled stand against business as usual in Washington, striking a blow for individuals against the malignancy of collectivism.

Individual economic liberty is the cornerstone on which America, the greatest country in the history of the world, was built. Our past achievements would not have been possible without both the incredible talents of the American people and our incredible systems of political and economic governance, which combined to unleash our full potential. As we continue making our way into the twenty-first century, we must not lose sight of the principles that have made us successful in the past, nor should we succumb to the attractive pitfalls that could lure us down a path to economic stagnation in the future.

Patrick Wetherille is Co-Founder and Chair of Students for Saving Social Security, a non-profit advocacy organization that fights for entitlement reform that is fair to younger generations (www.SecureOurFuture.org). Patrick double majored in Economics and Political Science at Haverford College and studied for a year at the London School of Economics. He has a Master of Public Policy degree from Georgetown University and will graduate with his MBA from Harvard Business School in 2010. Patrick has been featured by the Washington Post, Fox News, CNN. com, and C-SPAN.

REINVENTING THE RIGHT:
The Way Forward
by Robert Wheeler and John Amble

America is not a landmass that was simply smiled upon by Providence and endowed with innate greatness. There is nothing special in the water here that, over the last 200 years, created the single greatest engine of material and social change that the world has ever seen. America is an idea – a set of incredibly special principles that were articulated by our Founders and codified as the supreme law of the land in our country's founding documents. Throughout our history, men and women have fought and died to defend these values against the hostile intent of foreign enemies. Countless millions have endured unfathomable persecution domestically as they challenged America the country to live up to America the ideal. At the heart of the American experiment have been the three values that this book has hopefully made real to you: individual liberty, free market economics, and equality before the law.

These values have served us well over the years. First and foremost, they have effectively defined the scope of government within American society. A government dedicated to the purpose of securing, protecting, and promoting Americans' rights to life, liberty, and property is inherently one that creates the conditions for the values mentioned above to thrive. In fact, the four most enduring institutions within our governmental apparatus were designed to protect the rights that we, as Americans, were promised at our nation's founding: a strong military, an effective police force, a sovereign judiciary, and popular representation in government.

Our country has always fielded a military, unique in history due to its lack of a territorially expansionist mission and the fact that its underlying purpose was not the furthering of colonial ambitions. The military's true purpose has been to safeguard the interests of the American people, most basically by protecting Americans from foreign threats to our life, liberty, and property. Local governments in America have always provided a police force to protect the populace from domestic criminals who would infringe upon the most basic rights of their fellow Americans. More recently, the state and federal governments have stepped up their execution of the domestic policing function in the wake of increasingly complex and dispersed threats to the fundamental rights of Americans. The local, state, and federal court systems' purpose has historically been twofold – the prosecution of criminals and the adjudication of disputes between parties locked in good-faith disagreements. Although the law is often complex and unwieldy, until recently very few disagreed that its purpose is to ensure that Americans do not trample upon each others' rights and that binding agreements can be exercised and adjudicated between consenting parties. Finally, at all levels of government, our elected representatives have been charged to ensure that the military, police force, and court system were up to the challenge of effectively and efficiently executing their missions.

With the government's purpose thus established, ordinary Americans could undertake the task of embracing liberty and utilizing their lives as they saw fit – pursuing happiness in whatever personal form it might take. Some decided that their lives would be dedicated to the building of businesses. In so doing, they built truly magnificent organizations that make discoveries, commercialize innovation, and ensure that Americans have access to the material goods that make life more bearable, even truly enjoyable. America became a global innovation powerhouse – leading the world into a future where technological advances meant more effective medical treatments, more abundant food and water, better and more universal access to clothes and shelter, and a variety of luxuries that were unfathomable just years before. Some Americans chose to dedicate their lives to serving others. Locally and nationally, people banded together into voluntary associations with the means to care for the sick and forgotten, to feed the hungry, and to clothe the naked. We taught the world that a free man's conscience was the most powerful tool to bring to bear in defense of the truly destitute. Still others decided that their lives would be dedicated to ensuring that the individual liberty and equality before the law that America's founding documents embraced truly were unalienable. They fought to ensure that one's gender, race, or class determined neither how that individual was treated by his government nor the protections that his government guaranteed to his rights. America, although it has never achieved perfection in its promises of liberty and equality before the law, continues to move closer to the ideal thanks to the concerted efforts of individual Americans. And all of this occurred in one of the most ethnically, racially, and religiously diverse countries in the planet's history, a remarkable fact in which every American should take pride.

It was the government's respect for its limited mandate that made these achievements possible. A government dedicated to the preservation of free markets inherently stewards over an innovative and prosperous society. A society in which the government's responsibility to secure individual liberties is paramount is one where bigotry can harm no one, unless the government is derelict in its duties. And a government that does those two things offers true equality of opportunity, where free individuals may do what they will with their talents and property, supremely confident that they will be protected from anyone's interfering. There can be no more effective standard of justice.

We, as Americans, must recognize that the strength of our country lies in its adherence to these principles. The conservative philosophy outlined in this book is founded in the robust defense of these ideals, a claim no other movement can make. Our philosophy acknowledges proudly that America truly is an exceptional nation and we must understand the principles that have made it so. An honest assessment of the conservative movement recognizes that it has failed here in the past. When conservatives have come to power, they have been all too eager to utilize the contemporarily accepted powers of government to their advantage rather than question whether these powers were truly legitimate. The behemoth was not reigned in, but simply redirected toward different ends. Conservatism's electoral failure has been the price paid for betraying our nation's core principles.

But while rediscovery of the values of conservative philosophy is necessary, it is by no means sufficient to affect a restoration of our nation's most important and most abiding principles. Even those Americans who have remained steadfastly dedicated to the preservation of individual liberty are guilty of a failure of articulation. The evolution of the values that this book espouses, and for which this country has stood, are quite simply the best thing that ever happened to the world of men. The moral authority behind them as well as their historical impact has been clearly established through the American experiment. Yet the conservative movement today finds itself caricatured as corrupted by special interests, bigoted, and anti-intellectual. Nothing could be further from the truth. Corruption is only possible in a world where coercive force or the threat of it can be arbitrarily brought to bear in favor of one side in its struggle with another. But that is contradictory to the society we seek, in which the government has a monopoly on the use of coercive force and where the government is constitutionally bound not to play favorites. A movement that believes the government should treat all people equally and should protect their unalienable rights equally is also a movement that cannot be described as bigoted. Again, conservatism's detractors find themselves arguing for a contradiction. And how is it possible for our movement to be anti-intellectual when we believe that all people should be able to pursue whatever interests of the mind they have, as long as those interests do not infringe upon the fundamental rights of others? Again, no honest support for this misguided charge can be heard.

Sadly, it is not enough to point to the past and celebrate the unprecedented human progress that has been made because of the American government's embrace of the rights of man. For our conservatism to be a viable movement in the future we must clearly articulate not just how our values have succeeded in the past, but how they offer the best hope for a bright future. We must clearly articulate to all Americans, but to the younger generation in particular, that good intentions are neither sufficient to justify a government program nor a valid defense for trampling on any citizen's rights. Americans under thirty do not remember Carter's administration or the Reagan Revolution. Americans under thirty do not harbor the deep-seated fear of an omnipotent central government that was ingrained in our founders by the British Empire and in countless later generations of Americans by Nazi Germany and the Soviet Union. The future American leaders remember neither the liberation of Auschwitz nor perhaps even the fall of the Berlin Wall. Without the experience of tyranny it is hard to comprehend the enormous privilege of liberty. But the lack of a direct, omnipresent threat to our freedom does not mean that it cannot still be slowly eroded. Indeed, this threat, fueled by unwitting masses, is supremely dangerous precisely because it is obscured by good intentions.

But there is hope. With our generation's situational naiveté also come a respect for reason and a boundless optimism for America's future. It is to these qualities which the principles of our conservatism should appeal. As conservatives, our calling must be to articulate how free men, free markets, and equal justice can solve the greatest problems that our society faces, and how they can do so better than a bureaucracy that reaches beyond its appropriate bounds. We who believe in the supremacy of the individual and the power of liberty must understand our principles, study the issues, and learn our history. Then we must articulate the confluence of the three – recognizing that the most successful values of the past truly are our best hope for the future. We sincerely hope that this book provides an optimistic articulation of a just, prosperous, and happy future rooted in a firm belief in the power of freedom. We stand resolute, steadfast in the recognition that our country, our movement, and our principles deserve nothing less.

ACKNOWLEDGEMENTS

We would like to acknowledge the many people whose assistance and support made this book possible. The authors of all of the essays worked tirelessly on their contributions to *Reinventing the Right*. This extremely intelligent and thoughtful group made the editing process truly a pleasure. We have been honored to work with them.

Two authors in particular were instrumental in getting this project off the ground. Matt Obenhaus and Patrick Wetherille served as members of the initial editorial board, which laid the foundation for the project and created a roadmap toward its completion. Greg Reed also played a major role in the early development of this project, for which we owe him many thanks. Chris Tiedeman went beyond his responsibilities as an author, and the donation of his time, effort, and advice is immensely appreciated.

We must also thank the friends and colleagues who agreed to read multiple drafts of this book at various stages of completion. It was they who provided the honest feedback necessary to achieve the vision that we set out to create.

To our families we extend our deepest thanks. Their love and support gave us the confidence we needed to undertake this ambitious project.

Finally, we thank God for blessing us with the honor of being born in a nation where abundant opportunity has made this book possible.

NOTES

1. Liberty and Justice for All: Judicial Philosophy and Representative Government

1. Collins, B. (2009, July 14). The Supreme Court and the Minnesota smoking ban. *Minnesota Public Radio.* Retrieved September 7, 2009 from http://minnesota.publicradio.org/collections/special/columns/news_cut/archive/2009/07/the_supreme_court_and_the_minn.shtml

2. Sotomayor's resume, record on notable cases. (2009, May 26). *CNN.* Retrieved September 7, 2009 from http://edition.cnn.com/2009/POLITICS/05/26/sotomayor.resume/?iref=hpmostpop

3. Kang, C. (2008, July 30). Court Tells Sprint To Refund Fees for Early Termination. *The Washington Post.* Retrieved September 7, 2009 from http://www.washingtonpost.com/wp-dyn/content/article/2008/07/29/AR2008072901200.html

4. Avila, J. and Francescani, C. (2007, June 13). Tearful Testimony in $54 Million Pants Lawsuit. *ABC News.* Retrieved September 7, 2009 from http://abcnews.go.com/TheLaw/story?id=3269485&page=1

2. Permission to Speak Freely: The First Amendment as the Cornerstone of American Democracy

1. Kovash, B. and Rosenstiel, T. (2001). The Elements of Journalism: What Newspeople Should Know and the Public Should Expect. New York: Three Rivers Press. p. 10

2. Ibid., at 16

3. Pérez-Peña, R. (2008, November 17). Web Sites That Dig for News Rise as Watchdogs. *The New York Times.* Retrieved September 7, 2009 from http://www.nytimes.com/2008/11/18/business/media/18voice.html

4. Goldwater, B. (1960). The Conscience of a Conservative. Princeton: Princeton University Press. p. 3

5. Ibid., at 4

6. Jacobs, J. (2009, June 8). Chine Requires Censorship Software on New PCs. *The New York Times*. Retrieved September 7, 2009 from http://www.nytimes.com/2009/06/09/world/asia/09china.html

7. Kennedy, R.F., Jr. (2007). Afterword. In B. Goldwater, The Conscience of a Conservative. Princeton University Press. pp. 123-4

3. Disarmed is Dangerous: A Fresh Take on the Second Amendment

1. National Center for Injury Prevention and Control. (2009). WISQARS Injury Mortality Reports, 1999-2006. Retrieved August 27, 2009 from http://webappa.cdc.gov/sasweb/ncipc/mortrate10_sy.html

2. Malcolm, J. L. (2002, November). Gun Control's Twisted Outcome. *Reason Magazine*. Retrieved August 27, 2009 from http://www.reason.com/news/show/28582.html

3. Slack, J. (2009, July 3). The most violent country in Europe: Britain is also worse than South Africa and U.S. *Mail Online*. Retrieved September 9, 2009 from http://www.dailymail.co.uk/news/article-1196941/The-violent-country-Europe-Britain-worse-South-Africa-U-S.html

4. Blair Holt's Firearm Licensing and Record of Sale Act of 2009. H.R.45. 111th United States Congress. 1st Session. (2009).

5. Centers for Disease Control and Prevention. (2003, October 3). First Reports Evaluating the Effectiveness of Strategies for Preventing Violence: Firearms Laws. Retrieved August 27, 2009 from http://www.cdc.gov/mmwr/ preview/mmwrhtml/rr5214a2.htm

6. Extending a Hand: Strengthening Volunteerism in America

1. Demint, J. (2009, March 30). Discussion of Flaws in National Service Act in Congressional Record, Remarks from Senator Jim Demint (R-SC).

2. Matt, G.E, and Cook, T.D. (1993). The War on Fraud and Error in the Food Stamp Program. *Evaluation Review,* 17(1). pp. 4-26

3. Correa, V., Rossman, S., and Burke-Storer, M.R. The Public Housing Safety Initiative (PHSI): Strategic Crime Reduction and Prevention. Paper presented at the annual meeting of the American Society of Criminology (ASC). Retrieved September 3, 2009 from http://www.allacademic.com/meta/p126300_index.html

4. Riedl, B.M. (2005, April 4). Top 10 Examples of Government Waste. Retrieved September 3, 2009 from the Heritage Foundation website: http://www. heritage.org/research/budget/bg1840.cfm

5. The Brookings Institution. (2002). The Costs of the Manhattan Project. Retrieved September 2, 2009 from http://www.brookings.edu/projects/archive/ nucweapons/manhattan.aspx

6. Burke, K. (2009, January 7). Data Set of the Day: Who is More Generous? Republicans or Democrats? Message posted to http://blog.fortiusone. com/2009/01/07/dataset-of-the-day-who-is-more-generous-republicans-or-democrats/

7. Murtaught, D., Bridges, V., and Busby, G. (2005, September 21). In Wake of Katrina, Church Agencies Out-Quicked Government, Secular Groups. Religion News Service. Retrieved September 3, 2009 from Worldwide Faith News archives website: http://www.wfn.org/2005/09/msg00256.html

8. Bentley College and City Year Launch New Model for National Service. (2008, October 21). New England Cable News. Retrieved September 3, 2009 from http://www.necn.com/category/89/20021

7. True Multiculturalism: Shattering the Walls That Divide Americans

1. Miller, J. R. (2009, June 23). Kansas Teacher with Conservative Views Gets Job Back. Fox News. Retrieved August 28, 2009 from http://www.foxnews. com/story/0,2933,528484,00.html

2. Grant, A. (2002, May 22). Ventura Vetoes Pledge of Allegiance Requirement. Minnesota Public Radio. Retrieved August 28, 2009 from http://news.minnesota.publicradio.org/collections/session2002/ap_pledge.shtml

3. Temple-Raston, D. (2009, March 11). FBI Sheds Light on Missing Somali-Americans. National Public Radio. Retrieved August 28, 2009 from http://www.npr.org/templates/story/story.php?storyId=101808484

4. Public Agenda. (1998, November 23). Being an American is a Privilege, Say White, African American, Hispanic, and Foreign-born Parents [Press

Release]. Retrieved August 28, 2009 from http://www.publicagenda.org/ press-releases/being-american-privilege-say-white-african-american-hispanic-and-foreign-born-parents

5. Steinberg, J. (2003, June 24). The Supreme Court: University Admissions; An Admissions Guide. *The New York Times.* Retrieved August 28, 2009 from http://www.nytimes.com/2003/06/24/us/the-supreme-court-university-admissions-an-admissions-guide.html

6. Holmes, S. A. (1999, September 30). Fannie Mae Eases Credit to Aid Mortgage Lending. *The New York Times.* Retrieved August 28, 2009 from http://www.nytimes.com/1999/09/30/business/fannie-mae-eases-credit-to-aid-mortgage-lending.html

7. U.S. Census Bureau. (2000). Census 2000 Demographic Profile Highlights: Selected Population Group: Japanese Alone [Fact Sheet]. Retrieved August 28, 2009 from http://factfinder.census.gov/servlet/ SAFFIteratedFacts?_event=&geo_id=01000US&_geoContext=01000US&_street=&_county=&_cityTown=&_state=&_zip=&_lang=en&_sse=on&ActiveGeoDiv=&_useEV=&pctxt=fph&pgsl=010&_submenuId=factsheet_2&ds_name=DEC_2000_SAFF&_ci_nbr=022&qr_name=DEC_2000_SAFF_R1010&reg=DEC_2000_SAFF_R1010:022&_keyword=&_industry=

8. Voices of the Damned: A Rights-Based Analysis of Abortion in America

1. Jones, R.K., Zolna, M.R.S., Henshaw, S.K., and Finer, L.B. (2008). Abortion in the United States: Incidence and Access to Services, 2005. *Perspectives on Sexual and Reproductive Health,* 40(1). pp. 6–16. Retrieved from http://www.guttmacher.org/pubs/journals/4000608.pdf

2. Bankole, A., Singh, S., and Haas, T. (1998). Reasons Women Have Induced Abortions: Evidence from 27 Countries. *International Family Planning Perspectives,* 24(3). pp. 117-127 & 152. Retrieved from http:// www.guttmacher.org/pubs/journals/2411798.pdf

3. Finer, L.B., Frohwirth, L.F., Dauphinee, L.A., Singh, S., and Moore, A.M. (2005). Reasons U.S. Women Have Abortions: Quantitative and Qualitative Perspectives. *Perspectives on Sexual and Reproductive Health,* 37(3). pp. 110-118. Retrieved from http://www.guttmacher.org/pubs/psrh/full/3711005.pdf

4. Ibid.

NOTES

9. Liberty and Stewardship: Going Green the American Way

1. Fagan, B. (2002). The Little Ice: How Climate Made History, 1300-1850. New York: Basic Books. pp. 96-97

2. Crichton, M. (2004, March 1). Environmentalism as Religion Run Amok. *USA Today* (magazine), 132(2706). p. 22

3. Bender, F. On the Importance of Paul Shepherd's Call for Post-Historic Primitivism and Paleolithic Counter-Revolution against Modernity. *The Trumpeter*, 23(3). pp. 14-15

4. Ehrlich, A.H., Ehrlich, P.R., and Holdren, J.P. (1977). Ecoscience: Population, Resources, Environment. San Francisco: W.H. Freeman. pp. 786-788 & 837-838

5. Gray, H.F. (1940, September). Sewerage in Ancient and Mediaeval Times. *Sewage Works Journal*, 12(5). pp. 939-942. Retrieved from http://sewerhistory. org/articles/whregion/1940_as201/article1.pdf

6. Keller, K., Young, E., and Kronk, G. Cahokia Mounds State Historic Site. Retrieved September 8, 2009 from http://www.cahokiamounds.com/learn/

7. Seppa, N. (1997, March 12). Metropolitan Life on the Mississippi. *The Washington Post*. Retrieved September 8, 2009 from http://www.washingtonpost. com/wp-srv/national/daily/march/12/cahokia.htm

8. Federal Water Pollution Control Amendments of 1972§ 33 U.S.C. § 1251 (2008). Retrieved from http://straylight.law.cornell.edu/uscode/html/uscode33/ usc_sec_33_00001251_000-.html

9. Ohio History Central. (2005, July 1). Cuyahoga River Fire. Retrieved September 9, 2008 from http:// www.ohiohistorycentral.org/entry.php?rec=1642

10. Environmental Protection Agency Office of Water. (2009, January). National Water Quality Inventory: Report to Congress. Retrieved from http:// www.epa.gov/owow/305b/2004report/2004_305Breport.pdf

11. *Rapanos v. United States*, 547 U.S. 715 (2006). Scalia, J., Opinion. Retrieved September 9, 2009 from http://www.law.cornell.edu/supct/html/04-1034. ZO.html

12. Borsos, E., Makra, L., Beczi, R., Vitanyi, B. and Szentpeteri, M. (2003) Anthropogenic Air Pollution in Ancient Times. Acta Climatologica et Chorologica Tom. pp. 5-15

293

13. Hong, S., Candelone, J.P., Patterson, C.C., and Boutron, C.F. (1994, September 23). Greenland ice evidence of hemispheric lead pollution two millennia ago by Greek and Roman civilizations. *Science*, 265(5180). pp. 1841-1843

14. Environmental Protection Agency. (2009, May 21). Air Quality Summary Through 2005. Retrieved September 8, 2009 from http://www.epa.gov/airtrends/2006/aq_summary_2005.html

15. Ottaway, D.B., and Stephens, J. (2003, May 4). Nonprofit Land Bank Amasses Billions. *The Washington Post*. Retrieved September 8, 2009 from http://www.washingtonpost.com/wp-dyn/content/article/2007/06/26/ AR2007062600803.html

16.. Lubowski, R.N., Vesterby, M., Bucholtz, S., Baez, A., and Roberts, M.J. (2006, May 31). Major Uses of Land in the United States, 2002. U.S. Department of Agriculture. Retrieved September 9, 2009 from http:// www.ers.usda.gov/Publications/EIB14

17. Dahl-Jensen, D. et al. (1998, October 9). Past temperature directly from the Greenland Ice Sheet. *Science*, 282(5387). pp. 268-271

18. McIntyre, S., and McKitrick, R. (2003). Corrections to the Mann et.al. (1998) Proxy Data Base and Northern Hemispheric Average Temperature Series. In *Energy & Environment*, 14(6). pp. 751-771. Retrieved September 9, 2009 from http://www.climateaudit.org/pdf/mcintyre.mckitrick.2003.pdf

19. Carter, R.M., De Freitas, C.R., Goklany, I.M., Holland, D., and Lindzen, R.S. (2006, October-December). The Stern Review: A Dual Critique, Part 1: The Science. *World Economics*, 7(4). Retrieved September 8, 2009 from http://members.iinet.net.au/~glrmc/World%20Economics%20-%20Stern%20Review,%20Part%201.pdf

20. Nova, J. (2009, July 21). Climate Money. Science & Public Policy Institute. Retrieved September 8, 2009 from http://scienceandpublicpolicy.org/images/stories/papers/originals/climate_money.pdf

10. Powering America: Enduring Solutions to the Energy Problem

1. Institute for Energy Research. (2009). Petroleum (Oil). Retrieved September 2, 2009 from http:// www.instituteforenergyresearch.org/energy-overview/petroleum-oil/

2. Goldstein, M. and Rascoe, A. (2009, May 27). Global Energy Demand Seen Up 44 Percent by 2030. *Reuters*. Retrieved September 2, 2009 from http://www.reuters.com/article/GCA-GreenBusiness/ idUSN2719528620090527

NOTES

3. Buer, M.C. (1926). Health, Wealth, and Population in the Early Days of the Industrial Revolution. London: George Routledge & Sons. p. 30

4. Jefferies, J. (2005). The U.K. Population: Past, Present, and Future. Focus on People and Migration: 2005. Retrieved September 2, 2009 from U.K. Government Statistics website: http://www.statistics.gov.uk/downloads/ theme_compendia/fom2005/01_FOPM_Population.pdf

5. Crafts, N.F.R., and Mills, T.C. (1994). Trends in Real Wages in Britain, 1750-1913. *Explorations in Economic History,* 31(2). p. 176

6. As Gas Goes Up, Driving Goes Down. (2008, May 27). *CNN.* Retrieved September 2, 2009 from http:// www.cnn.com/2008/US/05/26/gas.driving/index.html

7. Ibid.

8. Valdez-Dapena, P. (2006, March 18). Toyota Tops Hottest Cars in America. *CNN.* Retrieved September 2, 2009 from http://money.cnn.com/2006/03/16/Autos/hot_cars/index.htm

9. Strassel, K.A. (2009, June 26). The Climate Change Climate Change. *The Wall Street Journal.* p. A13

10. Energy Information Administration. (2004, December). Trends in U.S. Carbon Intensity and Total Greenhouse Gas Intensity. Department of Energy. Retrieved September 2, 2009 from http://www.eia.doe.gov/oiaf/ 1605/archive/gg04rpt/trends.html

11. Institute for Energy Research. (2009). Nuclear. Retrieved September 2, 2009 from http:// www.instituteforenergyresearch.org/energy-overview/nuclear/

12. Institute for Energy Research. (2009). Coal. Retrieved September 2, 2009 from http:// www.instituteforenergyresearch.org/energy-overview/coal/

13. Nuclear Energy Institute. (2009). Plant Security. Retrieved September 2, 2009 from http://www.nei.org/ keyissues/safetyandsecurity/plantsecurity/

14. Ibid.

15. Yucca Mountain Nuclear Waste Repository. (n.d). Retrieved September 2, 2009 from Wikipedia: http:// en.wikipedia.org/wiki/Yucca_Mountain_nuclear_waste_repository

16. Nuclear Energy Institute. (2009). Repository Development. Retrieved September 2, 2009 from http:// www.nei.org/keyissues/nuclearwastedisposal/yuccamountain/

17. The Brookings Institution. (2002). The Costs of the Manhattan Project. Retrieved September 2, 2009 from http://www.brookings.edu/projects/archive/nucweapons/manhattan.aspx

18. Apollo Program. (n.d.). Retrieved September 2, 2009 from Wikipedia: http://en.wikipedia.org/wiki/ Apollo_program

19. Will, G. (2008, August 28). The Devils in His Details. *Real Clear Politics*. Retrieved September 2, 2009 from http://www.realclearpolitics.com/ articles/2008/08/obama_should_address_russian_a.html

20. The Tax Foundation. (n.d.). Gasoline Taxes, Tolls, and Transportation Charges. Retrieved September 3, 2009 from http://www.taxfoundation.org/ research/topic/124.html

21. Energy Information Administration. (n.d.). Gasoline – A Petroleum Product. Department of Energy. Retrieved September 3, 2009 from http:// www.eia.doe.gov/kids/energyfacts/sources/non-renewable/gasoline.html

11. Live Free or Die: Principles for a 21ˢᵗ Century Healthcare System

1. Tocqueville, A.D. Democracy in America. Retrieved September 2, 2009 from http://xroads.virginia.edu/ ~HYPER/detoc/ch4_06.htm

2. Ibid.

3. Marmot, M., and Wilkinson, R.G. (2006). Social Determinants of Health, Second Edition. Oxford: Oxford University Press.

4. Executive Office of the President Council of Economic Advisers. (2009, June). The Economic Case for Health Care Reform. Retrieved September 2, 2009 from the White House website: http://www.whitehouse.gov/ assets/documents/ CEA_Health_Care_Report.pdf

5. Obama, B.H. (2009, June 15). Obama Addresses Physicians at AMA Meeting: Transcript of President Obama's Remarks. Retrieved September 2, 2009, from American Medical Association website: http://www.ama-assn.org/ ama/pub/about-ama/our-people/house-delegates/2009-annual-meeting/speeches/ president-obama-speech. shtml

6. Cohen, J.T, Neumann, P.J., and Weinstein, M.C. (2008, February 14). Does Preventative Care Save Money? Health Economics and the Presidential Candidates. *New England Journal of Medicine,* 358(7). Retrieved September 2, 2009 from http://content.nejm.org/cgi/reprint/358/7/661.pdf

7. Tapper, J. (2009, August 9). Congressional Budget Expert Says Preventative Care Will Raise – Not Cut – Costs. Message posted to: http://blogs.abcnews.

com/politicalpunch/2009/08/congressional-budget-expert-says-preventive-care-will-raise-not-cut-costs.html

8. Elmendorf, D.W. (2009, June 15). Letter to Senator Edward M. Kennedy. Congressional Budget Office. Retrieved September 2, 2009 from http://www.cbo.gov/ftpdocs/103xx/doc10310/06-15-HealthChoicesAct.pdf

9. Of NICE and Men. (2009, July 7). *The Wall Street Journal.* p. A14

10. McCaughy, B. (2009, February 9). Ruin Your Health With the Obama Stimulus Plan. *Bloomberg.* Retrieved September 3, 2009 from http://www.bloomberg.com/apps/news?pid=20601039&sid=aLzfDxfbwhzs

11. Obama, B.H. (2009, July 1). Remarks From the President in an Online Town Hall on Health Care. Retrieved September 3, 2009, from The White House website: http://www.whitehouse.gov/the_press_office/ Remarks-of-the-President-in-an-Online-Town-Hall-on-Health-Care-Reform/

12. Crisis States Research Centre. (n.d.) Table 2: Medical Patents Granted by USPTO, 1996-2000. London School of Economics and Political Science. Retrieved September 3, 2009 from http://www.crisisstates.com/ download/others/shadlen(table2).pdf

13. Gazella, K. (2005, June 1). High Cost of Malpractice Insurance Threatens Supply of OB/GYNs, Especially in Some Urban Areas. Retrieved September 3, 2009 from University of Michigan Health System website: http:// www.med.umich.edu/opm/newspage/2005/obgyn.htm

14. Burd, S.A. (2009, June 12). How Safeway is Cutting Health-Care Costs. *The Wall Street Journal.* p. A15

12. Freedom to Choose: Reestablishing Excellence in American Education

1. McKinsey and Company. (2009, April). The Economic Impact of the Achievement Gap in America's Schools. Retrieved September 1, 2009 from http:// www.mckinsey.com/App_Media/Images/Page_Images/Offices/ SocialSector/PDF/achievement_gap_report.pdf

2. Gootman, E. (2008, March 7). At Charter School, Higher Teacher Pay. *The New York Times.* Retrieved September 1, 2009 from http://www.nytimes.com/2008/03/07/nyregion/07charter.html

3. Christensen, C.M., and Horn, M.B. (2009, June 2). Commentary: Don't prop up failing schools. *CNN.* Retrieved September 1, 2009 from http:// www.cnn.com/2009/US/06/02/christensen.schools/index.html

4. EDITORIAL: Per-pupil spending in D.C. (2008, June 25). *The Washington Times*. Retrieved September 1, 2009 from http://www.washingtontimes.com/news/2008/jun/25/per-pupil-spending-in-dc/

5. McKinsey and Company. (2009, April). The Economic Impact of the Achievement Gap in America's Schools. Retrieved September 1, 2009 from http://www.mckinsey.com/App_Media/Images/Page_Images/Offices/ SocialSector/PDF/achievement_gap_report.pdf

6. Calefati, J. (2008, November 28). Giving Students Cash for Grades. *U.S. News & World Report*. Retrieved September 1, 2009 from http://www.usnews.com/articles/education/2008/11/28/giving-students-cash-for-grades. html

13. Serve and Protect: A Federalist Approach to Police and Crime Policy

1. Burnett, H. S. (2000). Texas Concealed Handgun Carriers: Law-abiding Public Benefactors. National Center for Policy Analysis. Retrieved August 27, 2009 from http://ncpa.org/pub/ba324

2. Facts About Concealed Carrying of Weapons (CCW). Illinois Campaign to Prevent Gun Violence. Retrieved August 27, 2009 from http://www.icpgv.org/ccw.html

3. USMS Office of Public Affairs. (2006) More than 1,100 Sex Offender Arrests by U.S. Marshals' "Operation Falcon II": Among 9,037 Fugitives Apprehended in Nationwide Operation. United States Department of Justice. Retrieved August 27, 2009 from http://www.usmarshals.gov/falcon2/news_releases/national_news_release. htm

14. Yes, Unless: A Just Approach to Immigration

1. Hoefer, M., Rytina, N., and Baker, B.C. (2009). Estimates of the Unauthorized Immigrant Population Residing in the United States: January 2008. US Department of Homeland Security Office of Immigration Statistics Population Estimate. Retrieved September 9, 2009 from http://www.dhs.gov/xlibrary/assets/statistics/publications/ ois_ill_pe_2008.pdf

15. Navigating the Shoals: Building a Conservative Foreign Policy Worldview

1. Tanenhaus, S. (2009, February 18). Conservatism is Dead: An intellectual autopsy of the movement. *The New Republic*. Retrieved September 9, 2009 from http://www.tnr.com/article/politics/conservatism-dead

2. Nash, G. (1976). The Conservative Intellectual Movement in America Since 1945. New York: Basic Books. p. 127

3. Tanenhaus, S. (2009, February 18). Conservatism is Dead: An intellectual autopsy of the movement. *The New Republic*. Retrieved September 9, 2009 from http://www.tnr.com/article/politics/conservatism-dead

4. Kirk, R. (1993). The Politics of Prudence. Wilmington, DE: ISI Books. p. 20

5. Feulner, E. (1996, January 25). Remember the Victims of Communism. Retrieved August 31, 2009 from the Heritage Foundation website: http://www.heritage.org/Press/Commentary/ED012696b.cfm

6. Brooks, D. (2009, February 23). The Big Test. *The New York Times*. Retrieved September 2, 2009 from http://www.nytimes.com/2009/02/24/opinion/24brooks.html

7. Burnett, B. (2006, August 15). A New Liberal Foreign Policy. Message posted at The Huffington Post website: http://www.huffingtonpost.com/bob-burnett/a-new-liberal-foreign-pol_b_27292.html

8. Berger, S. (2004, May/June). Foreign Policy for a Democratic President. *Foreign Affairs*. Retrieved May 1, 2009 from http://www.foreignaffairs.com/print/59892?page=7.

9. Mandelbaum, M. (2005). The Case for Goliath. New York: Perseus Book Group. p. 68

10. Said, E.W. (2001, October 4). The Clash of Ignorance. *The Nation*. Retrieved September 2, 2009 from http://www.thenation.com/doc/20011022/said

11. Kaplan, R.D. (2001, December). Looking the World in the Eye. *The Atlantic*. Retrieved September 2, 2009 from http://www.theatlantic.com/doc/200112/kaplan

12. Mandelbaum, M. (2005). The Case for Goliath. New York: Perseus Book Group. p. 82

13. Reagan, R. (1990). An American Life. New York: Pocket Books. p. 437

14. Kissinger, H. (1994). Diplomacy. New York: Touchstone. pp. 20-21

15. Ibid., at 834

16. Scheuer, M. (2008). Marching Towards Hell: America and Islam After Iraq. New York: Free Press. pp. 172-174

17. Carafano, J., and Spalding, M. (2007, June 12). A New Strategy for Real Immigration Reform. Retrieved September 2, 2009 from the Heritage Foundation website: http://www.heritage.org/Research/Immigration/wm1499. cfm

18. Riedl, B.M., and Frasier, A.A. (2009, January 13). How to Reform Entitlement Spending: A Memo to president-elect Obama. Retrieved September 2, 2009 from the Heritage Foundation website: http:// www.heritage.org/Research/Budget/sr0043.cfm.

19. Wight, M. (1978). Power Politics. New York: Holmes & Meier. p. 294

16. Reclaiming our Foreign Policy: International Organizations and American Sovereignty

1. World Vision International 2008 Review: Hope for the Most Vunerable [online]. (2008). Retrieved August 28, 2009 from World Vision International: http://www.wvi.org/wvi/wviweb.nsf/C5C75B86935DAAA888257589

00751799/$file/WVI_2008_Annual_Review.pdf. p. 19

2. Senate Report 105-235. (1998). Retrieved August 28, 2009 from THOMAS database

3. Blair, D. (2006, September 2). Sudan Gets Set for Offensive in Darfur Region. *The Irish Independent*. Retrieved September 9, 2009 from http://www.independent.ie/world-news/africa/sudan-gets-set-for-offensive-in-darfur-region-76401.html

4. United Nations Secretariat. (2008, December 24). Assessment of Member States' contributions to the United Nations regular budget for the year 2009. p. 7

5. Ibid.

6. United Nations Secretariat. (2006, December 27). Implementation of General Assembly resolutions 55/235 and 55/236

7. Military spending estimates by nation are available in The World Factbook [online]. Retrieved August 28, 2009, from U.S. Central Intelligence Agency website: https://www.cia.gov/library/publications/the-world-factbook/

8. Fergusson, Ian F. (2007, May 9). The World Trade Organization: Background and Issues. Congressional Research Service. p. 2

NOTES

17. This We Will Defend

1. Atran, S. (2006). The Moral Logic and Growth of Suicide Terrorism. TheWashington Quarterly. Retrieved June 4, 2009, from http://www.twq.com/06spring/docs/06spring_atran.pdf

18. Free Men, Free Trade: Embracing the Virtues of Globalization

1. Los Angeles Times/Bloomberg Poll. (2008, May 1-8). Retrieved September 1, 2009 from http:// www.pollingreport.com/trade.htm
2. Roberts, R. (2006, October 8). The Choice: A Fable of Free Trade and Protectionism (3rd Edition). New Jersey: Prentice Hall.
3. Krol, R. (2008, September 16). Trade, Protectionism, and The U.S. Economy: Examining the Evidence. Retrieved September 1, 2009 from http://www.freetrade.org/pubs/briefs/tbp-028.pdf
4. Ibid.
5. Ibid.
6. Bartlett, B. (2004, July 27). Brief Analysis #480: How Outsourcing Creates Jobs for Americans. National Center for Policy Analysis. Retrieved September 1, 2009 from http://www.ncpa.org/pub/ba480

19. Dissolving Collectivism: Taxing, Spending, and the Rights of Man

1. Thirty-thousand.org. (2005, May 30). The Size of the US House of Representatives and its Constituent State Delegations. Retrieved September 9, 2009 from http://www.thirty-thousand.org/documents/QHA-02.pdf
2. Research and Innovative Technology Administration, Bureau of Transportation Statistics. (2004, December). Federal Subsidies to Passenger Transportation. Retrieved September 9, 2009 from http://www.bts.gov/publications/federal_subsidies_to_passenger_transportation/
3. Reynolds, P. (2006, January 4). The Hum You Hear is from Lobbyists. *BBC*. Retrieved September 9, 2009 from http://news.bbc.co.uk/2/hi/americas/4581298.stm

4. Walker, D. (2008, October 7). Commentary: America's $53 Trillion Debt Problem. *CNN*. Retrieved September 9, 2009 from http://www.cnn.com/2008/POLITICS/10/06/walker.bailout/index.html

5. Social Security Administration. (1996, July). Research Note #3: Details of Ida May Fuller's Payroll Tax Contributions. Retrieved September 9, 2009 from http://www.ssa.gov/history/idapayroll.html

6. Blahous, C.P. (2000). Reforming Social Security: For Ourselves and Our Posterity. Westport, CT: Praeger Publishers. p. 119

4400869

Made in the USA
Charleston, SC
14 January 2010